HUMOR AS AN
INSTRUCTIONAL DEFIBRILLATOR

Other books by Ron Berk:

Professors Are from Mars®, Students Are from Snickers®
War and Peace
The Grapes of Wrath
Hamlet
Catcher in the Rye
Don Quixote
The Writings of Sigmund Freud
Harry Potter & the Sorcerer's Stone
The Republic
Canterbury Tales
The Old Man and the Sea
Gray's Anatomy
Dave Barry Slept Here
A Beautiful Mind
Autobiography of Malcolm X
E.T.
Beloved
The Lord of the Rings
Les Misérables
2002 Physicians' Desk Reference
Jaws
A Tale of Two Cities
The Bible (NIV only)

HUMOR AS AN INSTRUCTIONAL DEFIBRILLATOR

Evidence-Based Techniques in Teaching and Assessment

Ronald A. Berk

Sty/us

STERLING, VIRGINIA

Published in 2002 by

Stylus Publishing, LLC
22883 Quicksilver Drive
Sterling, Virginia 20166

Library of Congress Cataloging-in-Publication Data

Berk, Ronald A.
    Humor as an instructional defibrillator: evidence-based techniques
in teaching and assessment/Ronald A. Berk.—1st ed.
        p. cm
Includes bibliographical references and index.
    ISBN 1-57922-063-0 (alk. paper)
    1. Teaching. 2. Humor in education. 3. Educational tests and
    measurements. I. Title.
    LB1027.B472 2002
    371.3'02'07—dc21   2002006866

First edition, 2002
ISBN: paperback 1-57922-063-0

Printed in the United States of America

All first editions printed on acid free paper

Dedication

TO MY STUDENTS, who energize and inspire me to aspire to new levels of whatever I do.

CONTENTS

Part II

Assessment

ACKNOWLEDGMENTS

Before you quickly flip over this page, you might want to scan it to see if your name is mentioned. I'm kinda sneaky. Check it out.

Since my last humor book, the new humor strategies and ideas I developed for my own classes have been kept alive and visible in the academic community through my presentations at conferences and universities and in research publications. I am extremely grateful to the following conference directors and journal editors for encouraging and challenging my imagination rather than squishing it. Their supportiveness has meant more to me than they will ever know.

- *Milt Cox,* Director, Lilly Conference on College Teaching
- *Gregg Wentzell,* Managing Editor, *Journal on Excellence in College Teaching*
- *Bill Gorth,* President, National Evaluation Systems
- *Dick Allan,* Vice President, National Evaluation Systems
- *Paula Nassif,* Vice President, National Evaluation Systems
- *Jack Chambers,* Director, International Conference on College Teaching and Learning
- *Joel Goodman,* Director, The HUMOR Project and the International Conference on Humor and Creativity
- *Ronald Harden,* General Secretary, Association for Medical Education in Europe Conference
- *Pat Lilley,* Administrator, Association for Medical Education in Europe Conference

To those colleagues who took the time to thoughtfully review several chapter drafts, I express my deepest appreciation for their highly constructive, very concrete, sometimes brutal, and always valuable feedback. They include three jocular psychometricians, *Jim Popham, Bob McMorris,* and *Irv Lehmann;* two computer whizzes, *Frank Hoey* and *Jesse Whittington;* a humor researcher/editor, *Larry Mintz;* a humorist, *Roz Trieber;* and a doctoral student, *John Hitchcock.*

At Johns Hopkins, I thank *Kate Lears* who has patiently listened to more humor material than any person should have to endure. Her sensitivity and insightful responses always improved my work. *Ellen Spies,* administrative assistant and word processor par excellence, prepared the entire manuscript and made a bazillion of my changes without resorting to controlled substances or violence. I am debted to her for all that she does for me. However, if you spot any errores or omis sions, none of the above mentioned people is responsible. Ultimately, there is only one person who should be held totally accountable for what appears in this book, and that person, of course, is: Wolf Blitzer.

These acknowledgments would be incomplete, in fact, nonexistent without *John von Knorring*'s willingness to take the risk of publishing this book. However, in all modesty, I did provide some rather compelling arguments, such as: "The prequel to this book sold more than 17 copies, 16 of which were purchased by my mother." John responded: "How did you get a job at Johns Hopkins?" I am extremely grateful to John (the one without the "s") and my editor, *Larry Goldberg,* for their humor, tender loving care of my manuscript, and highest standards of publishing quality, which give me hope that this book will go over the top and sell more than 18 copies.

Finally, none of this would mean anything without a family who recognizes my need for long-term therapy. Over the past year, my wife, *Marion,* and two daughters, *Corinne* and *Marissa* (a.k.a. *Boo Boo*), plus my son-in-law, *Chris,* and my *mommy* have actually attended one of my classes or workshops. After their five heads stopped shaking from side to side and 10 eyeballs stopped rolling, they still talk to me and provide humor support. They remain the greatest blessings in my life.

Ronald A. Berk

Warning: Although this book is written expressly for professors, teachers (K-12), and trainers, if you have the sense of humor of tile grout, then you should not read any further. This book's not for you. Certainly every academic discipline has its fair share of wingtipped professors who sport pocket protectors and Mr./Ms. Dork designer horn-rimmed glasses that come from the factory with the nose support pre-broken and white tape wrapped around it. They are usually extremely serious about how they present material. That is not the approach taken here. This book is intended to furnish the essential information on the various topics, but in a moderately amusing style so you don't conk out continuously, just occasionally. Since some of you may have the attention span of goat cheese, the text will be interrupted regularly by warnings such as this one to check if you're still awake. Are you? Terrific! Heeeere we go.

This book is the sequel to *Professors Are from Mars®, Students Are from Snickers®* (Magna Publications, 1998), hereafter abbreviated as *Gone with the Wind*. After you read the title of *this* book, I suspect there were several questions that immediately raced through your brain, such as:

1. "Are you nuts?"
2. "Unlike your first book, is this one going to be funny?"
3. "Is this a rehash of the same stuff?"
4. "Am I going to have to buy it or should I request it for the library and then copy theirs?"
5. "How funny could a test possibly be?"
6. "Where did I put my car keys?"

The answers are: Yup, Yup, Nope, Yup, Side-Splitting Hilarious, On the Kitchen Table Where You Left Your Glasses.

Now that your most important questions have been addressed, let's move on with the fluff. I asked myself: "Bucko, why write another book on humor?" To which I responded: "There are so many jokes, so little time; plus I need the royalties in order to replace the front tires on my SUV." This book also demonstrates that someone with a low score on the SAT can still be productive. Students with low scores often feel discouraged. To those students, I address the following:

NOTICE TO STUDENTS
Many of you believe that if you get a low score on the SAT, you will end up in some no-name college, such as _____?_____ College, and eventually get stuck in a reeeeaally boring low-life dead-end loser job, such as host of a "reality TV" program or bodyguard for Jennifer "J. Lo" Lopez. *Au contraire!* (French expression, literally meaning "Your shorts are on backwards"). Listen up for a moment and stop trying to figure out what body part to pierce next. A low SAT score does not necessarily mean you'll be a failure. There have been a few, well-known very successful people who performed poorly on the SAT just like you. For example, Albert Einstein scored only 201 on the quantitative section and, as we all know, he went on to invent Afro-Sheen®. So, take heart, there is hope for you too to make a name for yourself in haircare products. You never know what can happen until you try.

This is the sequel you've been anxiously awaiting. It is the only spinoff from an original work to have won the Pulitzer Prize in fiction, Nobel Prize in physics, Tony Award for best musical, and an Olympic Gold Medal in the shot-put. Now that's supernaturally amazing. It probably deserves a spot on the Fox TV network. Unlike other sequels, such as *Terminator 2, Jaws 2,* and *Scream 2,* this one doesn't contain expressions such as "girlie mon," a mechanical shark that explodes, or gratuitous violence. In fact, it's rated "PG."

Please take note that this book is "reality based," nonvirtual. You can feel this rectangular object in your hands, right? Welcome to the interactive World Wide World. This www can be found offline on the Outernet. The only memory you need is in your noggin. Softwear-wise, while reading this book, dress is casual. There's no scroll bar or hypertext link, not even a keyboard, mouse, or modem. To navigate this book, simply grasp the upper-right corner of each page and turn right to left. Not yet! Wait, I'm not finished. The writing, the research, the jokes, and the students with whom all of the methods have been tested are REAL. This page is real. Even your coffee cup sitting on this paragraph is real. Ouch! Wow, is that hot. *I'm* imaginary. Kinda Stephen Kingish, huh?

Over the four years since *Gone with the Wind* hit the streets, I have been deluged with feedback on the techniques and material from novice as well as veteran jocular professors. One of those three e-mails even asked me how to purchase a block of seats for the Super Bowl. I have also continued to test ideas that just keep pouring out of my twisted mind. The substance of this book contains that spillage.

This volume plugs gaps and extends humor strategies from my earlier work and adds completely new methods in the areas of music and demonstrations, Web-based and online courses, and student assessment. Approximately 95% of the content is new and 8% is review (Gotcha!). This book has "A Third More Jokes, Same Great Taste." The techniques have been tested for specific mirthful effects, side effects, and after effects based on research (*Emergency Bulletin:* Wait. This sounds like a clinical-trial study for a life-saving medication, not a teaching technique. Sorry for the interruption. We now rejoin the originally scheduled sentence already in progress) with my own undergraduate and graduate statistics classes over the past eight years. The material has also been presented in over 100 keynote addresses and training sessions to more than 12,000 educators, many of whom clearly communicated their likes and dislikes. Their constructive comments have been incorporated into the content in one form or another; their destructive ones are toast.

What remains unchanged in both books is the underlying purpose: to make me rich! Kidding. That purpose is to use humor to connect with our students and engage them in learning to facilitate their academic success. As we get older, which for me translates into grayer and fatter, a new crop of frisky students enters our classes just as young as the preceding year's crop. The differences in appearance are obvious: They wear logo-infested gear, cargo pants the size of tents with crotches three feet long (*Note:* These pants typically contain enough material to make all of the sails for every boat entered in America's Cup), oversized tees, shoes with foot-high elevator-lift soles, and, of course, the ubiquitous baseball caps worn backwards, plus giant spider tattoos, fluorescent-colored Mohawk-spiked hair, and enough rings in their nostrils, lips, ears, eyebrows, and tongues to set off an airport metal detector; I saunter into class looking suave and sophisticated like a Brooks Brothers® version of a Teletubby®. This gap seems to be constantly widening, especially with undergraduates, because we're the only ones getting older. Their definition of *old* is "before Ginger left the Spice Girls." They expect to live 50,000 years. A gap also exists with graduate students, but it's narrower.

This generational gap is due to our worldly differences. Many of our students cannot relate to nor do they have any interest in our world. We have to take the initiative to reach out to what's meaningful in their world if we are going to connect. Otherwise, the barriers that naturally exist, due to our title, age, clothing, eyesight, belt size, and medications, will remain.

We need to search for common denominators to connect with our students. One strategy is to pinpoint elements in both of our worlds that can bridge the gap. The primary source from which I have drawn joke material for both books is the cultural, common ground, nonacademic experiences in our lives. Examples include the broad culture-specific areas of TV programs, movies, plays and musicals, and music. Other more generic topics are computers, the airlines, food, books, sports, pets, power tools, and multitentacled, stalk-eyed aliens.

Although major life-changing phenomena throughout history have occurred in threes, such as *Three Blind Mice, Charlie's Angels,* and tic-tac-toe, this book is organized into only two parts. That's because this book won't change your life. It may not even make a dent in how you teach. In fact, if any of the methods actually seem useful, you may want to double your medication dosage. The two parts are teaching and assessment. Each consists of four chapters.

The *teaching* section (Part I) examines the various forms of humor used in teaching, the psychophysiological benefits of humor in teaching and assessment, the use of music and demonstrations to trigger laughter and facilitate learning, and the use of humor on a course Web site or in distance learning. These new outrageous techniques are designed ultimately to convert your classroom into an adult version of *Sesame Street.* Your students should be having so much fun that they probably will not even realize how much they're learning.

The *assessment* section (Part II) provides an overview of types of classroom assessment, a consumer's guide to selecting assessment methods, boring general rules for writing test items, even more boring rules for writing multiple-choice items, a free sample of No-Doz® before detecting internal item flaws, and eight techniques for injecting humor into your items. Before you gag at the seriousness of these topics, please know that there is nothing serious about how that material is presented. It is as sick and twisted as the preceding section, plus there are nearly 100 joke examples to illustrate the rules. In fact, you might want to ignore all of the text and just use the items in your classes.

Given the nature of the content in the eight chapters, I suggest beginning with any chapter you are willing to read. If the one you select is underwhelming or knocks you out cold, try another chapter. Hopefully you'll find something useful.

PART I

TEACHING

Warning: As you enter the first few pages of Chapter 1, please be aware that this is a SMOKE-FREE book. If you must inhale substances that would corrode your car's engine and will gradually turn your lungs into malignant lumps of carbon, I ask that you go outside to the designated penned off area to smoke. Ouch! Did you just put out your cigar in this warning box? If you think I'm being unreasonable here, just wait until you get to Chapter 2 where you will have to put on latex gloves to conform with OSHA Standards to protect yourself from the variety of bodily fluids used to measure the physiological effects of laughter. You can take them off in Chapter 3, which describes strategies for using music (Yes, music!) as a teaching tool to tap your students' multiple intelligences. Simply by pressing a button on a tape or CD player, you can elicit mirthful responses in your classroom, which can facilitate learning. Consider using the theme from *Star Wars* with light sabers to open the first class of the semester or the theme from *Cops* ("Bad Boys, Bad Boys, What Ya Gonna Do When They Come for You") with men or "Bad Girl" (Donna Summer) with women to begin a class demonstration. More than 40 different pieces of music are suggested. Finally, Chapter 4 presents more than a dozen online forms of humor that can be placed on any course Web site or distance-education course. A variety of print forms that can be inserted into standard comatose print material on the Web as well as visual and sound effects are described.

1

CREATING HUMOR
TO HOOK YOUR STUDENTS

Bored & Order: In the higher education system, the learning environment is supported by two separate yet kinda important groups: the professors who teach and publish lots of stuff and the students who try to learn. These are their stories. Ka Chung!

In the movie *Finding Forrester*, fictitious Pulitzer-Prize winning novelist William Forrester (a.k.a. James Bond) gave the following advice on writing to talented 16-year-old Jamal Wallace whose secret passion was writing:

> You write your first draft with your heart. You rewrite with your head. The first key to writing is to write. Not to think. If you try to write the perfect page one, you'll never get to page two.

When I heard this, my response was: "Like coool duuude. Awesome!" That rule of thumb applies to writing humor too, except in the reverse. You start with a twisted idea in your head, then develop it into an emotional chuckle-inducing joke.

The entire process of creating humor involves creative writing and releasing the childlike imagination that seems to get repressed as we age. Remember when you were an adorable tyke who engaged in playful shenanigins (you little rascal), risk-taking adventures, and fantasizing that one day, maybe, you might become Cokie Roberts, Alan Greenspan, or a Limp

Bizket? It appears that for *some* of us at least that spirit became squished inside of our bodies as a more dignified, proper, inhibited, and stuffy professorial self emerged instead. If this description sounds familiar, it's now time to set that imagination free. (*Note:* If you feel like breaking into the song "Born Free," don't do it, at least, not yet. You'll have the opportunity to sing later.)

This chapter furnishes the structural foundation for the entire book. It has six purposes: (1) to provide two instructional reasons for using humor in the classroom, (2) to present the basic formulas for humor and their relationships to teaching and learning, (3) to differentiate among five forms of humor used in teaching, (4) to examine five key factors that affect students' laughter, (5) to describe an evidence-based approach to how to be funny, and (6) to suggest methods for evaluating the effectiveness of humor strategies.

Why Use Humor in the Classroom?

Why do we do anything in the classroom? Hummm. I bet you guessed it. Yup. To get tenure. Bull's-eye, but it's also to facilitate learning. Among all of the instructional reasons for using humor in your classroom previously reviewed (Berk, 1998c), there are two that bubble to the surface: (1) it builds the professor-student connection, and (2) it instantaneously engages students in the learning process. Lowman (1995) insists these are the two most important ingredients in college teaching.

Professor-Student Connection

The professor-student connection was the focus of *Gone with the Wind* and continues to be the focus of this book. (*Reminder:* In case you skipped the "Introduction," *Gone with the Wind* is the abbreviation for the long-winded title of my previous book, *Harry Potter Gets a Humongous Royalty Check and Buys Edinburgh Castle.*) Humor can chop down, smash, demolish, even vaporize the pre-existing barriers that separate you from your students. It opens up communication that's not based on fear or intimidation. Instead, the communication is positive, constructive, and relaxed; it continuously ebbs and flows all over the classroom until the rockets' red glare with amber waves and purple mountains. A bonding or rapport develops between you and your students that is founded on respect, trust, and fun (Lowman, 1995). Research by Astin (1985) and Pascarella and Terenzini (1991) indicates that this connection is essential for student learning, satisfaction, and retention. In fact, one of the major reasons for the high student dropout rate in many distance-education programs is the lack of that connection. The chat room, or rather type room, is not an adequate proxy for the personal contact possible in and out of the classroom with a live or even semi-live professor.

Student Engagement

Student engagement is also a key factor in learning (Eble, 1994; McKeachie, 1994). Students enter our classrooms with their own baggage of personal distractions, or, as Professor Charles Kingsfield of the *Paper Chase* called it, "a skull full of mush." We do not know what is on their minds when they sit down. It could be a fight with a significant other, chapped lips, unwanted body hair, ruptured spleen, or a monkey named Jerome. Our job is to snap them to attention and concentrate it on the topic for the day—to be fully engaged in learning activities.

Announcement: I am proud to announce that the next paragraph was just chosen as the OFFICIAL PARAGRAPH OF THE 2012 WINTER OLYMPIC GAMES IN ANTARCTICA. Why? I have no idea!

In movies and the theater, the attention-grabber is called the *hook*. It is intended to pique interest quickly and whet curiosity. "Wait. Time out. I have a question. Bucko, are you sure that's how you spell 'whet'?" Yup, unless you prefer to have your curiosity drenched as in *The Perfect Storm!* I think we need to get back to the topic of this paragraph, which is George Clooney. In teaching, Hunter (1982) calls this *hook* the *set*—those actions, activities, or experiences that pull students into the learning process to engage their emotions and focus their minds. This is essential not just to open class, but throughout the class period because students can start squirming in their seats at any time or drift into thoughts about Jerome or turn off completely. From their perspective, some classes may seem to last longer than the Crusades. Others may tend to move at the speed of fingernail growth. Does the term *glacial thawing* come to mind? A professor must draw on a variety of techniques to hook his or her students and then sustain a high level of engagement until class ends. Few professors can deliver the drama and high-voltage, spine-tingling excitement that many students may need to keep them involved. If a traditional lecture format is used, multiple hooks, including a cattle prod, may be required to keep bringing the students back to attention. They may need to be constantly sucked out of passivity and then immersed in activity, over and over again.

Another variation on this function of humor is to see it as an *instructional defibrillator*. If the joke is represented by the paddles, when it is delivered, your students will be shocked into attention. The humor can not only bring your students back to life, but deadly, boring course content as well. So grab those paddles. Charge 300. Clear!

Regardless of what content you teach or how you teach, humor used as a systematic tool can serve as the hook or paddles of your dreams. "Excuse me for interrupting again, but isn't there a movie called Hook Dreams?" No. You're thinking of the basketball flick *Space Jam*. Anyway, there are 10 humor strategies previously described in *Gone with the Wind*. Plus there are new ones presented in this volume that can extend your humor repertoire to include music, class demonstrations, print and non-print Web site techniques, and testing approaches. They can supplement the student-centered and problem-based learning methods you may already be using. Humor can be planned and executed to rivet your students' attention in a nanosecond and sustain a level of engagement that can facilitate learning.

Basic Formulas for Humor

The most basic structure of the humor presented in this book is *incongruity* (a.k.a. "contrast resolution"). It consists of at least two elements:

1. EXPECTED CONTENT, which usually is serious material to set up the humor

2. UNEXPECTED TWIST or PUNCHLINE, which is an outrageous spin or a ridiculous outcome

This structure was formerly proposed by Raskin (1985), although others have tinkered with the notion of incongruity (Forabosco, 1992; Rothbart, 1976). This tinkering, in fact, dates as far back as the work of Kant (1790). Yes you can! I know what you're thinking right now: "It's lunchtime. Why am I reading about humor formulas when I could be eating Chinese food? I'm outta here."

When you return, you'll probably ask, "What the heck does this dumb incongruity formula have to do with teaching and learning?" Wow. What a great question. Interestingly, the cognitive process used to understand a joke is similar to that involved in problem solving. The mental processing of humor involves your noggin, especially the right hemisphere (Svebak, 1982), and is, believe it or not, similar to the processing of creativity (Derks, 1987; O'Quin & Derks, 1997) and problem solving (Goldstein, Harmon, McGhee, & Karasik, 1975; Johnson, 1990). They all require the novel and successful manipulation of ideas (Belanger, Kirkpatrick, & Derks, 1988). Suls (1972, 1983) identified two stages in the processing:

1. *Recognition* of the incongruity in the humor which resembles *identifying the problem.*

2. *Resolution* or understanding the punchline which is akin to *solving the problem.*

Electrophysiological evidence indicates it is the second stage that engages the right hemisphere. The resolution requires divergent thinking, creativity, and a playful Toys-R-Expensive® cognitive set (Forabosco, 1992; Ziv, 1976, 1983).

Since humor and problem solving involve the same basic cognitive process, one can prime the other. In teaching, humor can improve problem solving and performance on right hemisphere tasks, such as spatial temporal reasoning and recognition (Bihrle, Brownell, & Powelson, 1986; Brownell & Gardner, 1989; Brownell, Michel, Powelson, & Gardner, 1983). This linkage would be particularly valuable in problem-based learning (PBL) courses.

Trifecta Formula for Humor Delivered Orally

When you present humor in your class, most forms have three elements:

1. *Expected*—serious set-up with commonly understood situation or content

2. *Expected*—build-up of tension

3. *Unexpected Twist*—punchline

This is the *humor trifecta*. All three elements are required for maximum winnings.

When students anticipate a joke is coming, cued by your set-up, body language, or use of italicized words, you have the benefit of building tension before delivering the punch. It is a form of delayed gratification similar to hunger and sex. "Uh oh, I bet that was the hook. You have my attention, Bucko." In those areas, self-imposed tension in anticipation of the prize that awaits can produce greater heights of pleasure when that tension is released. Whoooa! That second element can really make the difference in the students' responses. Building the tension in your humor can significantly affect the pleasure your students derive from it. Your ability to coax them in your delivery will determine the type of laughter that results. It has been suggested that this effect is related to the amount of endogenous opiate-like neurochemicals released to pleasure sensors in the brain by the punchline (Perlmutter, 2000). This is just like using controlled substances, except without the "substances."

And, it is within *your* power to produce a laugher's "high" in *your* class. But try to wait and build some tension until you get to Chapter 2 where you and your students can explode with loads of physiological effects.

Formulas for Humor in Print

In contrast to the above, script humor (Attardo & Raskin, 1991) or humor that is embedded in text or a test, even in a humor column written by Dave Barry or Art Buchwald, has no build up of tension. The reader doesn't have a clue when the punch is coming. He or she is simply reading seriously, merrily along, when all of a sudden, your tea kettle starts screaming. Yiiikes! It scared me. You better go turn off the burner, but take this book with you so I can finish my sentence properly. What I was going to say before I was so rudely interrupted was that you are unexpectedly smacked with a punch of some kind. Whammo! Right between your eyeballs. The punchline in print is the point of collision between two conflicting trains of thought: *serious text meets unexpected twist.* CRASSSH! The resulting laughter is our response to the shock of recognizing the incongruity. Because there is less opportunity to build tension, except when the print form is a multipanel cartoon, the level of laughter is usually less than that elicited by live humor.

There are several formulas for written forms of humor presented in Chapters 4 and 8. All are derived from the basic two-element incongruity formula.

Forms of Humor in Teaching

Five categories of humor you should consider in your teaching include: (1) in-class forms that rely on delivery, (2) in-class forms inserted into print materials, (3) out-of-class forms on a course Web site, (4) out-of-class forms that should remain out of class, and (5) in-class topics that are not culture specific.

In-Class Forms That Rely on Delivery

The following forms of humor described and illustrated previously in *Gone with the Wind* depend on live delivery:

- Opening Jokes
  - Stand-up Jokes
  - Anecdotes
  - Quotations and Questions
  - Multiple-Choice Jokes

- Top 10 Lists
  - Cartoons (single- and multipanel)
- Skits/Live Dramatizations
- Spontaneous Humor
- Humorous Questions
- Humorous Examples
- Humorous Problems or Exercises
- *Jeopardy!* Reviews

In-Class Forms Inserted into Print Materials

There are several forms that involve systematic techniques for inserting humor into various course print materials:

- Syllabus
- Handouts
- Examples
- Assignments
  - Problems
  - Case Studies
  - Scenarios/Vignettes
  - Simulations
- Tests

All except the last were presented in *Gone with the Wind*. An extended treatment of methods for infusing humor in course tests is given in Chapter 8. Since these five print forms can be distributed in class or be made available on a course Web site, their potential as vehicles for humor and learning are greater. They can be mixed and matched between the two outlets. A further discussion of these options is given in the next section and in Chapter 4.

Out-of-Class Forms on a Course Web Site

In addition to the preceding forms are those that can take advantage of the unique characteristics of the technology. What can be presented on the screen that could not be presented in class? When students leave your class, what could motivate them to run to their computers? *Answer:* Printing the test key online by mistake. That'll do it. Otherwise, something that's funny, entertaining, and contains the element of surprise will get them there. The students should feel like they're rushing to open a birthday gift.

Just clicking on the list of course components to view the syllabus should be an experience. Not only is there humor laced throughout the syllabus, but as soon as it appears, the theme music from *E.R.* or *Friends,* one of the course prerequisites, begins to play.

The Web site contains two basic forms of humor: print and non-print. The print humor is inserted into the course components mentioned previously, which may have been presented in class, plus others that will only appear online, including:

- Course disclaimers
- Announcements
- Warnings or cautions

Further, any print information on the Web site may have humor inserts in text in the following:

- Lists
- Word derivations
- Foreign word expressions
- Acronyms and emoticons
- Locations of college/universities, institutes, agencies
- Serious-humor contrast table

Visual and sound effects can be used to embellish the print material. Visual effects may include:

- Pictures
- Graphics
- Animation
- Icons
- Movies

Sound effects may involve:

- Music
- Sounds/noises
- Voices

Techniques and barrels of resources are described in Chapter 4 to develop the quintessential, ultra-hysterical course Web site. The combination of in-class and out-of-class Web site humor can create a *Sesame Street*-type learning experience for college students that is within the grasp of any professor. I challenge you to employ every imagination gene in your skull to extend your teaching methods beyond the limits imposed by most books on teaching scholarship.

Out-of-Class Forms That Should Remain Out of Class

Have TV and movie writers lost their minds? Has Hannibal Lecter dined on their brains? Why do so many writers for these media as well as stand-up comedians seem addicted to humor that pushes the limits of profanity, vulgarity, and sexuality, or is just plain *out there* to offend? Rather than reflecting prevailing norms and tastes, the humor in these products of popular cultures seem to be lowering them. The producers have trained consumers to accept progressively lower standards of language and behavior. This sinking enables their work to stand out in an increasingly crowded field. Whatever criticism that results is far outweighed by the profits. Falling standards, consequently, become self-fulfilling. Each new breach of the existing "standard" establishes a new, lower standard that comes to be seen as the norm, at least until the next breach.

One example is gross-out body humor which is breaking box-office records. *There's Something About Mary* and *American Pie* struck a nerve because there was enough grotesque, low humor to ensure that every single viewer will be shocked by something. Keenan Ivory Wayans, director of *Scary Movie,* feels that you have to stay one step ahead, that is, take it up a notch. You can't settle for less, not in the number of laughs or in the gross factor. You have to push the envelope because the audience expects it. And he did in *Scary Movie 2. Freddy Got Fingered* also responded to this challenge with its relentless obscenity, crude and explicit sexual innuendo, including sex jokes involving a girl in a wheelchair and the molesting of children, an accident prone child injured over and over again for laughs, and depictions of animal abuse and disgusting, gross-out "comedy" designed to offend everyone. Ads for the movie billed it as the "Hannibal of Comedies" and the star Tom Green as "He doesn't cross the line . . . He stomps on it!"

The types of humor we see in the movies and on TV are out of control. That being said, as professors, where do we draw the line, set the standard, for humor in our classrooms? Despite what types of humor our students might enjoy outside of the classroom, you will have to determine the boundaries for what is appropriate and inappropriate humor in *your* classroom. Those boundaries must also be communicated to your students. If your humor is being used as a systematic teaching tool to facilitate learning, you need to lay out the rules.

Guidelines for offensive humor. How do we do that? The first step is to define *what is offensive.* It seems as though we should know it when we see or hear it. But it's not that simple. Humor that offends is based on an individual, subjective interpretation.

> *Rule of Thumb:* Any word, object, or action that violates a person's values, moral principles, or norms of behavior would be offensive (Veatch, 1998).

The operative word here is *violation.* A significant violation is what offends. For example, sexist jokes would offend feminists because they violate principles that feminists take very seriously. Racist humor is offensive to people who are strongly committed to the principles of human dignity. Belching and other bodily sounds in comedies such as *Shrek, The Nutty Professor,* and *Doctor Doolittle 2* are offensive to many adults because it is a violation of propriety; whereas other adults and children find that type of behavior hilarious.

The level of attachment or commitment to principles may determine whether the humor is offensive or funny. A violation that happens to others, such as *put-downs,* does not produce as strong an attachment as a violation that happens to oneself. People joke more easily at the expense of others than at themselves because they are committed much more to their own dignity and comfort than that of others. However, self-effacing or self-deprecating humor in the form of *self-downs* is not only an acceptable form, but a highly desirable one to break down barriers in the classroom. The self-down can even puncture professorial pomposity. Despite the fact that the self-down represents a "violation of self," it also provides an infinite source of humor material that can be extremely effective. It also means more than put-downs because it makes a powerful statement about the self-esteem of the person doing it.

The second step in drawing boundaries is to consider "offensiveness" in the professor-student context. To what extent do your values match those of your students? The greater the match and the consistency of your choice of humor with their values, the greater your chances of success. The generation gap between you and your students is a starting point to evaluate the match. What complicates this process is the diversity of backgrounds and, consequently, values and moral principles of our students that are at risk of being violated. This is a tightrope walk as we try to balance what is funny with what is violated. To minimize violation that can offend your students, I recommend a conservative standard. You must either share or at least understand the values and principles of your students. Arriving at that common denominator provides the path of least offensiveness. The humor you select should follow that path and be communicated to your students.

I suggest doing that in your first class of the semester. Simply present a list of the categories or types of humor that could offend your students. That list automatically affects the class atmosphere and tone right from the get go. For example, by saying I will try to avoid all forms of put-down humor, especially where a student could be the butt of the joke, I convey that put-down jokes by any student directed at other students are also out of bounds. After that first class, a few students regularly comment that those statements make them feel very comfortable and free to ask questions without fear of being whacked by me or their peers.

Since none of us can be perfectly sensitive to everything that could possibly offend our students, I conclude my remarks with the following *disclaimer:*

> You knuckleheads! Oops, wrong speech. Given the amount of humor infused throughout everything we will be doing this semester, from the syllabus to our problem assignments to the exams, I may unknowingly say or do something that offends you. Please know that it was never intended. If that happens at any time, please let me know.

This disclaimer both protects me as well as assures my accountability. If I slip, the students will catch me. Occasionally, I still commit infractions with the new material I'm testing. The offensive material may simply be a word or a phrase in an example, a problem description, or a test item. Any violation is corrected immediately. That is essential. I have never rationalized or ignored a comment by a student that identified humor content that was offensive. It is simple enough to correct.

Effects of offensive humor.   You're probably thinking by this point, "Why is he beginning another paragraph right here?" Because, otherwise, this section of the page would be buck naked. At the risk of reiterating my position on offensive humor in *Gone with the Wind,* say it with me: *"Humor that can potentially offend any student is inappropriate in the classroom."* Why? Because it can have the following negative effects on a student:

- Tightening up
- Withdrawal
- Resentment
- Anger
- Tension
- Anxiety
- Turning off/tuning out

After reading down this list, does the word *disconnect* come to mind? These physical and emotional effects can squash a student's motivation or spirit to learn, which results in a loss of spunk. Once you've lost spunk, it's over. More importantly, a single offensive joke can irreparably damage your relationship with the student. In other words, you quite possibly could lose that student for the entire semester. A student would usually stop coming to class to avoid the preceding feelings, the risk of a recurrence, or a confrontation with the perpetrator (YOU!). What is offensive is not determined by a majority vote of the students. It is an individual issue in many cases because humor is open to individual interpretation. However, your experience should weed out most of the offensive material so these individual cases are rare.

The above negative effects are exactly opposite of the positive effects for using humor in the first place. One primary goal is to *connect*. Nonoffensive humor can break down barriers, relax, open up, and reduce tension, stress, and anxiety to create the professor-student connection. In addition, it can grab and maintain the students' attention on learning. Furthermore, offensive humor is inconsistent with some of the characteristics of effective teachers, such as sensitive, caring, understanding, compassionate, and approachable.

If one were to study the humor that appears in the research literature, the joke types usually fit the following themes: superiority, aggression, hostility, malice, derision, cruelty, disparagement, stupidity, sex, and ethnic put-downs. Is there anything positive or nonoffensive in that list? I've identified seven major categories of offensive humor in the context of classroom usage, where humor may be presented in a variety of forms. They are inclusive of many of the above themes. Those categories are as follows: (1) put-downs, (2) sarcasm, (3) ridicule, (4) profanity, (5) vulgarity, (6) sexual content and innuendo, and (7) sensitive personal experiences. Before I continue with an examination of these categories, I know you have bottled up lots of opinions on this contentious topic. In order to avert an explosion of your brain all over this paragraph, here's your opportunity to vent.

Opinion Vent: Hold this box up to your mouth and express your opinions in the area in parentheses below in a loud and clear voice. Okay? Go.
(Express Your Opinions HERE)
Okay, that's enough. Stop already. Thank you. Thank you for your input.

Put-downs.   This is, perhaps, the most ubiquitous form of humor. Everywhere we look, from Leno and Letterman to images of professionals on sitcoms, such as the inept mailmen on *Seinfeld* and *Cheers* and dingbat social workers on *Norm,* to colleagues and even our closest friends and our family, the put-down is inescapable. Disparagement humor occurs when an individual or group is victimized, belittled, or suffers some misfortune or act of aggression (Zillmann, 1983). Sometimes it is rather harmless in the context of kidding around or teasing, while at other times it can be mean, cruel, and hurtful, albeit a powerful weapon for verbal abuse. Freud (1905) believed this to be an important function of humor, such that you can express aggressive and hostile feelings in a "socially acceptable" manner. This type of humor is called *tendentious.* There is even research evidence that people enjoy put-downs more when they have negative attitudes toward the victim (LaFave, 1972; LaFave, Haddad, & Marshall, 1974; Olsen, Maio, & Hobden, 1999; Wicker, Barron, & Willis, 1980).

At the 1998 Kennedy Center Honors in Washington, DC, which for more than 20 years has celebrated five artists each year for their "lifetime contributions to American culture through the performing arts," Bill Cosby was honored. Fewer than a handful of comedians have ever been so honored. The first person to speak on Cosby's behalf was Phylicia Rashad (a.k.a. Claire Huxtable). Her first words were: "It doesn't take a lot of intelligence to put people down. But it takes Bill's intelligence, his sensibilities, and his grace to embrace the whole world with humor and uplift it with laughter."

Although there may be a time and place for put-down humor, such as in those over-advertised videos of Friar's Club Celebrity Roasts emceed by the late Dean Martin and others, the college classroom is not the place. Creating humor that builds students up rather than tearing them down is not easy. However, yielding to the latter temptation can produce the consequences described previously.

One such temptation is after you have just finished explaining a concept or making a point, a student asks a question about that same concept or point, which suggests he or she simply wasn't paying attention. What an opportunity to slam dunk that student. But before you do, think about whether you have ever mentally drifted away during a presentation at your research conference, a seminar on financial planning or retirement at your institution, or a faculty meeting. Some of us may have the attention span of macaroni and/or may be coping with pressing personal issues. Well, so do your students. Hel-LO! We usually have no clue what is on their minds when they enter our classroom. It could be financial or romantic problems, illness or tragedy in the student's family, or ruminating over what to eat for lunch or what to do with Jerome.

When presented with this situation in your classroom, you have at least two options:

Stupid, Thoughtless Option 1: Make a joke about that student's not paying attention, so he or she is the butt of your put-down. This guarantees the student's embarrassment and humiliation. When do you think that student will ask another question? Maybe when your classroom freezes over!

Empathetic, Compassionate Option 2: Answer the question in a respectful tone without any negative comment.

The acid test of whether you executed Option 2 correctly is the reactions of students. After class or in the hallways, a few students will always approach and ask, "Why do you put up with those stupid questions in class?" (Similar comments are also given on my course evaluations.) My response: "If you drifted for a moment in class and asked that question, wouldn't you want me to respond to you respectfully instead of putting you down and humiliating you in front of the class? *(Incabod)* deserved that respect and so would you." The student's typical response to that explanation is: "You're an idiot. No wonder no one laughs at your jokes."

In addition to your students, I suggest you avoid the following *targets of put-down jokes* in your class:

- Colleagues or other co-workers
- Popular, entertainment, or political personalities
- Groups based on race, ethnicity, culture, nationality, gender, religion, or sexual orientation
- People with certain physical characteristics (e.g., fat, thin, short, tall, blonde, pregnant, bald, or all of the preceding)
- People with physical disabilities or handicaps
- People with mental handicaps or illnesses

Sarcasm. A sarcastic remark frequently is just another form of the ever popular put-down. Haiman (1998) notes that it expresses "the speaker's actual contempt, indifference, or hostility toward his or her target" (p. 19). Students often perceive sarcasm as a sign of intellectual wit or as an elite verbal art form, even when the comment is directed at them as a put-down (Nelms, 2001). Sarcasm "always has an edge; it sometimes has a sting" (Hutcheon, 1995, p. 15). It is usually cutting, caustic, biting, derisive, sneering, harsh, sardonic, or bitter. In the classroom, professors use it to taunt, deflate, scold, ridicule, and push students to perform. If you're not sure of its effect, check out the sarcasm (and other put downs) of the host/hostess of *The Weakest Link*. Also, the TV character Toby Ziegler, Director of Communications in President Josiah Bartlet's White House on *The West Wing*, inflicts his caustic remarks on everyone except the president.

In an extensive study of sarcasm in the college classroom, Nelms (2001) proffers a more neutral definition and balanced analysis than only the negative motivations above. She defines sarcasm as "a speech behavior in which the surface structure of a speaker's utterance does not match the speaker's intended meaning" (p. 11). Although she found many negative examples of sarcasm, the most frequent use by professors was positive, such as to build rapport, make a point, spark interest, and push students. One example was self-denigrating sarcasm by the professor. Even when the sarcasm served a negative function, students who were not the chosen targets found it extremely entertaining. There were also rare instances where the sarcasm was classified as neutral, such as an indirect reprimand, a reaction to a minor irritation, or in making a point.

Professors who regularly use negative sarcasm have asked me whether there is any way to justify or rationalize its use as appropriate in the classroom. Read my letters: NO! What makes sarcasm so dangerous is that it is spontaneous. It's highly risky because it's difficult to control the positivity or negativity of the comment when it comes out of our mouths so quickly. If the result is negative and directed at an individual student, the consequences can be so hurtful and damaging that a student may not recover from the wound (Nelms, 2001).

Ridicule. It doesn't get any nastier. According to Gruner (1978), "ridicule is the basic component of all humorous material" (p. 14). I don't think so. Ridicule may be a jest that makes fun of someone sportively or good-humoredly, but most often it is intended to humiliate. It may consist of words and actions, such as scornful or contemptuous laughter. It is usually mean and malicious, and may include sarcasm or other derisive, taunting, or jeering comments.

There are a variety of motives and functions of this type of insult-humor, which may range from the actual expression of hostility to self-deprecation to ironic reversal, where the insult is turned around and used against the attacker (Mintz, 1999). For example, in the popular comedy *Meet the Parents*, the character Greg Focker (played by Ben Stiller) was ridiculed throughout the movie by several hostile members of his fiancée's family for being a male nurse and, finally, at the end of the movie for his name, Gaylord ("Gay Focker").

Even Mel Brooks admits the power of ridicule in his smash Broadway musical *The Producers*. In an interview on *60 Minutes* with Mike Wallace (April 15, 2001), Brooks noted that the greatest form of revenge he could execute against Adolph Hitler is ridicule:

> How do you get even with him [Hitler]? There's only one way to get even. You have to bring him down with ridicule . . . . If you can make people laugh at him [Hitler], then you're one up on him. It's been one of my lifelong jobs to make the world laugh at Adolph Hitler.

Brooks does just that in the show's major production number, "Springtime for Hitler."

Any personal characteristic of a student can easily be held up to ridicule. A foreign accent, a lisp, a stutter, an unusual gesture, and a physical disability represent common targets. Please resist every temptation you see and hear.

Sexual content and innuendo.   This topic is the core of many stand-up routines by comedians who appear on HBO and Showtime specials and on Comedy Central. It is also the primary vehicle for many popular TV shows, such as *Friends, Ally McBeal,* and *Sex and the City,* and just about every movie with a PG rating or worse. Regardless of the gender composition of your class, sexual humor is out of bounds as a teaching tool, unless that's what you're teaching.

Profanity.   Expletives are heard just about everywhere. What the "&!%#" is going on? What used to be considered locker room language is now heard regularly by foulmouthed gangsters *(Sopranos),* cops *(NYPD Blue* and *The Shield*), lawyers *(The Practice),* doctors *(E.R.),* and school kids *(South Park)* on TV (Farhi, 2002). This coarsening of TV and our culture suggests nothing is sacrosanct anymore. However, despite the increasing frequency of profane language around us, its use in jokes in the classroom is inappropriate and unnecessary, plus it cannot be bleeped out of our presentation. Whenever it occurs, its crudity debases the level of discourse and the "discourser."

Vulgarity.   Creating vulgar images and sounds of anything for laughs, especially the flatulence and toilet humor in *Blazing Saddles,* the *Nutty Professor,* the animated PG-rated *Shrek,* and every Jim Carrey comedy, has no place in any classroom.

Sensitive personal experiences.   Jeno Leno's relentless series of jokes about former New York Yankee Darryl Strawberry's cocaine addition is representative of this target category of humor. Entertainment, political, and sports personalities are especially vulnerable to jocular barbs about divorce, abortion, sexual infidelity, cosmetic surgery, alcoholism, drug addiction, HIV/AIDS, and personal tragedies. This category is inclusive of what are called "sick jokes" in the humor literature, which make fun of death, disease, dysfunction, or deformity usually following a significant disaster or tragedy (Dundes, 1987a, 1987b; Mindess, Miller, Turek, Bender, & Corbin, 1985). Those who engage in humor on these topics exhibit screamingly bad taste. Do the jabs at Ted Kennedy, Bill Clinton, Betty Ford, Robert Downey, Jr., and Michael Jackson suggest examples of this type of derisive humor spewed by talk-show comedians? Steer clear of this category.

It is significant to note that after the terrorists' attacks on the World Trade Center in New York and Pentagon in Washington, DC, and crash near Pittsburgh on "9–11" 2001, there was no evidence of sick jokes that used the victims as punchlines. That tragedy had such a profound effect on everyone that comedy clubs shut down for a couple of weeks and Jay Leno and David Letterman went on hiatus. Lipman (2002) noted, "laughter seemed out of place, an irreverent form of disrespect to the memory of 1000s of victims" (p. 6). How do you laugh after a mass murder? As weeks passed, stand-up comics, talk-show hosts, Web sites, and political cartoonists decided the country was ready for humor, a respectful brand that was directed at the perpetrators rather than the victims. Professional comedians were careful and cautious in their jokes (Wooten & Dunkelblau, 2002). As our war on terrorism escalated, the targets of humor that emerged were the Taliban, Islamic/Afghan culture (especially, the oppression of women), and, of course, the elusive Osama bin Laden. One prime example of this humor was the opening monologue of Ellen DeGeneres who hosted the once postponed Emmy Awards in November 2001. Her first line was: "What would bug the Taliban more than a gay woman in a suit surrounded by Jews?" Her jokes were timely, appropriate, hilarious, and extremely well received.

Over the four years since *Gone with the Wind* hit the streets, I have received a lot of unsolicited feedback from both faculty and students regarding my position on offensive humor in the classroom. About 99.99% (margin of error = ± 3 feet) have affirmed that position. The .01% that didn't said, "You're a big fat idiot to ignore that disgusting cesspool of vulgar and profane material that could fill your classroom." I rest my case.

In-Class Topics That Are Not Culture Specific

The content of much of the humor in my books is culture specific. In searching for common denominators between professors and students, I have drawn heavily from material in TV shows, commercials, infomercials, movies, Broadway musicals and plays, and American products and services with which we're all familiar. That furnishes bushels of grist for my jocular mill.

Major limitation: You have to be American or be thoroughly familiar with our culture to understand the humor.

Problem: If you have foreign students in your class or teach courses or present papers at international conferences on foreign topsoil, culture-specific humor will not be understood or be misunderstood. A recent study by McMorris, Kim, and Li (2001) of international students in a large northeastern university found that they appreciated humor in instruction and testing, especially funny comments and stories. When the humor was culture-based, however, the language and cultural barriers often created misunderstanding, frustration, and confusion. When the humor was appropriate and understood, it was an effective tool for teaching.

Solution: Present culture-free humor or humor on topics that are universal, not culture or country specific. This criterion greatly restricts the available pool of material, but it is essential to be sensitive to your students' backgrounds to be successful with your humor. Generic, universal topics for humor would include the following:

- Academic experiences
    - Student life
    - Professorial habits
    - Types of courses
    - Coursework
    - Exams
    - Preparation for theses
    - Policies and practices
    - Technology problems, especially PCs
- Relationships
    - Marriage (Be careful!)
    - Being a parent
    - Living with teenagers
    - Professor-student

- Music
  - Songs by internationally known artists
  - Mega-hit movies (e.g., *Star Wars, Rocky, Titanic*)
  - Musicals on international tours
- Miscellaneous
  - Pets
  - Airlines (Be careful!)
  - Coffee
  - Food
  - Being young
  - Getting old

You need to carefully assess your students' or audience's sociodemographic profile and then select humor material that will be appropriate. (*Note:* If you need to explain a joke to an international student or your audience, that can be a learning experience itself that you may never forget.) It is certainly much more difficult to pick the right stuff for a culturally diverse audience than an American one. But the time invested in editing your material will yield laughter dividends. Several examples for all of the above topics are given in *Gone with the Wind* and in this book.

Before we leave this little section, I strongly caution you to avoid the universal topics of sex, male and female bashing, and spousal put-downs, plus attacks on politicians and international celebrities. Although these relatively culture-free topics often constitute the heart of many stand-up comedians' monologues, they are out-of-bounds offensive material for your students. Also, be especially careful with any airline jokes, particularly those related to security precautions.

Factors That Can Affect Laughter in the Classroom

Although there are several stages or levels of laughter that will be described in Chapter 2, don't lose sight of your goal for laughter in *your* classroom. Your students should be laughing so hard that they exhibit at least one of the following physical signs: (1) burst their guts, (2) rupture key internal organs, (3) wet themselves without the "h," or (4) spurt beverages from their nostrils.

Assuming your humor is thigh-slapping, roll-in-the-aisle, knock-down, drag-out, side-splitting hilarious, what characteristics of you, your class, and your classroom environment can affect the volume and duration of your students' laughter? There are at least five key factors to consider: (1) the physical arrangement of your classroom, (2) class size, (3) class atmosphere, (4) eye contact, and (5) gender. There is a smidgen of research evidence on the first, third, and fourth factors, and a moderate amount on the last.

Physical Arrangements

Professional comedians and psychologists have described the contagiousness of laughter and what some have called the *giggle-fest* phenomenon (Veatch, 1998). Laughter falls within the class of natural, social, following behaviors. That is, people will join in laughing when others in a group are already laughing; laughter feeds on itself and spreads contagiously in a group environment (Søbstad, 2001). It stimulates group imitation similar to smiling, yawning, and fighting (Provine, 1992, 1996).

So how can we infect everyone in our class with the contagion of laughter? Squish your students together. The closer everyone sits next to one another, as opposed to being spread out all over the classroom, the greater the chances of the infection spreading. This is known as the "Sardine-Can Theory of Laughter" (Berk, Is, Nuts, & Sick, 2002a). Physical proximity increases laughter (Aiello, Thompson, & Brodzinsky, 1983; Chapman, 1973, 1975; Søbstad, 1990, 2001). If the seats can be arranged around tables so that groups of students can look at each other, that's even better. Seeing the laughter of others in a close, friendly environment, enhances laughter (Chapman, 1975; Søbstad, 1990).

There are four categories of laughers: (1) those who will laugh at almost anything, (2) marginal laughers who need to be nudged, (3) tough laughers who rarely laugh at anything unless they're stricken by something exceptionally funny or weird, and (4) the nonlaughers who exhibit the emotional range of the zombies in Michael Jackson's video *Thriller*. All of those categories are probably represented in every college classroom.

Student laughter can be maximized by smushing your class into a smaller room that is nearly filled to capacity rather than half full. That physical proximity increases the probability that category one laughers can infect category two and possibly a few category three laughers. Category four is hopeless and unreachable.

Class Size

Laughter is an actively shared, social experience. "Social facilitation drive theory" (Zajonc, 1965) indicates that the reticular system of the brain is activated when other people are present. OWWW! Laughter is 30 times more frequent in social than in solitary situations (Provine, 2000). (*Pop Quiz:* How often do you laugh out loud when you're alone compared to when you're in the company of others? *Answer:* Will be printed upside down at the end of the chapter.) People receive signals or cues of appropriate behavior by seeing and listening to others. Those signals explain the contagiousness of laughter. However, you have to have someone to infect. A class size with $n = 1$ doesn't trigger laughter.

Consider the response difference you receive to a joke when you tell it to one person compared to a group of five. The contagiousness effect is a function of group size (Aiello et al., 1983). How many laughers and marginal laughers could there be even in a doctoral seminar with only 5 to 10 students? In other words, the larger the class, the higher the probability that there will be hordes of laughers spread throughout the class who can infect category two and three laughers. Try telling the same surefire joke to classes of 10, 50, 100, and 500 students. The volume and duration of laughter increases exponentially with significant increases in class size. This effect is generalizable to various sizes of professional audiences as well. Workshops of 30 or fewer participants cannot match the laughter potential of presentations to several hundred or several thousand people.

Classroom Atmosphere

The success of incongruity humor is contingent on a playful setting or context (Alden, Mukherjee, & Hoyer, 2000), mentioned earlier in this chapter. That is, a jocular, playful state of mind is an essential precondition for humor appreciation (McGhee, 1979). There is even evidence that the physical play, shouting, and running found on playgrounds and at sports events promote laughter (Ding & Jersild, 1932; Smith, Foot, & Chapman, 1977). The atmosphere you create in your classroom can significantly affect the students' responsiveness to your humor.

Laughter occurs in casual, relaxed, laugh-ready environments where people feel safe and free to be uninhibited. The tone and mood you set by your own demeanor will transfer to your students. For example, if you are constantly joking and laughing, then your students will react to your banter and playful behavior in kind. However, if you are formal, stiff, and officious, and then say something humorous, your students may not laugh because your inhibited behavior signals it may not be appropriate to laugh. If the joke is told out of context, coming out of nowhere like the *Star Wars* lexicon of "The Force," "Death Star," and "Licensed Merchandise," the students may not even recognize it's a joke.

You have to exhibit a playful state of mind by your actions and words before the students can join in with their minds. That sets the stage for an inhibition-lowered, chuckle-ready class atmosphere that is conducive to fun and plenty of laughter. You just have to bring the humor, your students will supply the laughs.

Eye Contact

Research with young children has demonstrated that eye contact increases laughter (Chapman, 1973, 1975). If those kids are in graduate school now, maybe their behavior is generalizable to college students. That is, student-to-student eye contact, where looking at each other conveys a shared experience, generates more laughter than if that eye contact were not present (Søbstad, 1990, 2001).

Similarly, your deliberate eye contact with your students is a critical physical and mental element in the professor-student connection. It creates a special bonding that can affect how your students respond to anything you do. Your eyeballs are the *plug;* each student's are the *outlet.* When they make contact, the electricity begins to flow. As you walk around the room, each momentary pause of eye contact sends a special psychic message:

What professor sends:	"I'm talking to *you.* This is my best joke material. So please laugh because I will grade your test by hand."
What student receives:	"Oh, you care. That is the sorriest excuse for a joke. It even borders on violating my values, you moron. But I'll laugh anyway because you control my destiny."

Need I say more? But you know I will. That personal connection via eye contact can facilitate positive feedback for your humor. Although laughter can occur in an impersonal, nonconnective relationship with a class, professor-student and student-student eye contact can maximize the laughter as well as other forms of humor support and appreciation (Hay, 2001).

Gender

The research evidence to date indicates that women laugh more than men in response to humor (Bogaers, 1993; Brodzinsky, Barnet, & Aiello, 1981; Cantor; 1970; Dreher, 1982; Easton, 1994; Hay, 2001; Makri-Tsilipakou, 1994; Provine, 2000). Laughter is an emotional response to a stimulus and, in general, women tend to be less inhibited in their display of emotions than men. Men are more guarded and reserved in their emotional reactions and may even intentionally stifle or internalize their responses. Barreca (1991) has gathered truckloads of evidence to explain this gender difference. One of her examples is that women who usually go into public restrooms with other women also exit that way, laughing. Rarely do you ever see men laughing when they walk out of a restroom. Don't even go there, figuratively or literally.

The classroom implication of this behavior is to recruit lots of women into your course if you want to increase the laughter to your jokes. The higher the proportion of women students, the greater are your chances of eliciting laughter.

May I ask you a question? "No!" Why not? "Because I'm a really manly man and I love to laugh." Thanks for that input. There are exceptions to the preceding observations. In fact, the same research that claims women are the laughers also reveals that men are the leading jokesters (Foot & Chapman, 1976). "You're joking." Would I joke in a paragraph like this? Although men laugh less than women, they are more likely to create the humor; they're the best laugh getters. That could explain why most stand-up comedians are men. Also, men usually like to tell formal jokes. A few are story-tellers, such as Bill Cosby and Sinbad. Women, on the other hand, rarely tell jokes; they typically describe situations and stories that are funny.

Now back to my attempted question before I was sidetracked: If women are the most responsive to humor, why are almost all humorous TV commercials directed at men? Aaha! Gotcha! Can you recall a single product for women that has used a humorous advertising strategy? The only semi-jocular one I can remember is Lubriderm®, which is a skin firming lotion. It shows an alligator exercising on a treadmill with several women.

Why doesn't humor sell with women? Advertising executives who test marketing strategies and would-be ads with panels of women or focus groups have found that the funny ad campaigns bombed. Women just don't want to watch them. This response is true even when the product is consumed equally by men and women. And that's not new. Advertising aimed at women has been constantly humorless for at least two generations over the past 50 years. There are at least three explanations:

1. *The products purchased by women aren't inherently funny,* such as household cleansers, packaged foods, body care soaps and creams, feminine hygiene products, and over-the-counter and prescription medications. Check out the ads on "Lifetime," the cable channel billed as Television for Women. They're super serious.

2. *The types of humor used in commercials for men are not appreciated by women.* Men's ads typically involve put-downs, ridicule, sexual innuendo, slapstick, and stupidity. What's wrong with that?

3. *The types of humor appreciated by women have not been tested in commercials.* Who dreams up the humor in TV commercials anyway— men or women? Maybe the humor writers need to be sensitive to non-insulting, non-offensive forms of humor to which women may respond positively.

So what makes men laugh? Talking frogs or lizards or guys who say, "Whassssup?" According to an analysis of men's ads by Forhi (2000), those ads frequently portray men as dorks, doofuses, losers, weirdos, and the butt of just about anything. Men will laugh at other men who fall on their heads or get poked in the eyes (a "Three Stooges" mentality). Women don't laugh when someone is embarrassed or hurt (Barreca, 1991). The men in these ads dress up as walking, talking fruit to sell underwear, parts of a pizza box to sell pizza, and fairies to sell toothpaste. In a Pepsi® commercial a guy is sucked up into a bottle on a beach; in a VISA ad another guy is sucked up into a vacuum cleaner. Commercials on "guy shows," which are those involving a ball, a babe, or bullets (known as "the 3 building blocks of guy humor"), often involve bawdy or rowdy humor. "Sports Center" and "The Man Show" ads as well as those for beer, chips, deodorant, automobiles, computers, and Internet companies may be idiotic, insulting, or utterly indecipherable, but guys seem to find them amusing. Maybe the women have a point!

These gender differences in commercial advertising suggest that what men and women find funny is at the heart of those differences. They're not a function of simply who laughs the most. Barreca (1991) has provided an in-depth analysis of these differences. Even one of America's greatest philosophers, Dave Barry (2000), has recognized that "females tend to reach emotional maturity very quickly, so that by age seven they are no longer capable of seeing the humor in loud inadvertent public blasts of flatulence, whereas males can continue to derive vast enjoyment from this well into their 80s" (p. 211).

Pertinent to the gender composition of college classes, the types of humor that men college students prefer include sexual, sick, cruel, hostile, aggressive, disparagement, and slapstick (Burns, 1998; Herzog, 1999; Herzog & Anderson, 2000; Herzog & Karafa, 1998; Herzog & Larwin, 1988; Mundorf, Bhatia, Zillmann, Lester, & Robertson, 1988; Prerost, 1984; Ruch & Hehl, 1988). There is evidence that women college students enjoy sexual (even private parts) and hostile humor when the male is the victim, but not when the female is the victim, and nontendentious jokes (as opposed to tendentious ones that express hostile and aggressive feelings) (Herzog, 1999; Herzog & Anderson, 2000; Herzog & Karafa, 1998). Women are especially and exclusively sensitive to any form of humor that is demeaning to their own gender.

Virtually all of these types of humor, except slapstick and nontendentious jokes, satisfy the previous criteria for offensive, out-of-bounds humor for the college classroom. Excluding the preceding gender differences in humor appreciation reduces the humor playing field to nonoffensive categories that *may* be preferred by women, but also appreciated by many men. Since women are the laughers, they may be the best gauge of our success with those categories of classroom humor.

Summary

This concludes my evidence-based review of the current state of the art of laughter in the college classroom. We have finally come to the *denouement* (a French word meaning, literally, "laughing makes me whet my curiosity"). What can be gleaned from our knowledge about the preceding five characteristics? How can we maximize the laughter response to our classroom humor?

> *Solution:* Smush a large class of thousands of women students into a room with just enough comfortable chairs, facing each other in small groups, peer into each one's eyeballs, and joke around until everyone's relaxed and in a playful, laugh-ready mood.

If any one of those characteristics is missing from your class, you're in trouble with a little "t." But that's okay. Rarely can you hand pick your students, classroom, and furniture. However, being sensitive to all of these characteristics and the types of humor you use can significantly increase your humor success.

Alternatively, there are only two other methods you might want to consider to produce hysteria in your classroom: (1) suck helium and deliver a lecture sounding like Cartman on *South Park* or (2) pump nitrous oxide (laughing gas) into your class. At least, that class will be memorable.

How Do You Learn to Be Funny?

After all that's been said so far about the formulas and forms of humor, the caveats regarding offensive humor, and the factors that affect laughter, now what you need is something funny to present. Much has been written on how to write and perform stand-up comedy. The excellent books by Steve Allen (1998), Mel Helitzer (1987), Gene Perret (1982a, 1982b, 1990, 1993, 1998), and Mary Ann Rishel (2002) provide practical guidelines, techniques, tricks of the trade, and resources derived from a zillion years of experience. But recently, there is a growing body of research that furnishes *evidence-based comedy techniques* for being funny. And the best part is that they can be learned. Now don't make the inferential leap or even hop that anyone can become the next Robin Williams, Steve Martin, Billy Crystal, or Anne "Weakest Link" Robinson. One's God-given gifts, talents, and creativity play a major role in your comedic potential. However, the strategy described in this section may provide the opportunity you've always wanted to take your sense of humor out for a spin.

Selectionist Approach

Several studies conducted by Dewitte and Verguts (2001) have tested a *selectionist approach* to producing jokes and being funny, which is kind of a "survival of the best jokes" evolutionary process. The approach boils down to the following steps:

1. Generate a large pool of jokes.
2. Practice them.
3. Test them out.
4. Fine tune them.
5. Select the best ones.
6. Get a job at a comedy club.
7. Leave academia.
8. Star in your own sitcom.
9. Become rich and famous.
10. Totally forget that this page was responsible for your success.

This process will yield a repertoire of jokes which are funny, plus a new career.

Frequency and sensitivity.   Two variables are critical to learning this process:

a. *Joking frequency*—making many jokes creates a large variety of jokes from which the good ones are retained and the bad ones eliminated; this facilitates the *quality* of the humor; and

b. *Sensitivity to social responses*—jokes are shaped according to the responses of the social environment, that is, positive and negative feedback, such as not violating the norms, values, and moral principles of your students.

The non-funny professor is often the one who produces and tells many jokes, but does not fine tune them based on students' responses. He or she is insensitive to feedback and will keep repeating the same dumb jokes year after year even if students do not smile or laugh.

Sensitivity to positive feedback or reinforcement of effective jokes enhances joking *frequency*. Those cartoons, multiple-choice jokes, and top 10 lists that elicit outbreaks of laughter in your class contribute to the select group of winners. On the other hand, *sensitivity to negative feedback,* such as no laughter, groans, total silence, complaints of offensiveness, or thrown fruit and vegetables, enhances joking *quality*. Be sensitive to your students' responses to each cartoon, each choice in the multiple-choice joke, and each entry in the top 10. You may need to duck occasionally to avoid being hit by flying objects. But based on the students' negative reactions, you will be able to revise and constantly try out new wordings or discard and substitute new material to test with your students.

This fine-tuning process can continue forever. I am never satisfied with the "quality" of the material I present. What complicates this process are the different responses to the same jokes you can receive from different classes. Creating universally hilarious jokes is nearly impossible. Among all of the material I've written and tested, very few jokes satisfy the "universal" criterion.

Dewitte and Verguts (2001) summarize their selectionist framework as follows: *"One can become a good joker only by trying out many jokes and being sensitive to negative social reactions"* (p. 51, ital added).

Classroom Application

Gone with the Wind supplies joke prototypes, techniques for writing and presenting humor in your classroom, and loads of pretested, surefire joke material. This chapter and the succeeding ones furnish humor formulas, examples, and over 100 pretested multiple-choice format jokes. All of this is designed to give you a jumpstart to test drive any of that material in your own classes. Using the selectionist approach, after you've tested something that hits your fancy, retain, revise, or reject it based on your students' reactions, positive and negative, then retest, retain, revise, or reject and so on, forever.

Eventually, you will build your own stockpile of jokes as you are honing your joke delivery skills. But I wouldn't quit my day job yet. Teaching and learning will take on completely new meanings. Writing humor and being funny are the mechanisms for bringing deadly content to life and making it palatable for the most motivationally challenged student in your class. They also make learning fun and effective for most everyone.

Evaluating the Effectiveness of Humor Strategies

Every humorous teaching and assessment technique described in this book and in *Gone with the Wind* has been evaluated by my undergraduate and graduate students over several years. Our students are in the best position to assess the effectiveness of *how* we teach and test. Since each humor strategy has a specific intended instructional outcome, its effectiveness can be measured.

Ideally, a randomized-groups design with a "serious" or traditional control can test the relative effectiveness of a humorous intervention. Pre- and posttesting both class samples can assess performance and attitude differences using analysis of covariance (ANCOVA). Essentially, this is an in-class "clinical trial" of a humor treatment.

Unfortunately, this control is rarely feasible due to course scheduling limitations, classroom unavailability, professorial resistance/reluctance, and/or inadequate class size ($n \leq 100$ before being randomly divided). There are two other more practical, though scientifically less rigorous, evaluation methods you might want to consider: (1) a pretest-posttest one-sample design without a control or (2) single-shot student ratings of effectiveness. The former involves administering pre and post measures related to the outcomes of the humor, such as achievement, attitude, and anxiety. My previous top 10 humor strategies (see Berk, 1997, 1998c) were designed to change performance and behavior on those constructs. A study was conducted to assess the statistical and practical/substantive significance of the gains in achievement and improvements in attitude and anxiety (Berk & Nanda, 1998). Determining the magnitude of the changes in terms of effect size is especially important to examine the impact of the strategies.

The simplest and most feasible approach to obtaining feedback on effectiveness is to ask your students directly. They will honestly tell you what works and what doesn't and throw in a few suggestions to boot. One method to gather this information is to build a formal rating scale with structured and unstructured items, assure complete anonymity and confidentiality of responses, administer it using standardized procedures, and analyze the results by item, subscale, and scale.

This procedure was used to evaluate the use of humor in teaching strategies (Berk, 1996b), music/music with demonstrations (Berk, 2001b), and humor in course tests (Berk, 2000a). A step-by-step description of how to construct an appropriate rating scale with examples from the three aforementioned studies is presented next.

Scale Construction

Given the time crunch of squeezing any in-class exercise into your class schedule and the need for valid and reliable ratings from which we can infer the degree of effectiveness of how we use humor, the following process is suggested.

Directions.   State the purpose of the scale in terms of measuring specific instructional outcomes. Indicate a commitment to anonymity and confidentiality of responses. Tell students how to respond or mark their answers. Consider the following examples:

Teaching Strategies

Directions: The purpose of this scale is to evaluate whether the Ronmeister's use of humor was effective in improving your ability to learn and perform in this course and reducing your anxiety about the subject matter. Please do not put your name or any other identifying information on this scale. All individual responses should be anonymous and will be kept confidential. Circle the number corresponding to your response from among the following categories:

Music

Directions: The purpose of this scale is to evaluate whether our hero's (Yeah right!) use of music was effective in grabbing your attention, increasing your interest, reducing anxiety/stress, and making class fun. Circle the number corresponding to your response from among the following categories:

Directions: The purpose of this scale is to evaluate whether my use of music and visual demonstrations helped you learn statistics. Rate the effectiveness of the music-demo in facilitating your understanding, memory, and application of the statistic by circling the number of your response from among the following categories:

Testing

Directions: The purpose of this scale is to evaluate my use of humor in your tests. Please indicate the degree to which you agree or disagree with each statement below. There are no right or wrong responses, so please answer honestly. Your answers should be anonymous and will remain confidential. Circle the number corresponding to your response from among the following:

Response anchors.   Since *degree of effectiveness* is being measured, a five-point anchored scale was used for most of the evaluations. It provided a high level of discrimination for determining effectiveness by college students. The anchors were introduced just below the directions as follows:

> 0 = Ineffective (**IE**)
> 1 = Somewhat Effective (**SE**)
> 2 = Moderately Effective (**ME**)
> 3 = Very Effective (**VE**)
> 4 = Extremely Effective (**EE**)

The teaching strategies, music, and testing studies used this effectiveness scale. The humor in testing studies also employed a four-point agree-disagree continuum to pinpoint particular uses and feelings about the humor. That anchor format is shown below:

> 0 = Strongly Disagree (**SD**)
> 1 = Disagree (**D**)
> 2 = Agree (**A**)
> 3 = Strongly Agree (**SA**)

Instructional outcomes.   In addition to briefly mentioning the outcomes in the directions, they need to be identified on the scale. To rate the effectiveness of the humor strategies, each outcome designated a separate subscale. So the strategies were rated based on the extent to which they were effective in achieving each outcome. The outcomes at the beginning of the three subscales appeared as follows:

Subscale 1:   How effective was each of the following in **REDUCING YOUR ANXIETY IN THE COURSE?**

Subscale 2:   How effective was each of the following in **IMPROVING YOU'RE ABILITY TO LEARN THE CONTENT?**

Subscale 3:   How effective was each of the following in **MAKING IT POSSIBLE FOR YOU TO PERFORM YOUR BEST ON EXAMS?**

The music effectiveness scales presented the outcomes across the top of the scale with the abbreviated anchors below. In this case every piece of

music or music-demo was rated for effectiveness according to each outcome. Examples are given below:

Grabbed Your Attention	Increased *Interest* in Class/Topic	Relaxed or Reduced *Anxiety/Stress* in Class/Topic	Made Class/Topic/Learning *Fun*
IE SE ME VE EE	IE SE ME VE EE	IE SE ME VE EE	IE SE ME VE EE

Facilitating your *understanding* of the statistic	Helping you to *remember* the stat. concept/process	Helping you to *learn* the stat. when you applied it to the problems
IE SE ME VE EE	IE SE ME VE EE	IE SE ME VE EE

The humor in testing scale outcomes were designated differently than the
preceding. Since an agree-disagree continuum was used, the items themselves
contained the criteria or outcomes being rated. The specific uses of humor and
the students' feelings about them will be illustrated in the next section on
"Items." The targets of the evaluation were embedded in the items.

Items.   The items for the scale are displayed as the list of strategies, music,
or statements about humor in the tests that students are asked to rate. The
items comprise *what* you are evaluating in your teaching or testing. They are
the humor techniques. A few examples are given next.

Teaching Strategies

1. How effective was each of the following in **REDUCING YOUR ANXIETY IN THE COURSE?**	IE	SE	ME	VE	EE
a. humorous material on syllabus	0	1	2	3	4
b. opening joke/skit in each class	0	1	2	3	4
c. in-class spontaneous humor	0	1	2	3	4
d. in-class humorous examples	0	1	2	3	4
e. in-class humorous questions	0	1	2	3	4
f. humorous problem sets	0	1	2	3	4
g. humorous material on covers of handouts	0	1	2	3	4
h. *"Jeopardy!"* type reviews	0	1	2	3	4
i. humorous material on exams	0	1	2	3	4
j. open-everything exam format	0	1	2	3	4
k. OVERALL EFFECTIVENESS in reducing your anxiety	0	1	2	3	4

Music

Music (Topic)	Grabbed Your Attention					Relaxed or Reduced *Interest* Increased *Interest* in Class/Topic					Your Anxiety/Stress in Class/Topic					Made Class/Topic/ Learning *Fun*				
	IE	*SE*	*ME*	*VE*	*EE*	*IE*	*SE*	*ME*	*VE*	*EE*	*IE*	*SE*	*ME*	*VE*	*EE*	*IE*	*SE*	*ME*	*VE*	*EE*
1. *Masterpiece Theatre* (Freq. Distrib.)	0	1	2	3	4	0	1	2	3	4	0	1	2	3	4	0	1	2	3	4
2. *The X-Files* (Central Tendency)	0	1	2	3	4	0	1	2	3	4	0	1	2	3	4	0	1	2	3	4
3. *The Odd Couple* (Correlation)	0	1	2	3	4	0	1	2	3	4	0	1	2	3	4	0	1	2	3	4
4. *Mission: Impossible* (Linear Regression)	0	1	2	3	4	0	1	2	3	4	0	1	2	3	4	0	1	2	3	4
5. *"YMCA"* (ANOVA)	0	1	2	3	4	0	1	2	3	4	0	1	2	3	4	0	1	2	3	4

Testing

Items	SD	D	A	SA
1. Humor in the test directions reduced my initial anxiety.	0	1	2	3
2. The humorous items helped me perform my best.	0	1	2	3
3. The humorous items were distracting.	0	1	2	3
4. The humorous items reduced my anxiety.	0	1	2	3
5. The humorous items were confusing.	0	1	2	3
6. Humorous items should be included on the next test.	0	1	2	3

Comments/suggestions.   In addition to the structured part of scale, there should be an unstructured, open-ended section to elicit comments about the humor or techniques and also suggestions for new methods, music, demonstrations, etc. This anecdotal information often explains high or low ratings and can guide changes in existing strategies or indicate some you may not have considered. This section should be tacked on the bottom of the scale after the last item. Either leave two open sections with the headings COMMENTS and SUGGESTIONS, or direct the students' responses more specifically with the following:

Comments on use of music:

Suggested music:

Scale Administration

The timing of the scale administration is crucial to the validity of the ratings. Two key concerns are response rate and accuracy of responses. To maximize the response rate, administer the scale on a day when you expect high attendance such as the first exam. Kidding. The next best choice is the day of the test review. Use class time and communicate how important the students' feedback is on planning your instructional techniques, use of music, or inserting humor in the test items.

Accuracy of the responses is a function of *when* the scale is administered, the students' truthfulness or honesty, and response bias, such as "acquiescence" or "halo." One problem with humor strategies, music, demonstrations, and other in-class experiences is that students may forget them or miss the class(es) when they were presented. Unless you are measuring strategies that are used throughout the course, an end-of-course administration only may be inadequate. To evaluate specific one-shot musical selections or skits, for example, I administer two scales, one before or after the midterm and the second before the final. Further, I identify each entry to be rated with the content topic with which it was associated. The previous listing of music items includes the topics in parentheses. This helps jar the students' memories.

As for the students' truthfulness and response bias, anonymity permits them total latitude and their comments usually suggest their "true" feelings. My students do not seem to hold back their opinions about anything I do. Although there may be a "halo" or *Touched by an Angel* effect from one activity they really like to another that may be less exciting, the variance in responses and the volume of comments and suggestions I receive indicate that bias may be negligible.

Scale Scoring and Analysis

Depending on class size, you can either manually score the scales ($n < 10$) or optically scan the scales using separate answer sheets by Scantron or NCS or a TELEform version of the scale. Using the latter makes it possible to scan the sheets and export the results to MS-Access, then to Excel, and open the data with numerical item responses, such as 0 to 4, so they can be analyzed with SPSS, SAS, or any other statistical package.

Since the anchors to which the students respond represent an ordinal, qualitative scale (*Note:* The quantitative scale is just a dummy numerical coding scheme to statistically analyze the anchor responses) and the item, subscale, and scale score distributions are typically skewed, the most appropriate statistics are percentages responding to each anchor and item, subscale, and scale median scores. It is the item anchor percentages and median that indicate the effectiveness rating for each teaching strategy or musical selection. Examples of how to present and interpret the statistics can be found in the articles cited previously and in Chapters 3 and 8.

2

THE ACTIVE INGREDIENTS
IN HUMOR AND LAUGHTER

> **Dedication:** This chapter is dedicated to the undergraduate men and women who unselfishly contributed their spit and blood for chemical analysis and their heart rate, blood pressure, temperature, respiration, brain, skin, and liver in the name of laughter research. Some were even asked to stick their hands in ice water until their digits became popsicles to measure pain thresholds. Special recognition should also be given to all of the control-group participants who had to endure boring, dreary films about rock formations or growing grass without time-lapse photography, or Bob Dole's home movies, while the treatment groups laughed their guts out watching Richard Pryor, Billy Crystal, Bill Cosby, Gallagher, or Lily Tomlin comedy tapes.

Much of the healthcare literature and popular media have communicated that many of the psychological and physiological benefits of humor and laughter are similar to the health benefits of aerobic exercise, such as sweating, gasping for air, athlete's foot, and getting to wear expensive sneakers. Unfortunately, those benefits still seem to be some of the best kept secrets from those of us who have so much to gain from that information—professors and students. The anxiety, tension, stress, and irregularity that we experience in academe can be decreased by using humor in and out of the classroom. Further, as the aging process takes its toll on our minds and bodies, we become geezoids, shriveled up caricatures of our former selves seeking new ways to "deal" because we will be experiencing more close encounters of the medical kind than any other. Seriously, professors and students who already must live with chronic pain, arthritis, rheumatism, emphysema, memory loss, and depression may be able to cope better with their conditions or find temporary relief by using humor and laughter.

The 1998 film *Patch Adams* (based on Adams, 1998) renewed interest in the effectiveness of laughter as a treatment for many psychological and physiological problems. However, Robin Williams' one fleeting line in the movie citing its therapeutic benefits was heard for less than five seconds. Similarly on TV when PBS (which stands for National Football League) programs their annual fund-raising campaign, occasionally they feature a humorist, such as Loretta LaRoche or Dom Perignon, who may refer to the stress-reduction benefits of lightening up and using humor. "Dom Perignon is a champagne, you idiot." Oops. Further, "health watch" newsletters published by healthcare systems, insurance companies, and hospitals, which are regularly mailed to the general public, rarely alert readers to the health benefits of laughter (Berk, 1999b). Occasionally though, an Internet newsletter for a professional readership, such as *WorldHealthNEWS,* will publish a monthly humor column that addresses those benefits (Berk, 2000b; *www.medcareers.com*). However, based on what is currently known about the health benefits of laughter, they are certainly worthy of more attention than they have received in movies, television, and healthcare publications.

The purpose of this chapter is fivefold: (1) to propose a model of humor research, (2) to provide an up-to-date, comprehensive synthesis of the research evidence on 15 psychological and physiological benefits of humor/laughter, (3) to describe the physiological risks, (4) to discuss the implications of the benefits for teaching and testing, and (5) to provide script material for my first sitcom, starring Steve Martin and Rosie O'Donnell. This chapter extends previous work (Berk, 2001a) that ranked 10 on the Berko *Snor-O-Matic®* scale.

Model of Humor Research

You probably remember that Chris Columbus rented three ships to sail to the New World: the Nina, the Queen Isabella II Royal Caribbean, and the Goodship Lollipop. After numerous stormy weeks on the Atlantic, Columbus and his mariners finally arrived at Plymouth Rock. One mariner suggested, "Hey, Bubba, maybe we should take a compass next time." The other mariners just dropped to their knees, and drawing on what inner strength they had left, threw up. A few years later, the Pilgrims, who used a different travel agent, sailed across the Atlantic searching for a place to starve to death. These events paved the way for the throbbing tourist industry in Williamsburg, VA. "Timeout. Bucko, that story was very informative, but what does it have to do with the topic of this section?" Hmmmmm. I forgot. Oh, it's the three ships. I guess I got a little carried away.

Coincidentally, the psychophysiological research on humor also partitions the "humor process" into three elements: (a) the stimulus (humor), (b) the emotional response (mirth), and (c) the physical response or behavior (laughter). The relationships among the elements of the S→R humor process and their psychophysiological effects are depicted in Figure 2.1.

Exposure to a humorous stimulus, such as a joke or funny situation, can produce two types of responses, one emotional and the other physical. The emotional responses are referred to as *mirth* (derived from the Greek word, "bonsai," meaning, "broccoli stuck in dirt"). They are measurable as psychological effects. The research on those effects is reviewed in the next section. The physical responses, which are the most visible, may range from a "smirk" to "die laughing." These responses are different forms or stages of *laughter*, which have been studied as physiological effects. Most of them are positive (i.e., benefits), but, believe it or not, a few are negative (i.e., risks), even dangerous. These effects will be examined in a subsequent section.

When we react to a joke or observe someone else's reaction, there is a complex set of psychophysiological responses occurring contemporaneously with pretentious polysyllabic words. How could anyone write a sentence like that? Some of these effects may be very dramatic, while others are very subtle. There is no consistent or predictable pattern of responses to a joke in any group of people or livestock. Consequently, we can expect to see a wide range of responses in our classes: one student may guffaw so hard that she hawks up a lung, while another student exhibits the emotional expression of plywood. The less visible psychological effects are described next.

FIGURE 2.1   The S→R humor process and its psychophysiological effects.

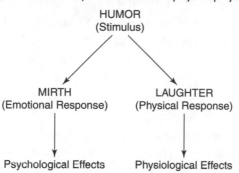

Psychological Benefits

Nearly a century ago, Kline (1907) stated that the largest psychological function of humor is

> [T]o detach us from our world of good and evil, of loss and gain, and enable us to see it in proper perspective. It frees us from vanity on the one hand and from pessimism on the other by keeping us larger than what we do and greater than what can happen to us. (p. 438)

Role of Detachment

First, you should know that *detachment* is derived from two Latin root words, "de," meaning, "remove," and "tachmentus," meaning, "this tire iron from my skull." It is one of the most effective techniques for coping with the day-to-day problems you must tackle as an academician. Using humor to distance yourself from professional as well as personal problem situations enables you to detach or disengage mentally, albeit temporarily escape from reality. It puts those situations into a proper perspective. However, this moment of fantasy doesn't mean it's okay to have an imaginary, inflatable, or stalk-eyed, oval-headed alien friend. So you're going to have to dispose of Orville.

This function of *detachment,* which considers humor as an adaptive coping mechanism, underlies the research on the psychological effects. It is also the conceptualization of humor adopted by psychological theorists such as Sigmund Freud, Gordon Allport, Rollo May, and Frasier Crane:

- Humor is "the highest of [the] defensive processes" (Freud, 1960, p. 233).

- "The essence of humor is that one spares oneself the affects to which the situation would naturally give rise and overrides with a jest the possibility of such an emotional display" (Freud, 1959, p. 216).

- "The neurotic who learns to laugh at himself may be on the way to self-management, perhaps to cure" (Allport, 1950, p. 92).

- Humor has the function of "preserving the sense of self . . . It is the healthy way of feeling a 'distance' between one's self and the problem, a way of standing off and looking at one's problem with perspective" (May, 1953, p. 61).

- "Humor has made it possible for me to make Dumpsters of dough over the past decade" (Frasier Crane, personal communication with Niles, June 2002).

Using humor involves a cognitive shift in perspective that allows one to distance oneself from the immediate threat of a problem situation; that is, view it from a different frame of reference, and reduce the negative feelings that would normally occur (Dixon, 1980; Kuhlman, 1984; O'Connell, 1976) Within this context, the humor serves both as a *response* to a problem stimulus and as a *stimulus* to trigger an emotional response, consistent with the S→R model of the humor process presented previously.

This psychological interpretation of humor consists of three components: (1) the *problem stimulus,* which is the problem situation or external stressor, (2) the *humor response,* which is the cognitive shift in perspective or cerebral process that enables one to separate mentally from the problem, and (3) the *emotional response,* which is the outcome feeling from that separation. A more detailed description is given next.

Problem Stimulus

The problem stimulus may be any uncomfortable or threatening situation encountered inside or outside the classroom. From a student's perspective, that stimulus may be *you,* the topic being covered, a test, projects due or past due, other students, or bats flying around the room, as well as the day-to-day stressors of life, such as a deranged roommate or significant other, wild and crazy children, tuition bills larger than the GNP of Bolivia, or a pile of dirty laundry the height of Everest. The most important question is not whether these "realities" of life will occur, but how will we respond to them?

Stimuli in the classroom that can shoot students' anxiety, tension, and stress levels through the roof include simple expressions we use, such as:

- Don't worry . . .
- It's only . . .
- You need to memorize . . .
- This assignment should only take ? hours to complete
- I don't give "As"
- I usually grade on a curve
- I will assign you into groups of four for the next project
- I'm not pleased with the grades on the exam/projects/essays
- You will be responsible for all of the readings . . .
- Next Wednesday will be your first test
- This exam/project is only 50% of your grade
- You will be sequestered until . . .

We, of course, have our own list of stimuli that can produce anxiety, tension, stress, and even burnout:

- Teaching load
- Publishing
- Presenting
- Obtaining external funding
- Attending meetings
- Chairing meetings
- Student evaluations
- Peer evaluations
- Annual review/evaluations for promotion
- Being traded to the Washington Redskins

Humor Response

The humor response is the adaptive detachment or coping mechanism that permits one to deal more effectively with the preceding aversive experiences. Wooten (1996) views humor as a self-care tool to cope with life stressors. Stepping back and seeing humor in a situation liberates you from your own emotional reactions to that situation. It promotes a sense of objectivity that buffers the negative emotional responses (Galloway & Cropley, 1999). Although humor may not always eliminate the responses, at least it can temporarily help you suppress them.

You can easily test your ability to use humor to detach the next time you attend a meeting. You do go to meetings, right? Try having an out-of-meeting experience. I don't mean drifting or sleeping. Imagine yourself levitating above your colleagues, looking down below at them, and observing how hilarious they can be as they "seriously" argue, complain, whine, scream, and smack each other. This source of entertainment is our secret, so please don't tell anyone.

Emotional Response

The emotional response to an uncomfortable or threatening situation is typically negative. There may be feelings of shame, embarrassment, anxiety, tension, stress, depression, helplessness, loneliness, escape, anger, frustration, hostility, low self-esteem, grief, and incontinence. These undesirable negative feelings can be very scary, in fact, similar to that experienced while watching a colonoscopy being performed on a 500-pound Sumo wrestler who had just won a burrito-eating contest. The intervening humor response to problem stimuli can significantly reduce the impact and possibly paralyzing effects of those negative reactions.

Frequently, we can become submerged so deeply IN the problem that we can't even see the problem. We can drown in the problem without being aware of any visible means of escape. We can only respond with negative feelings. Those feelings can cripple our ability to function (a.k.a. "do our job"). In fact, psychiatrists like Dr. Niles Crane report that people with severe mental disorders, such as Michael Myers, Norman Bates, and the guests on *The Jerry Springer Show,* usually lack a sense of humor. They can't detach from their immediate problems.

Humor can jolt us out of our habitual frame of mind, thereby decreasing or eliminating the negative feelings. Humor can be a powerful antidote. In this case, being "out of your mind" promotes a sense of control, self-protection, empowerment, and superiority OVER the problem. In other words, *you* rule. *You* da man or woman. You're Rambo in the classroom.

This effect of humor has been adapted by some psychiatrists in their therapeutic treatment of people with a variety of mental disorders. One technique is called "paradoxical therapy." It has been used with people who are locked inside their problems, unable to look at their problems from a distance, much less laugh. The psychiatrist uses hyperbole, exaggerating the person's problem to such an extreme that he or she will eventually laugh at the problem. This technique creates the detachment between person and problem necessary to begin working toward a solution.

Using humor in your academic life can even help prevent burnout. Burnout is caused by a sense of powerlessness, such as when your teenage daughter goes on vacation with *her* friends and *your* credit cards. That is just the right time you need to laugh. Ha ha ha. Then the detachment mechanism kicks in and you're able to gain control over the situation, at least mentally. Your ability to detach can increase your resilience to the dangerously high levels of stress that lead to burnout (Talbot & Lumden, 2000). *Remember:* Although you may not be able to control what's thrown on your academic plate, you don't have to swallow everything. You *can* control how you view and respond to every entrée. If you don't, some institutions known for devouring their young will eat you up and spit you out.

Consider the following graphic example to illustrate the preceding three stages:

1. *Problem stimulus*—Prostate Exam
2. *Humor response*

   Patient: "Yiiikes! Is it still the size of the Goodyear Blimp?"

   Urologist: "Oh, it's not that large."

   Patient: "Duuuuuh!"

3. *Emotional response*—Reduces anxiety, tension, loneliness (kidding!), and hostility, but doesn't put a dent in embarrassment

If you can't relate to this example, try this less formal one. Imagine playing the jester role of Hawkeye Pierce on *M*A*S*H* in your department or school. Some of you may have already assumed that role. Hawkeye's constant joking with his colleagues and patients, even the banter in the operating room, permitted him to distance himself from his primary stressor, the Korean War. (*Note:* "banter" is derived from the French word, *kibbitz,* meaning literally, "to torment Frank Burns.") You too can derive that coping benefit from banter with your faculty, administrators, secretaries, and students. Although your banter may be annoying to a few of the bantees, especially those who are humor impaired, its therapeutic value to you may be worth that cost.

In summary, there are eight major psychological benefits of humor for which there is quantitative and/or qualitative research evidence. There are five that lessen negative reactions by reducing anxiety, tension, stress, depression, and loneliness. Three benefits have positive effects by improving self-esteem, restoring hope and energy, and providing a sense of empowerment and control. (See research citations on these benefits at the end of the chapter.)

Physiological Benefits

In addition to all of the psychological benefits, there are significant physiological benefits. Before examining those benefits, however, let's consider why professors and students laugh.

Reasons for Laughter

Laughter is an instinctive behavior (Provine, 2000). No one taught us how to laugh. "But why do we laugh?" It's a vocal signal to communicate *safety*. A smile is a derived visual symbol with the same meaning. In other words, when we laugh or just smile, the message we convey is: "Relax, have no fear, I like you and I will not hurt you unless you don't return my Weedwacker® by tomorrow."

There are at least six different reasons people laugh, each one of which says: It's safe to laugh—the coast is clear. Laughter may be provoked by any of the following:

1. A joke, story, anecdote, or hilarious situation, such as the following: Which T-shirt expression should be worn by your dean?

    A. Objects Under This T-Shirt Are Larger Than They Appear

    B. Don't Sweat the Petty Things or Pet the Sweaty Things

    C. Since I Gave Up Hope, I Feel Much Better

    D. No, I'm Not on Steroids, But Thanks for Asking

    E. The Beatings Will Continue Until Morale Improves

    F. All of the Above

2. Triumph or victory in a competitive event that evokes a feeling of superiority, such as the Aussie Olympic triathletes' in the 2000 Olympics triumphant swim to avoid being consumed as buffet entrées by Great Whites in Sydney Harbour (now that is cause for chortling)

3. Play activities or relaxation, such as vacationing in Kuala Lumpur or rock climbing like Tom Cruise at the beginning of *Mission: Impossible 2* (*Note:* I am actually somewhat of a climber myself. On occasion, at the risk of considerable personal discomfort, I have bypassed elevators in my building and ascended to the second or even third floor via the stairs. "You're mother must be very proud." She is.)

4. Artificial kiss-up or face-saving response to an unfunny joke by a person in a "superior" position, a colleague, friend or relative, significant other, or mafia boss

5. Concealing shyness or embarrassment or expressing nervousness, contempt, or hostility in the course of a conversation (laughter that seems to occur for no apparent reason)

6. Tickling those parts of the body that have protective reflexes, such as the sole of your foot, armpit, kneepit, wattle, gizzard, or bladder

Laughter may also be produced (or reproduced) by hearing other people laugh, unprovoked, like yawning (see Chapter 1). It's contagious. Simply the sound of laughter triggers others to laugh. Ed McMahon on the previous edition of the *Tonight Show* with Johnny Carson and Kevin Eubanks on the current Jay Leno version stimulated laughter because their laugh was infectious. The early use of laugh tracks on TV sitcoms was designed to make us laugh. Now we hear the laughter from live studio audiences.

Stages/Grades of Laughter

Provine and Fischer (1989) have defined a *laugh* as "an explosive and often recurrent exhalation that produces a loud and destructive sound, usually as an expression of merriment" (p. 296). But this may be an oversimplification. For example, humorist James Thurber noted that "there are a dozen different kinds [of laughter], from the inner and inaudible to the guffaw" (Rosen, 1989, p. 229). Stages and numerous, distinct grades of laughter have been identified.

The physical act of laughing can affect the entire body. Consider Kuhn's (1994) surgical dissection of laughter into the following 15 stages:

1. **Smirk:** Slight, often fleeting upturning of the corners of the mouth, completely voluntary and controllable.

2. **Smile:** Silent, voluntary and controllable, more perceptible than a smirk.

3. **Grin:** Silent, controllable, but uses more facial muscles (e.g., eyes begin to narrow).

4. **Snicker:** First emergence of sound with facial muscles, but still controllable (if you hold in a snicker, it builds up gas).

5. **Giggle:** Has a 50% chance of reversal to avoid a full laugh; sound of giggling is amusing; efforts to suppress it tend to increase its strength.

6. **Chuckle:** Involves chest muscles with deeper pitch.

7. **Chortle:** Originates even deeper in chest and involves muscles of torso; usually provokes laughter in others.

8. **Laugh:** Involves facial and thoracic muscles as well as abdomen and extremities; sound of barking or snorting.

9. **Cackle:** First involuntary stage; pitch is higher and body begins to rock, spine extends and flexes, with an upturning of head.

10. **Guffaw:** Full body response; feet stomp, arms wave, thighs slapped, torso rocks, sound is deep and loud; may result in free flowing of tears, increased heart rate, and breathlessness; strongest solitary laughter experience.

11. **Howl:** Volume and pitch rise higher and higher and body becomes more animated.

12. **Shriek:** Greater intensity than howl; sense of helplessness and vulnerability.

13. **Roar:** Lose individuality; audience roars!

14. **Convulse:** Body is completely out of control in a "fit" of laughter resembling a seizure; extremities flail aimlessly, balance is lost, gasp for breath, collapse or fall off chair.

15. **Die laughing:** Instant of total helplessness; a brief, physically intense, transcendent experience; having died, we are thereafter "reborn" in a refreshing moment of breathlessness and exhaustion with colors more vivid and everything sparkling; everything is renewed. (Adapted from pp. 34–35).

Another physical partitioning of laughter has been presented by Kehl (2000) who delineated six categories of laughter and diversified grades within those categories. A full spectrum of grades is described in terms of tenor and intensity within the context of modern American literature. Those grades are briefly defined below:

1. **Inner and Inaudible Laughter**

   Simper: smile in a silly, self-conscious way; incipient laugh about to break forth into sound.

   Smirk: similar to a smile, but carries smugness and offensive familiarity.

   Sneer: derisive smile, showing scorn and contempt with a curling of the upper lip.

2. **Half-Suppressed, Restrained Laughs**

   Snicker/Snigger: sly, covert or partly stifled, indecorous, disrespectful, snide, even derisive laugh.

   Titter: half-suppressed, restrained laugh usually suggestive of nervousness, silliness, self-consciousness, or affectation.

   Giggle: series of rapid, usually high-pitched, convulsive, uncontrollable, short catches of breath or gasps when one is nervous, embarrassed, or attempting to suppress mirth.

3. **Soft and Subdued Laughs**

   Chuckle: quiet, low-toned, sometimes barely audible laugh of mild amusement, suppressed mirth, or satisfaction; laugh softly, often inwardly to oneself, objectifying personal, private conditions.

   Chortle: combination of chuckle and snort; a gleeful, chuckling, snorting sound, suggesting satisfaction, even exultation.

4. **Loud, Excessive, Unrestrained Laughs**

   Cackle: loud, excessive, unrestrained laugh.

   Cachinnation: long, hard, excessively loud, immoderate and convulsive laugh.

   Bellow: a loud, heart burst of laughter, similar to the boff or boffo.

   Bellylaugh: hearty as the boffo, but deeper, more resonant and jovial, less explosive.

   Guffaw: loudness and heartiness of the bellylaugh, the explosiveness of the boffo, but possesses boisterousness and coarseness, unrestrained.

   Horselaugh: crude, gross, usually derisive, often bitter edge.

5. **Laughs Associated with Black Humor**

   Crack-up: laugh out loud unrestrainedly; to roll in the aisle uncontrollably.

   Howl/Yowl: loud, scornful laugh.

Roar: loud, prolonged burst of boisterous laughter.

Hoot: laugh or shout derisively in association with scorn, disapproval, or objection.

Shriek: loud, high-pitched, piercing, shrill sound, usually wild and involuntary, of a person in terror, anguish, pain or laughter.

6. **Louder-Than-Life Olympian Laugh**

Olympian Laugh: gargantuan laugh, unrestrained and long-sustained, exalted, majestic, grand, imposing, deific. (Adapted from pp. 382–389).

Although all of these descriptions appear as discrete stages/grades, the actual response to humor may be anywhere along the underlying laughter continuum represented by those points. Also, they provide a snapshot of the potential physical effects laughter can have on the entire body.

These physical descriptions of laughter translate into seven specific physiological benefits that involve the central nervous, muscular, respiratory, circulatory, endocrine, immune, and cardiovascular systems (Fry, 1986, 1992), plus some minor effects on your gums, hair, sinus cavities, lips, and toe nails (Berk, Needs, & Help, 2002c). Those benefits, extracted from the accumulated research evidence, and their implications for teaching and learning are presented next.

Caution: In-depth, autopsies of the studies in this area by Martin (2001), McGhee (1999, 2002), and Provine (2000) have concluded that much of the accumulated evidence to date is sparse, weak, inconclusive, and absolutely putrid. They actually ripped the methodology of each study to smithereens. It got ugly! Consequently, the enthusiastic claims about some of the physiological benefits of laughter (Clay, 1997; McGuire, 1999; Zand, Spreen, & LaValle, 1999; Ziegler, 1995) are premature and exaggerated. This review proceeds under that black cloud of doom by tempering the statements about many of the alleged benefits as merely *suggestive* at this point. Further research and tankers of bodily fluids have yet to be collected and analyzed before sufficient evidence can substantiate the claims already being made.

Improves Mental Functioning

The mental processing of humor and its relationship to creativity and problem solving was reviewed in Chapter 1. The importance of this linkage to learning right hemisphere tasks, such as spatial temporal reasoning and recognition, is that humor can systematically be incorporated in problem-based learning (abbreviated ACLU) activities.

Other physiological evidence has found that laughter increases cate-cholamine (pronounced "kil bas′ sa") levels in the body, which improve over-all mental functioning (Fry, 1984). Whoooa! In fact, the postlaugh euphoric experience is associated with the functioning of the left and right hemispheres of the brain (Derks, Bogart, & Gillikin, 1991; Goldstein, 1976; Svebak, 1982). These effects can have a direct impact on learning. Inducing laughter prior to and during coverage of a specific topic in class can prime students' brains so they have increased alertness and memory. That laughter can also produce greater interpersonal responsiveness in Q & As and cooperative learning activities.

Exercises and Relaxes Muscles

A hearty guffaw requires the coordinated movement of 15 facial muscles plus spasmodic skeletal muscle contractions, which involve globs of muscle tissue. As Kuhn's (1994) description of the stages of laughter indicates, laughing cre-ates a total body response that is clinically beneficial. A "belly" laugh can exercise chest and abdominal muscles and improve their tone (Paskind, 1932), which can be particularly important for bedridden or wheelchair-bound peo-ple, or students who are held hostage in class hour after hour and then must study on their posterior for interminable time periods. However, despite these callisthenic effects, don't expect laughing by yourself to produce washboard abs. You'll need an expensive personal laugh trainer to get that kind of result.

Cousins (1979) has described laughter as "a form of jogging for the innards." (*Digression Alert:* Consider the visual image of your spleen jogging, in its teensie weensie CoolMax® non-chafing shorts with a Nike® swoosh on the side, red headband, and Gel-lite, less filling running shoes. What a sight! *Digression Ends.*) The research reports that even the muscles of the gastroin-testinal system are affected so that the digestion rate is improved.

In addition to these exercise effects of laughter, there are muscle relax-ation effects throughout your body. A "belly laugh" can produce this relax-ation automatically (Prerost & Ruma, 1987) in two phases: when you laugh and after you laugh. First, the muscles not involved in laughter relax while you're laughing. For example, your legs may get weak. You've certainly heard of people who fall down with laughter. Picture someone "rolling in the aisles." Unless you laugh with your femur or patella, collapsing during a fit of laughter is one form of relaxation. The second phase occurs after you laugh. All of the muscles used to laugh naturally retire to a condo in Miami. Kidding! Actually, they relax by crawling into a Barcalounger®, flipping on a football game or golf tournament with "Tigger" (Wait. I think there's only one "g.") decimating his competition, and glugging a bottle of Gatorade®. After all, they're pooped out from all of that exercise. The therapeutic benefit is to decrease muscle tension in the neck, shoulders, and abs, which can break up the spasm-pain cycle some people frequently experience with neuralgias and rheumatisms (Cushner & Friedman, 1989; Fry, 1986, 1992).

Improves Respiration

As an extension of the muscle contractions mentioned above, laughter exercises the lungs and chest muscles, thereby conditioning the lungs, which improves respiration (Lloyd, 1938). A laugh disrupts the normal cyclic breathing pattern, increases ventilation, clears mucous plugs and phlegmwads (EWWW!), and accelerates the exchange of residual air, which enhances blood oxygen levels (Fry & Rader, 1977). The increased pulmonary ventilation causes a blowing off of the excess carbon dioxide and water vapor which builds up in residual air. More oxygen is available for red blood cell uptake and there is less excess moisture to encourage pulmonary bacterial growth (Fry, 1994). These effects of laughter can help some of us with chronic respiratory conditions, such as emphysema, and can reduce the chances of bronchial infection and pneumonia in all of us.

Stimulates Circulation

Laughter initially produces an increase in heart rate (HR) and blood pressure (BP), which exercises the myocardium and increases arterial, venous, and mars circulation. This exercise can have a distinctly beneficial effect for the heart muscles, similar to any common aerobic exercise (Fry, 1994), such as kayak sprinting, mud wrestling, or rock-paper-scissors. Laughter causes increased movement of oxygen and bloodborne nutrients to tissues (Fry & Savin, 1988; Fry & Stoft, 1971). These effects can be especially beneficial to couch potatoes and others who lead sedentary life styles. After a laugh subsides, a brief relaxation phase occurs, during which the HR and BP drop below the prelaugh baseline levels. However, this drop is short-lived.

Empirical research to substantiate these effects is needed. One experimental study by White and Camarena (1989) examined the effects of laughter from humorous videos on HR and BP. No significant decreases occurred, although such changes did result from the relaxation-training comparison group. A correlational study by Lefcourt, Davidson, Prkachin, and Mills (1997) investigated the relationship between sense of humor and BP. There was no relationship between humor and diastolic BP, but inconsistent sex difference relationships were found with systolic BP. Females with high humor scores had lower SBP, while males with high humor scores had high SBP. These differences were explained by the different types of humor preferred by men and women (see Chapter 1).

Another experimental study by Tan et al. (1997) explored the effectiveness of laughter in the cardiac rehabilitation of patients who experienced myocardial infarctions (post-MI). After one year of bimonthly treatments that included standard cardiac medications plus a humorous video compared to medications alone, the med-humor group exhibited fewer arrhythmias, lower BP, lower urinary and plasma catecholamines (see previous section on stress hormones), required lower dosage of beta blockers, less frequent NTG, and significantly fewer recurrent MIs. The researchers concluded that laughter attenuates catecholamines and is a useful adjunct in post-MI cardiac rehabilitation.

The evidence reported in the investigations is slightly encouraging, though underwhelming due to small sample sizes, weak experimental controls, and/or inconclusive findings. But hold onto your handle bars; there's more.

Decreases Stress Hormones

When you are stressed, your body goes sour. There is considerable evidence that stress can suppress the immune system (Adler & Hillhouse, 1996; O'Leary 1990) and increase the risk of infectious diseases (Cohen & Williamson, 1991; Cohen et al., 1998) and heart disease (Esler, 1998). The use of humor as a coping strategy for daily life stressors was mentioned previously. Physiologically, stress increases the secretion of hormones, such as corticotropin, cortisol, catecholamines, beta-endorphin, growth hormone, and prolactin. You're probably secreting right now as you try to pronounce these hormones. These are sometimes referred to as "stress hormones."

Since laughter is regarded as a type of stress, *eustress* (we stress, we all stress for I stress), which is healthy stress (Milsum, 1985), researchers have been able to quantify the effects of laughter on the neuroendocrine and stress hormones. Investigations of those responses to stress have measured decreases in (here we go again) serum cortisol, dopac, epinephrine, and growth hormone levels in the blood, but no effects on norepinephrine, prolactin, beta-endorphin, and gamma-interferon levels (Berk et al., 1988a, 1988b; 1989a; Berk, Tan, Napier, & Eby, 1989b; Fry, 1971, 1984, 1992). One study by Berk, Felten, Tan, Bittman, and Westengard (2001) did find increased levels of gamma interferon. This substance contributes to the growth of T-cells and activation of natural killer cells essential for our immune system to function

(Berk & Tan, 1996) (see next section). Unfortunately, several methodological weaknesses in these studies, especially very small samples sizes, plus unpronounceable hormones render this physiological evidence for the stress reduction benefit of laughter as inconclusive or tenuous at best.

Despite this paucity of evidence, one of the latest techniques for stress management developed by Madan Kataria, known as the Guru of Giggling or laughing doctor from Bombay, is called "laughter yoga." During a seminar designed to reveal the Inner Spirit of Laughter, he shows slides, video clippings, and demonstrations of a variety of laughter exercises followed by a 20-minute group laughter session where all participants laugh together without jokes (Kataria, Wilson, & Buxman, 1999) (check out *http://www.laughteryoga.com* or *http://www.worldlaughtertour.com*). A documentary film of this phenomenon, titled *The Laughing Club of India,* premiered in August 2001 on CINEMAX.

Increases Immune System's Defenses

> **Bodily Fluid Alert:** The next few paragraphs contain a lot of bodily fluids. In order to conform with the Occupational Safety and Health Administration (OSHA) Standards, you should probably don latex gloves, gown, and mask now. This is for your own protection. If you are contaminated, don't blame me. In fact, I feel your thumb on this box right now and it isn't covered in latex.

Immunoglobulin A.   Several studies have attempted to investigate the effects of laughter on the immune system. One index of immune functioning is secretory immunoglobulin A (IgA), which is the predominant antibody in saliva, tears, and yucky intestinal secretions. IgA, in fact, is the type of abbreviation that I bet immunologists would put on their vanity license plates, such as I WUV IG A. It is also the primary defense against viral and bacterial infections in the upper respiratory and gastrointestinal tracts (Tomasi, 1976). Low levels of IgA have been associated both with high levels of self-reported life stress and increased illness, particularly upper respiratory infections (McClelland, Alexander, & Marks, 1980).

Experimental studies using college students over the past 20 years have investigated whether IgA in loogies increased as a result of watching comedy videos. All of the studies found significant increases (Berk et al., 2001; Dillon, Minchoff, & Baker, 1985; Labott, Ahleman, Wolever, & Martin, 1990; Lefcourt, Davidson-Katz, & Kueneman, 1990; McClelland & Cheriff, 1997; Njus, Nitschke, & Bryant, 1996). Even a small study with fifth-grade students reported a significant increase (Lambert & Lambert, 1995). Despite methodological weaknesses in most of this research and the failure to link laughter to those increases, the consistency of the findings is encouraging.

A few correlations between trait measures of sense of humor and IgA have been significant (Dillon et al., 1985, McClelland & Cheriff, 1997), but most have not been (Dillon & Totton, 1989; Labott et al., 1990; Lefcourt et al., 1990; Martin & Dobbin, 1988). In a study by Martin and Dobbin (1988), differences in IgA only appeared when sense of humor interacted with stress. It was concluded that individuals with a strong sense of humor experience less impairment in immune functioning following stress, and, therefore, would be less prone to infectious illnesses under those conditions. As laughter stimulates the immune system, it offsets the immuno-suppressive effects of stress.

Violence Warning: The next two paragraphs contain gratuitous cell violence. They graphically depict microscopic *Terminator*-type killer cells committing murders of viral and cancerous cells. It can get pret-ty gory. This section is not for the faint of heart.

Natural killer cells/T-cells.   Another line of research has examined the relationship of natural killer cell activity (NKA), which is responsible for the early recognition and removal of virus and tumor activity cells, and mirthful laughter (Berk et al., 1984, 1989b). Can you imagine that there are little cells with prison numbers imprinted on them running through your body killing other cells? How do they do that? Do they use really tiny guns supplied by Charlton Heston? Do they have a "license to kill" from James Bond? It is possible that there may be even serial killer cell activity (SKA)?

Natural killer cells are a type of immune cell that attacks viral and cancerous cells. Increases in NKA and in the number of activated T-lymphocytes (also called T4 or CD4 cells, which are a type of white blood cell) stimulate the immune system's defense against a variety of infectious diseases (Locke, 1984). These effects are especially important in preventing and fighting cancer (Dowling, 2001). Unfortunately, only Berk et al. (1989b, 1993, 2001) found increases in NKA and the T-cell ratio with exposure to a comedy video. One study by Kamei, Kumano, and Masumura (1997) reported no T-cell effect and NKA actually decreased significantly. Other studies have not demonstrated any changes in those indices to corroborate results found by Berk et al. (1989b, 2001) (Bennett, Zeller, Rosenberg, & McCann, in press; Itami, Nobori, & Teshima, 1994; Mittwoch-Jaffe, Shalit, Srendi, & Yehuda, 1995; Wise, 1989; Yoshino, Fujimora, & Kohda, 1996).

This research trend is particularly discouraging in view of what we know about the human immunodeficiency virus (HIV). It infects and destroys T4 cells, thereby gradually weakening immune system functions. In fact, the decreases in the T4 cell count provide an index of the progression of the infection. (For example, symptoms typically begin when the count is below 500 [a normal count is 700–1300/mm^3 of blood] and the average count for an AIDS-defining diagnosis is 50–100.) It is premature, given the lack of evidence, to be able to say that the positive effects of laughter can fight the negative effects of the HIV on the immune system.

Other measures.   In addition to IgA, NKA, and T-cell ratio, there have been a couple of studies that have examined the effect of laughter on immunoglobulin M (IgM) and G (IgG), B-cells, and Complement B (Berk et al., 1993, 2001). Increases were found for all four indices. These measures contribute in different ways toward improving both short- and long-term immunity to disease.

Considering all of the research in this section that sought to establish that laughter can boost immune system functions as measured by increases in IgA, NKA, T-cell ratio, IgM, IgG, B-cells, and Complement B, the evidence is uneven and, in some cases, weak, but seems to clearly suggest an effect using IgA. Laughter *may* increase the immune system's ability to fight viral and bacterial infections and buffer the immunosuppressive effects of stress. But don't pump your fists just yet. Future research with adequate controls and large sample sizes are desperately needed before firm conclusions can be drawn. In the mean time, while we wait for that, can you believe that laughter . . .

Increases Pain Threshold and Tolerance

Me neither! This physiological effect has been inferred from anecdotal evidence that has been collected from the personal pain reduction experiences of patients and from laboratory experiments in the 1990s. The first significant evidence of this type was reported by the late Norman Cousins, a former editor of the *Saturday Review.* He described how he used humor for healing and controlling pain in a 1976 article, "Anatomy of an Illness," which was expanded into his 1979 best-selling autobiographical book, *Anatomy of an Illness as Perceived by the Patient.* He suffered from a serious collagen disease, ankylosing spondylitis, that involved severe inflammation of his spine and joints as the connective tissue was disintegrating. He experienced intense pain and was given a 1-in-500 chance of full recovery.

Cousins surrounded himself with humor books and started watching films of "The Three Stooges" and "Marx Brothers." He improvised a therapeutic humor regime. It decreased his pain and helped him sleep easier without any analgesic medications. He recounted that "10 minutes of genuine belly laughter had an anesthetic effect and would give me at least 2 hours of pain free sleep" (p. 39). When he awoke and felt pain again, he turned on the films again. He continued this "humor therapy" and witnessed gradual improvement. After a few weeks, the doctors found that the connective tissue in his joints was regenerating. Cousins also observed that a drop of at least five points in the sedimentation rate (an indicator of the severity of inflammation or infection) occurred during episodes of laughter. Soon he was able to go back to work full-time, but it took several years for his condition to completely reverse itself. According to Cousins, he used laughter to heal himself, leading to his total recovery from the disease. However, it is not known whether that recovery could have been attributable to the vitamin C he was taking, personality traits such as optimism or a will to live, or to some other factor (Martin, 2001).

Cousins' (1979) documented experiences brought the therapeutic effects of humor and laughter to the attention of the medical community. Those experiences suggested that laughter may have a stimulatory effect on endorphins and other endogenous substances within the brain that results in decreased pain and a sense of euphoria. Subsequent studies using blood samples to measure change in levels of beta-endorphin after participants viewed a comedy video or performance have yielded no significant effects (Berk et al., 1989b; Itami et al., 1994; Yoshimo et al, 1996). Consequently, there doesn't seem to be a shred of physiological evidence that quantifies any significant change in endorphin levels with laughter (Fry, 1992). This may be due, in part, to difficulties in measuring endorphins. Fry (personal communication, July 6, 2001) suggests that the levels present in the blood may be too low to detect noticeable changes. Alternative bodily fluidwise, he noted that drawing spinal fluid through a needle stuck in someone's back while he or she laughed hysterically at Gallagher smashing watermelons is also problematic. Ouch!

Another more promising line of research is the series of laboratory experiments, many involving college students, that have investigated the analgesic effects of laughter on discomfort threshold (Cogan, Cogan, Waltz, & McCue, 1987; Hudak, Dale, Hudak, & DeGood, 1991), pain threshold and tolerance (Adams & McGuire, 1986; Nevo, Kienan, Teshimovsky-Arditi, 1993; Rotton & Shats, 1996; Weisenberg, Tepper, & Schwartzwald, 1995; Weisenberg, Raz, & Hener, 1998; Weaver & Zillmann, 1994; Yoshino et al., 1996; Zillmann, Rockwell, Schweitzer, & Sundar, 1993), and survival of patients with end stage renal failure (Svebak, Christioffersen, & Aasarød, 2001). Overall, Martin (2001) concluded from this body of evidence that exposure to comedy results in subsequent increases in pain threshold and tolerance, which do not appear to be due to distraction. A survey of 35 patients with traumatic brain injury, spinal cord injury, arthritis, limb amputations, and other neurological and muscular disorders found that 74% agreed with the statement, "Sometimes laughing works as well as a pain pill" (Schmitt, 1990). In fact, laughter has been systematically used as a pain management technique for terminally ill cancer patients and persons with AIDS (Peterson, 1992), burn patients (Kelley, Jarvie, Middlebrook, McNeer, & Drabman, 1984), and dental patients (Trice & Price-Greathouse, 1986).

Interestingly, the preceding *suggested* physiological benefits of laughter are similar to those experienced during intense exercise. (*Reminder:* There is still barely a smidgen of evidence to support these benefits.) The reduction of pain and sense of euphoria felt at a certain point in aerobic exercise, such as running, has been referred to as a "high," as in "runner's high." Fry (1992) claims that several minutes of intense laughter produce results similar to those of exercising on a rowing machine or stationary bicycle for about 10 to 15 minutes. That laughter also produces a "high." That's why we feel so great after a belly laugh. It's those endorphins; at least we believe that's the explanation. For those of you who refuse to exercise or simply can't, laughter can provide a limited proxy for exercise that is within everyone's reach. That's right! YOU can produce endorphins without even putting down your Power-Point remote. (*Tidbit:* Make sure you switch your remote from one hand to the other so one hand doesn't become over developed.) Although the aerobic value of laughter pales by comparison to full-blown exercise, it can probably be increased by engaging in convulsive laughter (see Kuhn's stage 14) for sustained periods of 20–30 minutes at least three times a week (Berk, Made, That, & Up, 2002b).

Laughter does offer sedentary folk an alternative. Even those of you who exercise regularly should seriously consider adding a daily dose of laughter to your routine. Many professors and students walk or jog, take exercise classes, or hop on their favorite piece of equipment, such as a treadmill, stationary bike, trampoline, Ab Rocker®, or Al Roker. (*Wait:* The treadmill tells you how many calories you burn as you walk or jog, but it doesn't know about the grilled cheese sandwich and chips you're eating as you walk!) This equipment is usually next to the water heater in the basement, being used as a clothes rack in the bedroom, or housed in an exercise room of an athletic club. Some even exercise while watching Billy Blanks punch and kick air. Maybe some of you should consider inserting your favorite comedy into the VCR/DVD player or flipping on "Comedy Central" and going on a laughing binge until you're totally loopy. Only then can you truly experience a "jocular high." As my mother (now 84 years old) advises still, "It couldn't hurt." Or could it?

MEMORY JOGGER 2.1   Suggested physiological benefits of laughter.

Benefits	Examples
1. Improves Mental Functioning	Increases interpersonal responses, alertness, and memory
2. Exercises and Relaxes Muscles	Exercises facial, chest, abdominal, and skeletal muscles; improves muscle tone, decreases muscle tension, and relieves discomfort from neuralgias and rheumatism
3. Improves Respiration	Exercises the lungs and improves breathing and blood oxygen levels; relieves chronic respiratory conditions; reduces chances of bronchial infection and pneumonia
4. Stimulates Circulation	Exercises the heart like aerobic exercise, followed by decreases in heart rate and blood pressure
5. Decreases Stress Hormones	Reduces stress
6. Increases Immune System's Defenses	Fights viral and bacterial infections
7. Increases Pain Threshold and Tolerance	Decreases pain and produces a euphoric state without liquor, drugs, or aerobic exercise
8. Kills Common Viruses and Bacteria	Relieves hemorrhoids, psoriasis, gangrene, gingivitis, and malaria

Summary

Given the number and complexity of the preceding suggested physiological benefits of laughter, Memory Jogger 2.1 was assembled to summarize the effects with specific examples based on the research evidence. Pass this jogger on to your colleagues and students. Perhaps, eventually, these health benefits will be as familiar to academia as the risk factors associated with heart disease and smoking. Speaking of risks . . .

Physiological Risks

Caution: Laughter may be hazardous to your health. Can you imagine that? Although the U.S. Surgeon General is probably unaware of this, you should know that if you laugh too hard, a vein in your forehead could explode resulting in a seizure, narcoleptic attack, or myocardial infarction. If you have any of the medical conditions described in the next paragraph, you better be careful.

Despite all of the benefits described previously, the profound physiological effects of laughter on the body can also be risky for people with serious medical conditions. A few risks cautioned by Fry (1992) relate to the central nervous, muscular, respiratory, circulatory, and cardiovascular systems. For example, a small number of people have experienced neurological reactions to laughter, including seizures and cataplectic and narcoleptic attacks. Large increases in abdominal and thoracic pressure are ill-advised following abdominal or pelvic surgery, after acute orthopedic distress, such as rib or shoulder girdle fractures, and acute respiratory diseases, such as asthma (Fry, 1986). The strong sudden increase in blood pressure of relatively brief duration can produce cerebrovascular accidents and even myocardial infarction.

Despite the anecdotal evidence of these negative effects of laughter, which have occurred in only rare cases, it is highly unlikely that the FDA (which stands for Internal Revenue Service) will require a warning label on laughter anywhere anytime soon, except on this page. With the exception of the extreme conditions just identified, the benefits seem to provide overwhelming evidence in favor of laughing. In fact, the late veteran radio comedian, Fred Allen, cautioned against not laughing. In other words, you should not stifle, suppress, or internalize the impulse to laugh. He warned: If you do, "it goes back down and spreads to your hips." Probably none of us needs that.

Implications for Teaching and Assessment

The preceding psychophysiologcal benefits of humor and laughter can have a significant impact on the health and well-being of just about every member of our species as well as Furby's new best friend, Shelby, an interactive clam in a shell. The eight psychological and seven physiological benefits have an accumulated research base of scientific thought that dates back nearly a century and empirical evidence over the past 30 years. What has not been considered are the specific implications of these benefits for teaching and assessment, independent of the research on humor in the college classroom (see *Gone with the Wind*). The benefits can have an impact in five areas: (1) professor-student connection, (2) classroom atmosphere, (3) student responsiveness, (4) test performance, and (5) student attendance.

Professor-Student Connection

This hyphenated topic has been the underlying theme of both of my humor books. It's because the research indicates *that* connection is critical for learning (Astin, 1985; Pascarella & Terenzini, 1991). As noted in Chapter 1, humor can break down the barriers that naturally exist between "us" and "them." For example, it is not unusual for students to fear a particular professor and, as a consequence, to hesitate to approach simply because he or she is reeeaally weird and wears a black cape and sunglasses to class. My suggestion to those students is usually to try garlic and a wooden stake or, if that doesn't seem to work, try using humor which can serve as a coping mechanism to knock down their anxiety and tension levels a few notches. (*Paragraphus Interruptus:* Speaking of notches, Chef Emeril Legasse kicks up a lot of notches with spices on his *Food Network* cooking programs. Can you believe that a live studio audience so desperate for entertainment actually applauds and cheers at the sight of cayenne pepper being thrown into a pot? BAM!). For example, an ice-breaker, humor-breathed conversation between student and professor might proceed as follows:

Student: "Yo, prof!"

Professor: "Are you calling me?"

Student: "Yup! By the way, did you see *Buffy the Vampire Slayer* last night?"

Professor: "Ha Ha. Yes, wasn't it delicious?"

Student: "If you say so. What type of toothpaste do you use to brush your fangs?"

Professor: "You're soooo funny. Are you getting these ideas from Berk's humor book?"

Student: "Who's Berk?"

I think it's time to move on to the next paragraph.

A professor, either one-on-one with a student or in class, can also take the initiative to drop anxiety levels by using self-effacing humor or humor as a systematic teaching tool (see *Gone with the Wind* or Berk, 1996b, 1997; Berk & Nanda, 1998). These various psychological effects can facilitate the professor-student connection.

Classroom Atmosphere

Building on the preceding connection, the entire atmosphere of each class can be changed by infusing humor into any instructional strategy, such as lecture, discussion, Q & A, cooperative learning exercises, student panels, role playing, and demonstrations. One of humor's most significant benefits is to create a relaxed, fun, and playful, but also intellectually stimulating environment conducive to learning. This is accomplished by its anxiety, tension, and stress reduction effects on just about everyone in the classroom—professor and students alike. Even if negative baggage is lugged into the room, the humor can detach a person's focus from that baggage and redirect it on classroom activities.

Student Responsiveness

In addition to the above psychological benefits, humor can increase a student's self-esteem, sense of empowerment, and confidence in conquering the subject matter. There are also a few physiological benefits that can markedly affect a student's in-class performance. Humor can facilitate problem solving and performance on spatial temporal reasoning and recognition tasks. Laughter can grab and maintain a student's attention and increase memory, alertness, and responsiveness in Q & A sessions, discussions, and debates. Use of hilarious illustrations in the form of case studies or hypothetical scenarios in small group assignments can improve a student's motivation, interest in the topic, and interpersonal responsiveness. Finally, if all else fails, at least laughter can increase the students' mental and physical pain tolerance for sitting through our classes. In fact, it induces a euphoric state without booze, drugs, or exercise, but it only lasts for a short time; so you better hurry and make your point before students lapse back in to their normal mental state, which I can't even imagine.

Test Performance

Probably a student's peak levels of anxiety, tension, and stress during any course occur when he or she walks into the classroom to take a test. Talk about aversive stimuli. Whoa! Injecting humor into course tests can trigger that "detachment" mechanism in students' brains to reduce those negative responses and to increase test performance (Berk, 2000a). Humor in the test directions can prime a student's problem-solving abilities for the actual test questions. For additional research evidence on these effects and specific techniques for developing mirthful tests, check out Chapter 8.

Student Attendance

Correlational studies examining sense of humor and self-reported illness symptoms using male and female undergraduates have produced zilch (Anderson & Arnoult, 1989; Korotkov & Hannah, 1994; Labott & Martin, 1990; McClelland & Cheriff, 1997; Porterfield, 1987). However, the health benefits of humor and laughter described throughout this chapter can have a positive effect on student attendance. Chortling regularly in class *might* decrease the risk of illness by fighting viral and bacterial infections, relieve chronic respiratory conditions, improve one's ability to cope with physical disabilities, and provide aerobic exercise while stuck in those hard, uncomfortable seats. Of course these benefits can not accrue if students do not come to class due to non-health-related reasons, such as laziness, studying for a test in another class, writing a paper that's already overdue, or attending a Backstreet Boys or Janet Jackson concert.

Research Citations for Eight Psychological Benefits

1. *Reduces Anxiety* (Cann, Holt, & Calhoun, 1999; DeSpelder & Strickland, 1983; Doris & Fierman, 1956; Dworkin & Efran, 1967; Hedl, Hedl, & Weaver, 1981; Liechty 1987; Nezu, Nezu, & Blisset, 1988; Singer, 1968; Smith, Ascough, Ettinger, & Nelson, 1971; Yovetich, Dale, & Hudak, 1990)

2. *Reduces Tension* (Brill, 1940; Goodheart, 1994; O'Connell, 1960; Wooten, 1996)

3. *Reduces Stress* (Bennett et al., in press; Bizi, Keinan, & Beit-Hallahmi, 1988; Dixon, 1976, 1980; Labott & Martin; 1987; Lefcourt, Davidson-Katz, Shepherd, & Phillips, 1995; Lefcourt & Martin, 1986; Lefcourt & Thomas, 1998; Lehman, Burke, Martin, Sultan, & Czech, 2001; Martin, Kuiper, Olinger, & Dance, 1993; Martin & Lefcourt, 1983; Nezu et al., 1988; Prerost, 1988; Rosenberg, 1991; Trice & Price-Greathouse, 1986; White & Camarena, 1989; White & Winzelberg, 1992; Wooten, 1996)

4. *Reduces Depression* (Danzer, Dale, & Klions, 1990; Deaner & McConatha, 1993; Leiber, 1986; Overholser, 1992; Porterfield, 1987)

5. *Reduces Loneliness* (Overholser, 1992)

6. *Improves Self-Esteem* (Frecknall, 1994; Kuiper & Martin, 1993; Kuiper, Martin, & Dance, 1992; Martin et al., 1993; Overholser, 1992)

7. *Restores Hope and Energy* (Bellert, 1989)

8. *Provides a Sense of Empowerment and Control* (Sherman, 1998; Thorson, 1985; Wooten, 1996)

3

LIGHTS, CAMERA, ACTIVE LEARNING!

> **Distraction Alert:** As I begin this chapter, to avoid any annoying unimportant interruptions that could break your concentration on this material, please turn off your pager, cell phone, shaver, hair dryer, jackhammer, and cement mixer. Your compliance with this request is greatly appreciated.

Let's chat for a moment, *professor-à-professor*. When you walk into your classroom to teach, do you see yourself as a "performer"? Before you answer, consider the following behaviors:

- lecture from a script (notes or memory)
- direct and choreograph planned active/cooperative learning activities
- improvise activities and learning exercises
- demonstrate concepts or processes with props or students
- direct role-plays, simulations, or dramatizations
- use lights, visuals, and/or a microphone
- manipulate your voice (volume, pitch, inflection, intonation) and body (gestures, postures, movements)
- inject humor in course materials and lectures
- add music, singing, or dance to presentations
- wear costumes or a pinwheel hat
- invite Mel Brooks or Susan Stroman *(The Producers)* as a guest lecturer

If you exhibit at least three of those behaviors when you teach, guess what? You're in trouble! Wait until your promotion's committee finds out. Just joshing. You are probably a *performer*. Teaching and performing have many parallels (Timpson, Burgoyne, Jones, & Jones, 1997). In fact, you may be a star, director, choreographer, writer, musician, or lighting and audiovisual technician, and don't even know it. We use theatrical techniques in teaching all the time.

At the beginning of a semester, as I prepare for my first class, I'm thinking: "This just isn't a class; this could be my big break! Who knows, there may be an agent from William Morris sitting out there." I have to remember my props, music, tape players, transparencies, flashlight, class lighting, projector, and humility, as well as the content I'm going to present. My first 8:30 a.m. Monday class is a "Broadway opening." My students' impressions of that class can make statistics a hit or a flop. Of course, if it's a hit on opening morning, I need to sustain those impressions for an entire semester to be nominated for a Tony Award.

Perhaps most significant in this theatrical approach to teaching is its instructional soundness. It is firmly planted in Multiple Intelligence Theory (MIT) and neurophysiological, psychological, educational, and TV advertising research on humor and cognition. Those plants will be described in the next section.

The starting point for building on what you are already performing in your class is music. By a show of hands, how many of you are currently using music as a teaching tool in your course? That's what I thought. Me neither. Kidding. It may seem rather nontraditional. In fact, the word that comes to mind is RIDICULOUS! When students reminisce about statistics courses they were forced to take, the type of music used to teach analysis of variance or multiple regression usually does not creep into their conversation.

Before I proceed any further, you should know that I'm not a professional musician. I have never been a musician. I don't want to be a musician. I don't even know a musician. Further, I can't carry a tune or anything else. I'm probably tone-deaf. Oh, I did play a red recorder really badly in the third grade and I took two piano lessons when I was 10, but my teacher, Mrs. Attilla Goldberg, threatened to smash my fingers with the keyboard cover if I ever returned.

Now that you know that I am musically challenged beyond hope, you may be able to appreciate the ease with which the techniques described in this chapter can be executed. If you have just one finger or a nose to push a button on a tape recorder or CD player, you're all set. You will not be performing the music.

What makes music so effective at facilitating learning is a combination of four factors: the instructional set-up, the element of surprise, the emotional impact, and the coupling of the music to a simple skit or class demonstration. It can be applied to any course content, discipline, or fat-free dessert. Consistent with the other chapters, this one is also organized as a trio of sections: (1) theoretical and research evidence base for the techniques, (2) guidelines for selecting the music, and (3) techniques for infusing music in college courses. More than 40 examples are described. Five appendices are even provided to summarize, identify, and locate the music, and furnish several step-by-step examples of the techniques.

Theoretical and Research Foundation

This section is designed to convince you that the theatrical use of music and skits/demonstrations in the classroom can actually improve learning. The compelling evidence is derived from Multiple Intelligence Theory, the incongruity formula for humor, and classroom research.

Multiple Intelligence Theory

The world of teaching and testing in college has been dominated primarily by two intelligences: *verbal/linguistic* and *quantitative/analytical*. Consider the tests that are used to guide admissions decisions. Although a variety of information may be considered in the decision process, one cannot diminish the weight that the SAT/ACT and GRE have in undergraduate and graduate admissions, respectively. Their subtests require abilities in only two or three areas. Although they're far from perfect as predictors of academic success, they strongly indicate the intelligences students are expected to apply to succeed in college.

> **Dinosaur Alert:** This next paragraph describes teaching methods that date back to the Voracious Period when prehistoric critters tried to enroll in our courses. Of course, we didn't let them and the consequence was *Jurassic Park III: The Same Plot Again*. More *dino-à-mano* violence. Those dinos *are* The Weakest Link. The T-rexes and raptors keep chasing a bunch of tourists, who are having a difficult time just harnessing enough strength to speak lines of really bad dialogue without laughing. In the mean time, the brontos roam the landscape, talk on their cellular phones, and devour everything in their paths, except Brussels sprouts, which were repulsive even then.

The first two intelligences mentioned above have provided the bases for how most professors teach and how most students are forced to learn since *Jurassic Park*. The majority of college courses are either verbally or quantitatively based and the teaching methods have conformed to the natural format of the subject matter. For example, literature is usually taught verbally and statistics is taught mathematically. Those methods restrict the intelligences that students can use to learn the content. For example, a student who has strong visual/spatial intelligence but has a weaker mathematical intelligence will probably struggle to succeed in a statistics course that is presented only in mathematical form.

Using music in conjunction with physical demonstrations (e.g., skits, dramatizations) to teach concepts and processes is grounded in Gardiner's (1983, 1993, 1995) Multiple Intelligence Theory (MIT). Only recently, however, has MIT been applied to college teaching by Díaz-Lefebvre (1999). His description of the neurological and learning characteristics of students framed within the eight intelligences of MIT is displayed in Table 3.1.

The application of MIT to college teaching can best be expressed by Díaz-Lefebvre's (1999, p. 25) metaphor of a 10-speed bike: *"Our students have several gears we've never asked them to use."* Teaching strategies that permit students to apply one or two of the gears other than the "natural" one for the course can significantly improve their chances of success. Perhaps the most pervasive set of strategies over the past decade to engage students in the learning process is active/cooperative learning activities, through which students can solve problems in dyads, triads, or larger groupings within the classroom. Depending on the structure of the various activities, those experiences provide students with opportunities to exercise their *interpersonal intelligence* as well as other intelligences.

The techniques described in this chapter which use music and demonstrations represent a package of teaching strategies aimed at higher-order thinking skills. They require students to draw to varying degrees on three relatively untapped intelligences: visual/spatial, bodily/kinesthetic, and musical/rhythmic.

Visual/spatial. This intelligence relates to being able to visualize and manipulate mental models in the "mind's eye." Spatial learners think in images and pictures. They use their eyeballs a lot to visualize concepts and problems in order to create solutions. Usually a skit or dramatization, especially with student actors, creates a concrete visual image of content that previously may have been presented to them in verbal or quantitative form. The demo can paint a picture in the students' minds that they may never forget. It provides a connection between traditional classroom materials and the real world. "The

TABLE 3.1   Neurological and learning characteristics of Gardiner's multiple intelligence theory.*

Intelligence	Neurological system	Students who	Learn by
Verbal/Linguistic (Word Smart)	Left temporal and frontal lobes	Verbalize	Reading, writing, speaking, listening, playing word games
Quantitative/ Analytical (Logic Smart)	Left parietal lobes; right hemisphere	Conceptualize	Abstracting, deductive reasoning, solving problems, experimenting, interacting with computers
Visual/Spatial (Picture Smart)	Posterior regions of right hemisphere	Visualize	Seeing, imagining, drawing, creating mental pictures
Bodily/Kinesthetic (Body Smart)	Cerebellum, basal ganglia, motor cortex	Dramatize	Touching, moving, feeling, role-playing, hands-on experiences, physical activities
Musical/Rhythmic (Music Smart)	Right temporal lobe	Harmonize	Singing, humming, drumming, listening to music
Interpersonal (People Smart)	Frontal and temporal lobes; limbic system	Fraternize	Relating, cooperating, teaching, emphathizing, social activities
Intrapersonal (Self Smart)	Frontal and parietal lobes; limbic system	Internalize	Self-reflection, planning, individuating, independent study, metacognition
Naturalist (Environment Smart)		Recognize	Observing, identifying, and categorizing elements in the environment, seeing patterns in the natural world

* Adapted from Díaz-Lefebvre (1999), pp. 17–28.

MTV program?" No! The words aren't even capped. Students *see* real problems or situations in which they are active participants in their analysis and resolution. The demo may be performed by one or more professors, a professor and one or two students, one or two groups of students, a seal and a bird, two seals and a monkey with a bird, or any combination of these. The entire class can also be involved in the performance. The demonstration may be structured as a simulation or relatively unstructured.

When the purpose for using music in the classroom is not to create humor, its impact on learning is more ambiguous. There have been several studies that have investigated the effects of listening to instrumental music on spatial-temporal reasoning. Couched within the context of neurophysiological theory (Leng & Shaw, 1991), one study by Rauscher, Shaw, and Ky (1993) found that listening to music and executing spatial tasks share neural pathways in the brain's cortex. The music serves to "prime" these neural pathways for the subsequent execution of spatial reasoning tasks. This finding was referred to as *"the Mozart Effect"* (Newman et al., 1995), named after Beethoven's "Fifth Symphony" used in the study. "Wrong! That was Mozart's piano sonata, you idiot." Oh. College students listening to the first movement of Mozart's "Sonata for Two Pianos" (K. 448) had a significant, but short-lived (10 minutes), improvement in spatial reasoning. This study was followed by another one by the same researchers (Rauscher, Shaw, & Ky, 1995) that produced similar results.

Two other investigations by Rideout and Laubach (1996) and Sarnthein et al. (1997) confirmed those findings with an EEG (electroencephalographic) coherence study which found that the presence of right frontal and left temporo-parietal activity induced by listening to Mozart carried over into spatial-temporal tasks.

Another series of studies by Stough, Kerkin, Bates, and Mangan (1994), Kenealy and Monseth (1994), and Newman et al. (1995) found no Mozart Effect. All three concluded that a brief listening to classical music, specifically a Mozart piano sonata, does not enhance the spatial problem-solving of college students. No other researchers have been able to replicate the Mozart effect in a rigorous control-group study.

Warning: This next paragraph describes bodily movements that may be too sensual or intense for some of you to handle. You might want to keep a glass of ice water at your side to throw in your face if it gets too steamy. You may now proceed slowly to the paragraph heading.

Bodily/kinesthetic.   This intelligence is associated with physical movement and bodily sensations of the touchy-feely kind. "Wow. This is HOT!" The key function is learning by doing. "You bet." Classroom strategies would include hands-on, manipulative tasks, role-playing, simulations, and physical activities. "Wow. This is NOT hot; this is boooring." As noted above, class demonstrations afford students the opportunity to tap this intelligence. Instead of just verbally describing and discussing a case study or an event in history, ask the students to *act* it out (Fancy, 1999; Sarason, 1999; Timpson & Tobin, 1982; Timpson et al., 1997). Let their performance serve as the springboard for discussion. The operative word here is "act." Students assume the role of actors in the learning process. *They* are "center stage." Where possible, use music to introduce the demonstration and include props and costumes to simulate the real experience.

Musical/rhythmic.   This intelligence involves the ability to produce and appreciate music, especially rhythm, pitch, tonal patterns, and timbre. Learning activities prompted by or accompanied by music raise the interest level and engagement of students with musical/rhythmic intelligence. Their talents heighten their sensitivity to a variety of musical forms. Although all of us appreciate music to different degrees, those students who are especially gifted in this intelligence probably value it second only to oxygen.

The use of music in teaching strategies, whether to set a tone for class, trigger laughter, or accompany a skit, will have more meaning to those students than to the ones who are musically challenged. In particular, the music used to introduce a skit can grab the students' attention. It can serve as a hook at the beginning and, later, accompany the drama. The emotional effects can be strong. In fact, the psychological research on the impact of music on mood suggests that music, with or without lyrics, can have a significant effect on mood change (Sousou, 1997; Stratton & Zalanowski, 1994).

Application of the Humor Incongruity Formula to Music

So far, I know this chapter has not really been hilarious. In fact, you're probably thinking, "Show me the funny! How does music relate to humor?" The linkage is the basic incongruity formula applied previously to verbal material (see Chapter 1). It can be applied to music and demonstrations in two steps:

1. An *expected* serious premise, statement, or context related to course content

2. The *unexpected* jolt of music

The music serves as the unexpected twist, the PUNCH! It may take three forms:

1. Music or melody

2. Title suggested by the music

3. Lyrics accompanying the music

Consistent with verbal punchlines, the music punch must have the element of surprise. Unless students are in a music or performing arts course, they do not expect to hear music of any kind in the middle of class. Niepel, Rudolph, Schützwohl, and Meyer (1994) found that the emotional arousal accompanying surprise typically results in "an interruption of ongoing activities and a spontaneous focusing of attention on the eliciting stimulus" (p. 434). In other words, they're hooked. The music punch hits like an accidental ambush. Surprise alone is a strong determinant of the humor (Brownell, Michel, Powelson, & Gardner, 1983; Deckers & Winters, 1986; McGhee & Johnson, 1975).

Within this context, the music takes on an essential role in the incongruity formula, the resolution of the humor. As explained in Chapter 1, this formula involves cognitive processes similar to problem solving. Consequently, the music "punch" can prime students' brains for problem solving activities and increase performance on right hemisphere tasks.

The effectiveness of this technique is primarily a function of the visual imagery and emotional arousal evoked by the music. There is an individualized jukebox full of memories inside every one of us. Hearing a piece of music automatically brings those special memories into focus like a photograph. Hearing the music alone triggers a response similar to what has been called a "flashbulb memory" (Brown & Kulik, 1977; Sierra & Berrios, 1999; Winograd & Neisser, 1992). When the music is juxtaposed against the serious set-up, various mental associations are stimulated in the students' brains which trigger the physical response of laughter. In other words, the music serves as a retrieval cue.

When the play button is pressed, our mental picture button is pressed into action. A snapshot image suddenly pops into our minds. This picture or image may provide vivid recollections of any of the following: (a) the person performing the song or composition; (b) the person with whom we associate a scene from a particular TV program, movie, or musical; (c) the person with whom we heard it; or (d) the time and place where we heard it. Other details may be recalled as well. All of this occurs in a nanosecond. The image creates feelings, emotions, and moods related to that previous experience. They may be positive or negative. It is essentially music-induced nostalgia.

This individual, very personal experience by each student is then linked to an image in class. The strength of the contrast in imagery between the first one created in the students' minds by the music and the second "real" one observed in class has a significant effect on the humor. For example, suppose you play the theme from *Rocky* ("Gonna Fly Now") in class. The first image that pops into my mind is Dustin Hoffman in a dress. Wait. That's *Tootsie*. I keep getting those images confused. Seriously, typical first images may be Rocky running through the streets of Philadelphia or up the museum steps. Then five male students, planted throughout the classroom, wearing hooded sweatshirts, stand up in your class. This extreme contrast between the first Rocky image in the students' minds and the second one of the five guys that they see triggers the laughter. The humor escalates as the five "Rockys" jog to the front of the room to prepare for the demonstration. This in-class form of parody creates maximum student engagement, plus plenty of laughter. And the demonstration has not even begun.

Once the demonstration is completed, the students are left with a whole new set of visual images linked to the music from *Rocky,* images that they now associate with the demo. The trick is to create such a concrete dramatic image in the students' minds that they will remember it vividly. In fact, when they hear the theme from *Rocky* again, the in-class image may very well displace the original one. It may be nearly impossible to erase the images created in class without sophisticated brainwashing methods.

This humor technique underlies many of the humorous ads on TV. An ad that evokes imagery, in fact, is likely to achieve greater comprehension of the details of its humorous contrast through enhanced incidental learning (Alden, Mukherjee, & Hoyer, 2000; Bower, 1972; Sheehan, 1972). The strength of the contrast in incongruity in a humorous ad is manipulated by contrasting the elements, such as the situation, visuals, music, or color scheme. Alden et al. (2000) found that juxtaposing sharply distinct versions of these elements in the same ad creates surprise, which, in turn, is the key antecedent of the humor. Ads that utilize imagery-evoking elements, such as those in many Pepsi® and Budweiser® spots during the Super Bowl, will produce higher surprise responses and greater humor.

The mental processing and laughter produced from the music and demonstration can be a powerful learning tool. The music association with the visual demonstration of a process, case study, or other content application makes it possible to anchor all subsequent verbal or quantitative examples in the demonstration.

Classroom Research Evidence

Based on MIT, the justification for using music and demonstrations as a systematic teaching tool can be best summarized by the old adage: "5 intelligences are better than 1." Rather than forcing students to apply only their verbal or quantitative intelligence to learning the material in your course, create presentations and activities that provide opportunities for them to draw on as many intelligences as possible. Díaz-Lefebvre (1999, pp. 57–58) compiled a list of 24 learning options with affected intelligences that were field-tested as part of his Multiple Intelligence/Learning for Understanding (MI/LfU) pilot project:

1. Sculpture (bodily/spatial/intrapersonal)

2. Poetry (linguistic/intrapersonal)

3. Video Review (spatial/intrapersonal)

4. Journal Writing (linguistic/intrapersonal)

5. Charades (linguistic/bodily)

6. Computer Application (linguistic/logical/intrapersonal)

7. Chapter Collage (spatial/logical/bodily/intrapersonal)

8. Oral Presentation (linguistic/intrapersonal)

9. Video Project (spatial/bodily)

10. Interview (linguistic/bodily/interpersonal)

11. Creative Dance (bodily/logical)

12. Oral Presentation-Dyad (linguistic/interpersonal)

13. Drawing/Sketching/Painting (spatial/bodily/intrapersonal)

14. Applied Term Paper (linguistic/intrapersonal)

15. Mime (bodily/logical)

16. Experiment (linguistic/logical/bodily/intrapersonal)

17. Musical-Rhythmic Application/Appreciation (musical/bodily/intrapersonal)

18. Book Report (linguistic/intrapersonal)

19. Acting/Role-Playing (linguistic/bodily)

20. Independent Project (linguistic/bodily/intrapersonal)

21. Computer Simulation and Graphics (logical/spatial/intrapersonal)

22. Article Review (linguistic/intrapersonal)

23. Cooperative Learning Project—2 to 3 Learners (bodily/linguistic/interpersonal)

24. Traditional Tests (linguistic/logical/intrapersonal)

At this point you're probably thinking, "Does any of this stuff work? As far as the application of MIT to college teaching, Díaz-Lefebvre furnishes students' anecdotal evaluations and reflections on the application of the preceding 24 learning options to specific coursework.

Students' ratings of effectiveness.   Student feedback on the effectiveness of teaching strategies is critical to gauge their success. It may be qualitative, quantitative, or both. In order to assess the impact of my somewhat bizarre uses of music and demonstrations, formal evaluative surveys were administered in seven courses—two undergraduate and five graduate statistics classes ($n = 385$) over two and a half years (1999–2001). Details on this study can be found in Berk (2001b). A brief summary of the results is given next.

The students were asked to evaluate the effectiveness of nearly 40 musical selections and eight class demonstrations in all seven classes. They rated the extent to which each piece of music was effective in attaining specific outcomes using a five-anchor qualitative scale ("Ineffective," "Somewhat Effective," "Moderately Effective," "Very Effective," "Extremely Effective"). There were four outcomes rated on this scale:

1. To grab your *attention* and *focus*

2. To increase your *interest* in the topic/class

3. To relax or reduce your *anxiety/stress* on the topic/class

4. To make the topic/class/learning *FUN!*

The first two outcomes measured the degree of student engagement, the third addressed the students' fear or anxiety related to a particular statistical topic, and the fourth assessed the global effect related to fun.

The median class rating was computed for each selection and outcome. The music chosen for inclusion in this chapter were those selections rated "Very Effective" or "Extremely Effective" consistently across undergraduate and graduate classes for all four outcomes. Clearly, the music significantly increased the students' levels of engagement, reduced their anxiety on various topics, and made learning fun.

In addition to these survey results, a separate survey was conducted in four of the classes (one undergraduate and three graduate; $n = 232$) to determine whether the music in combination with a demonstration was effective in helping the students *learn* the statistics material. In other words, did the spatial/verbal/bodily/musical/interpersonal intelligences have any impact on understanding quantitative concepts and processes? Did the music's visual imagery increase the students' memory of the demo and the statistic? Five to six music-demos per course using 10–12 musical selections were rated for effectiveness in achieving the following outcomes:

1. Facilitate your *understanding* of the statistic

2. Help you *remember* the statistical concept or process

3. Help you *learn* the statistic when you applied it

The students' median ratings of the three outcomes for all of the music-demos were "Very Effective." Up to 74% of the undergraduates rated them as "Very" or "Extremely Effective," compared with 62% of the graduate students. Overall, 86% or more of each class felt the music-demos improved to some extent ("Somewhat Effective" or higher) their understanding, memory, and learning of the respective statistics topics.

These findings from this preliminary self-report study are very encouraging in providing empirical classroom evidence that music alone and in combination with demonstrations can make a marked difference in the students' affect and learning, at least according to their perceptions. (See Berk, 2001b, for further discussion).

Guidelines for Selecting the Music

If the music is to create the desired visual, emotional, and learning effects on the students, *it must be familiar to everyone*. This criterion is similar to the first element in the structure of most humor—the commonly understood situation. In order for the music to trigger laughter, it has to stir an emotional response. If the students have never heard the music, the only response will be puzzled looks. Meeting this criterion, however, is not easy.

The most accessible sources of music, albeit culture laden, are TV programs, movies, Broadway musicals, and popular and classical music. My students' ratings in terms of impact and effectiveness favor the first three sources. What we experience on TV and in theaters is packed with both visual and auditory stimuli. The characters, actors/actresses, and scenes frequently create a very strong association with the music. This association may even be stronger than that of a pop music performance by a single artist, unless, of course, that artist is a superstar such as Mariah Carey or Elton John, or a group like the ever pubescent Destiny's Child, Backstreet Boys, or 'N Sync. I bet you're already having an emotional reaction to the previous sentence. That's the point. Use music that produces a major emotional experience in your students. The sudden, strong, and shock impact of the music is what triggers the laughter and the association with the class demonstration and course content.

Sources for Music Ideas

To determine students' familiarity with different types of music, there are four options: (1) conduct a formal survey, (2) conduct an informal survey, (3) obtain media survey information, or (4) all of the above.

Conduct a formal survey.   At the beginning of the semester, usually the first class, you can ask students to write down their three to five favorite TV programs, movies, musicals, pop songs, or artists. Distribute one or two 3 × 5 cards and ask them, for example, to jot down their three favorite TV programs on side one and three favorite movies seen over the past year on side two. It takes about five minutes to complete this exercise. It is an effective ice-breaker and tone-setter for the first class. The students are immediately engaged. They're being asked what they think about something to which they can relate.

This survey can produce top 10 lists for the categories requested that will provide a pool of potential music choices. A class size of at least 30 is needed to generate enough frequencies for the students' favorites. Once the results are tabulated in the form of one or more top 10 lists, read them to the students. Tell them you will be using that information during the semester, but don't tell them how. The element of surprise must be preserved.

Alternatively, you can hand out a list of music and request students to check those with which they are familiar and "Really Like," "Like," or "Hate." One possible problem with this survey is that reading the list could cue students about the music you will be using during the semester/quarter and partially remove the element of surprise. This disadvantage should be weighed against the useful information the survey provides. Plus, it need not be administered in every class every year.

Conduct an informal survey.   Another less formal and less systematic approach is to simply chat with the students in between classes, in your office, at lunch, or by e-mail. They love to discuss their "favorites." Obviously it would be too time consuming to contact every student in large classes, although e-mail may produce a high response rate. However, it's the personal face-to-face contact that counts. The problem is that the feedback is not representive of the class and less comprehensive in terms of the information it yields. Despite these limitations, this strategy is still useful and can be effective with smaller classes.

Obtain media survey information.   A third choice is to not ask the students at all, but instead, use media surveys of viewer demographics to guess the TV programs and movies your students watch and the music to which they listen. Such surveys can be extremely informative, although not tailored to your specific class profile. Nielsen Media Research survey results on TV programs will be presented in the next section to furnish insight into what adults at different ages and races watch most frequently.

All of the above.   Among the three preceding sources of music informa-tion, I suggest using all that you have time to obtain. Each option furnishes slightly different answers to the music questions. Once you've field tested the music in class, the students are even in a better position to evaluate its effec-tiveness, plus they can still recommend other music favorites.

Impact of Student Characteristics

Underlying your choice of any piece of music are the characteristics and pref-erences of your students. You need to at least profile your students. Three characteristics that are critical to the selection of appropriate music are age, race/ethnicity, and gender. The distribution of your students according to each of those factors can influence your selection.

Age.   The TV programs our students probably watch, if they have any time, could be a galaxy away from what we watch. Surveys conducted in fall 1999 by Nielsen Media Research report the median ages of the audience watching primetime TV broadcast series. Programs for median ages of 22 to 39.9 are listed in Table 3.2. Those for median ages of 40 to 57.2 are shown in Table 3.3.

How many of you view any of the 20–25 programs at the beginning of the 22–39.9-year-old list? The only network that has focused programming on younger audiences is UPN. The major networks of NBC, ABC, and CBS have median age viewers of 45 to 50+. Drawing ideas for music and class demon-strations from TV programs that "everybody watches" is getting extremely difficult.

A better bet may be the movie box office blockbusters. The biggest money makers of the past three decades are listed in Table 3.4.

It may be safer to build instructional strategies on some of these films, because many people are familiar with the music and plots of movies due to the bombardment of advertising, even if they don't get the chance to see the movies.

Another option is to consider Broadway musicals. In addition to Broad-way and national touring road companies, musicals are performed regularly in most high schools, dinner theaters, and some colleges. During this past decade, we have even seen numerous revivals of musicals from the '50s, '60s, and '70s. Students have been exposed to many musicals by the time they enter our class-rooms. In fact, several have been also made into movie versions. We need to build on those "musical" experiences. A comprehensive list of musicals is pre-sented in Table 3.5, which may suggest a few ideas pertinent to what and how you teach.

TABLE 3.2 Median age of primetime TV broadcast series (22–39.9 years).

Program	Network	Median age
Mission Hill	WB	22.4
Dawson's Creek	WB	22.9
WWF Smackdown!	UPN	23.2
Moesha	UPN	24.9
The Parkers	UPN	25.6
Grown Ups	UPN	27.1
Roswell	WB	27.2
Family Guy	FOX	27.4
Buffy the Vampire Slayer	WB	27.7
Futurama	FOX	27.9
Malcolm & Eddie	UPN	28.0
Shasta McNasty	UPN	28.4
The Simpsons	FOX	28.4
Angel	WB	28.6
Felicity	WB	28.8
Get Real	FOX	28.9
Jack & Jill	WB	29.1
The Jamie Foxx Show	WB	29.6
Sabrina the Teenage Witch	ABC	30.1
Party of Five	FOX	30.1
Odd Man Out	ABC	30.1
Charmed	WB	30.2
Dilbert	UPN	30.4
Time of Your Life	FOX	30.5
That '70s Show	FOX	30.5
For Your Love	WB	30.6
Action	FOX	31.4

Continued

TABLE 3.2 *Continued*

Program	Network	Median age
The Steve Harvey Show	WB	31.5
King of the Hill	FOX	31.5
Boy Meets World	ABC	31.9
Wonderful World of Disney	ABC	32.8
Redhanded	UPN	33.6
7th Heaven	WB	33.6
7th Heaven: Beginnings	WB	33.6
The Hughleys	ABC	34.3
X-Files	FOX	34.5
Ally McBeal	FOX	35.3
Safe Harbor	WB	35.4
Whose Line Is It Anyway?	ABC	36.4
Wasteland	ABC	36.5
Friends	NBC	36.5
Oh Grow Up	ABC	36.7
Norm	ABC	36.7
Greed 1	FOX	36.8
Jesse	NBC	36.9
World's Wildest Police Videos	FOX	37.1
Drew Carey Show	ABC	37.1
The Strip	UPN	37.2
Two Guys and a Girl	ABC	37.6
Harsh Realm	FOX	37.7
Will & Grace	NBC	38.4
World's Funniest!	FOX	38.7
Mike O'Malley Show	NBC	38.9
Veronica's Closet	NBC	39.0
Star Trek: Voyager	UPN	39.9

Source: Nielsen Media Research

TABLE 3.3   Median age of primetime TV broadcast series (40–57.2 years).

Program	Network	Median age
Stark Raving Mad	NBC	40.1
Just Shoot Me	NBC	40.5
Dharma & Greg	ABC	40.5
Greed 2	FOX	41.1
Once and Again	ABC	41.2
Suddenly Susan	NBC	41.2
E.R.	NBC	41.3
Cops 2	FOX	41.4
Frasier	NBC	41.4
Blockbuster Cinema	UPN	41.5
Cops	FOX	41.7
3rd Rock From the Sun	NBC	41.9
Ryan Caulfield: Year One	FOX	42.5
Cold Feet	NBC	42.6
7 Days	UPN	42.7
America's Most Wanted	FOX	42.8
ABC Saturday Night Movie	ABC	43.0
NBC Sunday Night Movie	NBC	43.1
NFL Monday Night Football	ABC	43.7
Pretender	NBC	44.4
20/20 (Wednesday)	ABC	44.8
Profiler	NBC	44.8
The Practice	ABC	45.3
Third Watch	NBC	46.7
Dateline NBC (Tuesday)	NBC	46.8
20/20 Downtown	ABC	47.3
Law and Order	NBC	47.7
Dateline NBC (Monday)	NBC	48.0

Continued

TABLE 3.3 *Continued*

Program	Network	Median age
20/20 Friday	ABC	48.6
King of Queens	CBS	48.7
Law and Order SVU	NBC	48.9
Nash Bridges	CBS	48.9
Everybody Loves Raymond	CBC	49.0
Ladies Man	CBS	49.1
Law and Order (Friday)	NBC	49.4
Now and Again	CBS	49.5
The West Wing	NBC	50.4
Walker, Texas Ranger	CBS	51.1
Becker	CBS	51.1
20/20 (Monday)	ABC	51.2
Early Edition	CBS	51.2
Family Law	CBS	51.4
Martial Law	CBS	51.4
Dateline (Wednesday)	NBC	51.4
Providence	NBC	51.5
CBS Wednesday Movie	CBS	51.5
Work With Me	CBS	51.9
Dateline (Sunday 7 p.m.)	NBC	52.1
Judging Amy	CBS	53.3
48 Hours	CBS	53.4
Dateline NBC (Friday)	NBC	53.4
CBS Sunday Movie	CBS	53.7
Touched by an Angel	CBS	53.7
Chicago Hope	CBS	53.8
JAG	CBS	54.1
Who Wants to Be a Millionaire	ABC	54.5

TABLE 3.3 *Continued*

Program	Network	Median age
Candid Camera	CBS	54.5
Love & Money	CBS	54.7
Kids Say the Darndest Things	CBS	56.0
60 Minutes II	CBS	56.2
60 Minutes	CBS	56.6
Diagnosis Murder	CBS	57.2

Source: Nielsen Media Research

TABLE 3.4 Box office top 10 American films for the '70s, '80s, and '90s.

Rank	Decade		
	1970s	1980s	1990s
1	Star Wars (1977)	E.T.: The Extra-Terrestrial (1982)	Titanic (1997)
2	Jaws (1975)	Return of the Jedi (1983)	Jurassic Park (1993)
3	Grease (1978)	The Empire Strikes Back (1980)	Forrest Gump (1994)
4	The Exorcist (1973)	Batman (1989)	The Lion King (1994)
5	The Sting (1973)	Raiders of the Lost Ark (1981)	Independence Day (1996)
6	Close Encounters of the Third Kind (1977/80)	Ghostbusters (1984)	Home Alone (1990)
7	National Lampoon's Animal House (1978)	Beverly Hills Cop (1984)	Men in Black (1997)
8	Saturday Night Fever (1977)	Back to the Future (1985)	Twister (1996)
9	The Rocky Horror Picture Show (1975)	Indiana Jones and the Last Crusade (1989)	The Lost World: Jurassic Park (1997)
10	The Godfather (1972)	Indiana Jones and the Temple of Doom (1984)	Mrs. Doubtfire (1993)

Source: Tim Dirks (*tdirks@filmsite.org*)

TABLE 3.5   Broadway musicals.

Aïda	Forever Plaid	On the Town
Ain't Misbehavin'	Forever Swing	Once upon a Mattress
Annie	Fosse	Pajama Game
Annie Get Your Gun	42nd Street	Passion
Anyone Can Whistle	The Full Monty	The Phantom of the Opera
Anything Goes	A Funny Thing Happened on the Way to the Forum	Pippin
Aspects of Love		Porgy & Bess
Beauty and the Beast	Godspell	The Producers
Bells Are Ringing	The Goodbye Girl	Promises, Promises
Big	A Grand Night for Singing	Purlie
Brigadoon	Grease	Ragtime
Bring in 'da Noise, Bring in 'da Funk	Guys and Dolls	Redhead
	Gypsy	Rent
Bye Bye Birdie	Hair	Riverdance
Camelot	Hello, Dolly!	Saturday Night Fever
Carousel	How to Succeed in Business without Really Trying	The Scarlet Pimpernel
Cats		The Secret Garden
Chess		Seven Brides for Seven Brothers
Chicago	Into the Woods	
A Chorus Line	Jane Eyre	1776
Cinderella	Jekyll & Hyde	Seussical
City of Angels	Jelly's Last Jam	She Loves Me
The Civil War	Jesus Christ Superstar	Show Boat
A Class Act	Joseph and the Amazing Technicolor Dreamcoat	Singin' in the Rain
Company		Smokey Joe's Cafe
Contact	The King and I	Song & Dance
Crazy for You	Kiss Me, Kate	The Sound of Music
Damn Yankees	Kiss of the Spider Woman	South Pacific
Dancin'	La Cage aux Folles	Starlight Express
The Dead	Les Misérables	Steel Pier
Dreamgirls	The Lion King	Sunset Boulevard
Evita	A Little Night Music	Sweeney Todd
Fame	Little Shop of Horrors	Titanic
The Fantasticks	Mame	Victor/Victoria
Fiddler on the Roof	Mamma Mia!	West Side Story
Fiorello	Man of La Mancha	The Who's Tommy
Five Guys Named Moe	Me and My Girl	Will Rogers Follies
Flower Drum Song	Miss Saigon	The Wiz
Follies	The Music Man	You're a Good Man, Charlie Brown
Footloose	My Fair Lady	
Forbidden Broadway	Oklahoma!	Zorba
Forbidden Hollywood	Oliver!	

The trick in choosing music or building a demonstration based on a TV program, movie, or musical is to search for that common denominator with which the majority of the students are familiar. If you're in doubt, ask them. Otherwise, the music and demo could easily bomb.

Race/ethnicity.   If you thought the gap between your students' ages and yours needed a major suspension bridge, the ethnicity factor may require something even longer. A comparison of the top 20 primetime TV programs watched during the 2000–2001 season in African American, Hispanic/Latino, and Caucasian households is displayed in Table 3.6. In general, TV viewing appears to be an ethnically segregated experience. Following *Monday Night Football,* the most watched programs by African Americans are six "black-cast" sitcoms and one drama which ranked near the bottom of 120 programs watched by Caucasians. This trend continued for the 2001–2002 season with *Bernie Mac* in the number one spot, followed by four "black cast" sitcoms and *Monday Night Football* at number six. Five of the six most watched sitcoms among Caucasian viewers are the lily-white *Everybody Loves Raymond, Friends, Will & Grace, Frasier,* and *Just Shoot Me.* They do not even appear in the African Americans' top 20.

That pattern is upheld in Hispanic/Latino households as well. The 20 most-watched programs among Hispanic viewers are on the Spanish-language network Univision. The No. 1 English-language program was *Temptation Island.* However, despite the fact that only one FOX program made the two other top 20 lists in Table 3.6, 12 appear on the Hispanic top 20 list. This may be due to the high concentration of younger viewers in Hispanic homes. FOX is the youngest-skewing of the major networks.

The problem is that TV's much criticized "virtual whitewash" is real world TV and real world. Each race tends to watch casts on TV programs who are entirely or mostly made up of its respective race. This practice is also generalizable to movies. This segregated pattern follows the racial stratification in society (e.g., colleges/universities, organized religions, social clubs, vacation resorts).

There is some common ground, however, in the top 20. Nine shows appeared on the African American and Caucasian lists: *Millionaire* (Tues. and Wed.), *E.R., Monday Night Football, The Practice, Law & Order, C.S.I., Survivor II, and Temptation Island.* Four of these programs—*E.R., Monday Night Football, Survivor II,* and *Temptation Island*—are also on the Hispanic/Latino top 20. This is the greatest common viewing experience ever. Unfortunately, except for those of us who teach graduate students, those programs are in the 40+ age group.

The popularity of the "reality TV" shows, especially *Survivor II* and *Temptation Island,* across ethnic groups seemed to breakdown the ethnically

TABLE 3.6 Top 20 primetime broadcast series for African American, Hispanic/Latino, and Caucasian households (2000–2001).

African American households			Hispanic/Latino households (English-language programs only)			Caucasian households		
Rank	Program	Network	Rank	Program	Network	Rank	Program	Network
1	Monday Night Football	ABC	1	Temptation Island[3]	FOX	1	Survivor II[3]	CBS
2	My Wife & Kids[1]	ABC	2	Simpsons	FOX	2	E.R.[3]	NBC
3	The Parkers[1]	UPN	3	Monday Night Football	ABC	3	Millionaire (Wed.)	ABC
4	The Hughleys[1]	UPN	4	WWF Smackdown!	UPN	4	Everybody Loves Raymond	CBS
5	Girlfriends[1]	UPN	5	Malcolm in the Middle	FOX	5	Millionaire (Tues.)	ABC
6	Moesha[1]	UPN	6	Boot Camp[3]	FOX	6	Friends	NBC
7	City of Angels[1]	CBS	7	E.R.[3]	NBC	7	Millionaire (Sun.)	ABC
8	Steve Harvey[1]	WB	8	Survivor II[3]	CBS	8	Millionaire (Thurs.)	ABC
9	Temptation Island[3]	FOX	9	Dark Angel[2]	FOX	8	Law & Order[3]	NBC
10	The Practice[3]	ABC	10	Friends	NBC	10	West Wing[3]	NBC
10	The District[1]	CBS	10	Grounded for Life	FOX	11	Monday Night Football	ABC
10	WWF Smackdown!	UPN	10	That '70s Show (Tues.)[3]	FOX	12	The Practice[3]	ABC
13	Millionaire (Wed.)	ABC	13	Titus	FOX	12	Becker[3]	CBS
14	C.S.I.[3]	CBS	14	X-Files	FOX	12	Will & Grace	NBC

15	E.R.[3]	NBC	15	That '70s Show (Wed.)[3]	FOX	15	C.S.I.[3]	CBS
15	Law & Order[3]	NBC	15	Wonderful World of Disney	ABC	16	60 Minutes	CBS
17	Survivor II[3]	CBS	17	King of the Hill	FOX	17	Frasier	NBC
18	Millionaire (Tues.)	ABC	17	Will & Grace	NBC	18	Millionaire (Fri.)	ABC
19	Touched by an Angel[1]	CBS	19	Millionaire (Sun.)	ABC	18	Just Shoot Me	NBC
20	Judging Amy[1]	CBS	20	America's Most Wanted	FOX	20	Temptation Island[3]	FOX

Source: Nielsen Media Research
[1] African American cast or lead character(s)
[2] Hispanic lead character
[3] Multi-ethnic ensemble program that features African Americans

segregated pattern of TV viewing. Unfortunately, this pattern didn't last long. In the 2001–2002 season, only *Survivor* survived the top 20 of Caucasian households and no "reality" program appeared in the African American top 20.

So far, considering three racial/ethnic groups, our best bet for music and demonstrations is *E.R.* or *Monday Night Football.* Not a big selection. But we haven't considered gender yet.

The last source to review for musical material is the Broadway musical. Over the past half a century there have been only a handful of musicals with mostly black or all black casts, including the following:

- Ain't Misbehavin'
- Bring in 'da Noise, Bring in 'da Funk
- Jelly's Last Jam
- Porgy & Bess
- Purlie
- Smokey Joe's Cafe

Unfortunately, there is no available ticket-goer evidence to determine whether African Americans supported these musicals more than any others.

Gender.   According to Nielsen Media Research, women dominate prime-time viewing. Of 116 regularly scheduled TV series, 95 attracted more females than males week after week. For example, *E.R.,* the most watched series, attracts nearly twice as many women as men. Network schedules are larded with programs like *Providence, Judging Amy,* and *Felicity.* Even programs designed to lure men, such as *Baywatch* (where, incidentally, I learned CPR) and *Charlie's Angels* of yesteryear, had a larger following among females in their heyday. Only two programs during 2000–2001 had a 50-50 male-female balance: *Boston Public* and *Temptation Island.*

The testosterone-driven programs focus on sports, action movies, and the raunchy and ribald. Men consistently prefer to watch other men playing games, talking, and doing anything considered manly. Comedian Rob Becker in his long-running Broadway show *Defending the Caveman* says: "A guy wants three things: something exploding, a beautiful woman, or sports. If he finds a program in which a beautiful women in shoulder pads is exploding, he's there." The top primetime programs with the highest percentage of male viewers by type of program are as follows:

Sports
Monday Night Football
Fox NFL Sunday

WWF Smackdown!

NFL Monday Showcase

CBS NFL Today

Animated

Futurama

King of the Hill

The Simpsons

South Park (Comedy Central)

Drama

Dark Angel

Cops

Police Videos

The X-Files

Star Trek: Voyager

Sitcom/Fluff

Malcolm in the Middle

Titus

The Man Show (Comedy Central)

The gender gap also needs to be addressed in the choice of music and demonstrations related to movies and Broadway musicals. There is a clear gender break in the preference of males for movies about sports and action with gratuitous violence, while females tilt toward romantic dramas and comedies, especially stories about terminally-ill ice skaters. Women also tend to be more interested in theater and the performing arts. Depending on your class gender distribution, be careful and sensitive in your selection of music and development of skits from the preceding sources.

Techniques for Infusing Music in College Courses

Based on the preceding guidelines for selecting music and generating class demonstrations from TV programs, movies, Broadway musicals, and popular music, I have tested nine techniques in my classes over the past 15 years. Those techniques are: (1) pre-class warm-ups, (2) first-class blockbusters, (3) class openings/topic introductions, (4) demonstrations/skits, (5) written activity interludes, (6) test reviews, (7) post-review send-offs, (8) post-test pick-me-ups, and (9) holiday frolic. The remainder of this chapter is devoted to these techniques. A description, rationale, and step-by-step procedure for executing each one is presented. A summary of the more than 40 pieces of music cited throughout the chapter along with the artists and CD titles and catalogue numbers are listed in Appendix A. Although only one detailed example per technique is outlined in the text, several others are given in Appendices B–E in an easy to copy format.

Pre-Class Warm-Ups

If your schedule permits you to arrive at class at least five to ten minutes early, you should consider some warm-up music. While you are preparing your class materials, setting up audiovisual equipment, passing out handouts, and/or performing any other pre-class activities, press a button on your CD or tape player with classical, popular, jazz, rock, or country and western selections that will prime your students and set the tone and mood for class. "What type of music?" you query. It depends on the mood you want to create. One option is any type of music that will not incite your students to riot. Ask them for music choices or choose some of your favorites. How many Gen-Xers are familiar with Mozart, Bach, Bizet, etc.? Only play the music for three to five minutes before class. When you stop the music, class begins. Since students tend to wander into class like it's a buffet over 15–20 minutes after class has begun, it may stimulate students to be on time. At least the music can provide a break in the typical "chatter" noise and permit students to relax, unwind, or get an emotional lift for a few minutes in between classes.

First-Class Blockbusters

The first class of the semester/quarter in any course is the tone-setter for all other classes. A student's first impressions of you, the content (what you teach), your method(s) of presentation (how you teach), course requirements, and your expectations are frequently highly predictive of the rest of the course. From a student's perspective, it could be the 4th of July or Armageddon. Since the students often do not expect any fireworks, any effort to jumpstart their motivation to be in the course will be appreciated. So get ready to turbocharge your students.

If you're concerned about the time this "blockbuster" will consume, most require about 1–1.5 minutes. The duration of its impact is immeasurable. Students will continue to discuss the blockbuster long after the course is over. It succeeds because (1) it catches the students off-guard (i.e., totally unexpected), (2) it's based on a common denominator, bigger than life movie or TV experience, (3) it's a parody of that movie or TV program, (4) it's visual and auditory, and (5) it requires the students' involvement.

Each blockbuster I present describes only one classroom application (my statistics courses), which can be adapted easily to a variety of class as well as professional presentations. The humor is inserted into the script via transparencies accompanying the music. The music in all cases has been recorded on high quality audiotapes from an original CD and is played on a Radio Shack cassette tape recorder (CTR-116, 14-1122). This recorder provides adequate volume for most class sizes up to 100. Placing the recorder near a lectern microphone or dangling a lavaliere on the speaker will furnish enough sound for the Roman coliseum. You can certainly use a much larger boom box, but the compactness and volume of the small recorder can't be beat, especially when you have a variety of props and materials to carry to class.

Here is one sample course opener:

Star Wars
   a. *Music:* Theme from *Star Wars*
   b. *Time:* 1 minute
   c. *Props:* 2 light sabers
      mini-flashlight
   d. *Preparation:* Light sabers should be covered on a table and easily accessible
   e. *Transparencies:* 3 are required to simulate beginning of movie

A long time ago at a School of _____
far, far away . . .

STAT WARS:
The Empire Installs Indoor Plumbing

EPISODE 90210
"The VICTORY"
It is a period of strife, skirmishes, and bloodshed. And that's just in the parking lot. During one of the battles, rebel students managed to steal secret plans to the School's ultimate weapon:
ROBO-PROFESSOR
The students responsible were captured,
smacked with a broom,
and sent to the School of Medicine
for future draft choices to be named later
when the print on this transparency is enlarged
because it's now becoming an eye test . . .

f. *Execution:*
   1. Test projector with a different trans, focus, and align image on screen
   2. Turn off projector light
   3. Place first trans on projector
   4. Blackout room (Needed for physical effects to contrast with light sabers and transparencies, but has significant emotional effects as well. At the beginning when the room is in total blackout, students feel tension, excitement, and anticipation until something happens. Laughter in response to steps 8, 11, or 13 serves as a release valve for those emotions.)
   5. Use mini-flashlight to find transparencies
   6. Turn on projector light
   7. Place second trans on projector
   8. Press button to begin music
   9. Pick up light sabers, extend, and turn on
   10. Move to right or left side of screen behind you so background is totally black
   11. Movements with light sabers to music can mimic beach lifeguard signals, air traffic signals to guide aircraft to the gate, and fencing or sword fighting (about 30 seconds total)
   12. Place third trans on projector with paper cover over entire trans except first line
   13. Scroll trans slowly, revealing one line at a time
   14. After last line, turn off projector light
   15. Turn off music
   16. Turn on room lights

Additional blockbusters, including *Mission: Impossible* and *Home Improvement,* are described in Appendix B at the end of the chapter.

Class Openings/Topic Introductions

Using music with a minimal visual demo (you and a transparency, not a sparkler) can be very energizing to students at the beginning of class or to introduce a new topic. The techniques described in this section are simpler to plan and execute than the preceding blockbusters. They fall into two categories: generic and content specific. The former can be used in almost any context or with a wide range of topics; the latter is more restrictive to only certain types of content.

Generic Techniques

Psycho

a. *Music:* Shower music from *Psycho,* plus a blood curdling scream
b. *Time.* 10 seconds
c. *Props:* large plastic (toy) carving knife
d. *Preparation:* Conceal knife in inside breast pocket or in a large handbag
e. *Execution:*
   1. Say "Whenever I teach this topic, I know what my students are thinking. There is one visual image that pops into your minds and one typical reaction."
   2. Press button to begin music
   3. Pull out knife and make large stabbing movements
   4. Stop stabbing when music stops
   5. After scream, stop the tape

Five other generic examples are given in Appendix C at the end of the chapter, such as *Star Trek, Mister Rogers' Neighborhood, 60 Minutes, Masterpiece Theatre, The Odd Couple, The Good, the Bad, and the Ugly,* and *Evita.*

Content-Specific Techniques

The X-Files

a. *Music:* Theme from *X-Files* TV series
b. *Time:* 40 seconds
c. *Props:* Inflatable alien (or alien mask)
d. *Preparation:* Hide the largest alien you can locate (2'–3' is adequate) in a large black plastic bag. (Or, hide mask in a small bag.) Leave it on the floor near the overhead projector.
e. *Transparencies:* 1 trans should be a parody of the *The X-Files,* such as $\overline{X}$-Files, which is the statistical symbol for average, the *XL-Files* or *XXL-Files, X–Y Files,* etc; the second trans should be a parody of the paranormal, such as paranormal distribution, paranormal personality, etc.

$\overline{X}$-Files

f. *Execution:*
   1. Test projector procedure
   2. Turn out projector light
   3. Place first trans on projector

4. Say, "Today, those of you who answer all of the central tendency homework problems correctly will have the opportunity to appear in the brand new (fall or spring) TV series, *The X̄-Files*"
5. Turn on projector light
6. Press button to begin music
7. Pull alien out of bag and slowly raise him, with his head peaking over the projector, until he is sitting or standing on top of the projector (*Note:* Total room blackout cannot be used if students are supposed to see the alien. Projector light by itself is inadequate.)

   or

   Bend down, pull mask out of bag, and put it on. (*Note:* Use total room blackout if mask is glow in the dark.)
8. After a few moments, remove alien
9. Say, "In this new series you will be able to study paranormal distributions"
10. Place second trans on projector
11. When music ends, stop the tape
12. Turn off projector light

Two other examples of content-specific techniques, including "YMCA" and *Sesame Street,* are presented in Appendix D at the end of the chapter.

Demonstrations/Skits

A visual demonstration of a theory, process, or application of a concept can be a powerful vehicle for learning. Frequently the demonstration requires students to think through a process rather than memorize it. Higher-order thinking skills are needed for understanding, application, analysis, and evaluation. Students actually *see* the process, *solve* the problem, or *critique* the encounter. The demonstration can train their eyeballs and minds differently from other teaching techniques. What they read on paper may be verbal or quantitative, but when it is acted out by the Not-Ready-for-Classtime Players, it can take on a whole new meaning and have a major impact on learning. The demonstration can be instructional CPR, by resuscitating a dead topic or pumping life into boring content, figuratively, and literally if you teach courses in the healthcare professions.

Creating a demonstration involves transforming a verbal or quantitative concept, process, or problem into a visual image. The techniques borrow heavily from the experience and craft of theater (Timpson et al., 1997). What would it be like to sit in the students' seats and *see* and *participate* in how to solve an equation or to respond to an angry client?

The effectiveness of the demonstration hinges on the students' level of engagement. There are four stages in the execution of the demonstration that can maximize engagement: (1) pre-demo set-up, (2) grabbing the students' attention, (3) seeing or walking through the demo, and (4) post-demo Q & A follow-up.

Pre-demo set-up. Prior to the demo, introduce the topic and briefly describe the theory, process, or application. A list of rules or step-by-step procedure can prepare the students for the content and context for the demo.

Grabbing the students' attention. Now that the students have a serious preview of the content, it's time to introduce the demo. This provides the opportunity to use music to trigger laughter in the class. The music is the hook to grab the students' attention and prime their minds for the demonstration; the demonstration itself maintains their attention. Proceed as follows:

1. Prior to the demo class, usually the class before, pre-select a group of men or women or both to participate in the demo. I usually select a dozen of one gender or half and half. The primary skill requirement to participate in my demos is the ability to ambulate, so hardly anyone can weasel out of the demo. (I also joke with the students that once they participate in a demo, they can list their roles on their resumés. That'll certainly distinguish their resumés from the competition in applying for a job. For example, "I was an outlier in a skewed distribution" or "I was a significant predictor in a multiple regression equation." You never know how valuable that can be.) When I ask the students to participate, I tell them exactly what I want them to do and assure them I will not embarrass them. Obtaining the students' trust is critical. If any student is embarrassed during a demo, that could be the end of all demos. Request the students to sit all the way in the back of the room. That physical distance permits a looooong entrance when they are asked to come to the front of the class for the demo. (*Note:* Select a different group of students for each demo to get as many students as possible involved.)

2. Say, "It's now time to demonstrate this process," or "It's now time for our Not-Ready-for-Classtime Players to demonstrate this process." This statement will immediately get the students' attention and generate interest in anticipation of what's going to happen next.

3. Say, "Who are the women participating in the demo?" After they raise their hands, say, "Please come forward and line up on the right side."

4. As the women stand up, press button to begin the music.

   Choose from the following:

   "I'm Every Woman" (Whitney Houston)

   "She's a Lady" (Tom Jones)

   "Survivor" (Destiny's Child)

   "I Will Survive" (Gloria Gaynor)

   "What a Feeling" (Irene Cara)

   "Wanabe" (Spice Girls)

   "Bad Girls" (Donna Summer)

   "She Works Hard for the Money" (Donna Summer)

   "Friends" (Bette Midler)

   "Simply Irresistible" (Robert Palmer)

   "Stayin' Alive" (Bee Gees)

5. Once they are lined up, stop the music. Change tapes, if necessary.

6. Repeat steps 3 and 4 for the men, except ask them to line up on the opposite side.

   Choose from the following:

   "Gonna Fly Now" (Theme from *Rocky*)

   "Bad Boys" (Theme from *Cops*, Inner Circle)

   "Bad" (Michael Jackson)

   "Do You Hear the People Sing" (*Les Misérables*)

   "Olympic Fanfare" (Noel Leon Arnaud)

   "Born to Be Wild" (Steppenwolf)

   "Hawaii Five-O" (The Ventures)

7. Once the men are lined up, stop the music (15–30 seconds).

8. Begin the demo.

The effect of the music on the class is similar to that of a dynamite stand-up joke. And steps 2–7 require less than 90 seconds of class time. Because the music serves as the punchline to the serious set-up, the choice of song is crucial to its impact. Pick music that is immediately recognizable. Try any of the titles suggested above, choose one of your own, or ask the students for their preferences. My students' suggestions have been incorporated into my list. Just use your imagination. You are the "disc jockey" in charge. [*Caution:* If you use current pop songs, such as "Lady Marmalade" (Christina Aguilera,

Lil' Kim, Mya, & Pink) from the movie *Moulin Rouge* and "Oops! . . . I Did It Again" (Britney Spears), they may need to change every semester or year depending on what's popular at the time. In fact, as you read this page, those songs are no longer current. That's the problem. Most current hit songs do not have staying power. Also, they're usually appropriate only for younger undergraduates, not older graduate students.]

The title, the lyrics, the melody, and the visual and emotional association of the music with each student's personal experience have an instantaneous effect. The extreme contrast between the expected serious introduction of the women and men and the unexpected music are the ingredients in the humor formula that create the laughter. Although using only women or men in a demo is effective, including both genders is often more effective. If large numbers of women and men are present, there's a greater identification and, consequently, a greater impact. As the two groups of students stand in front of their classmates, the level of engagement hits a climax. The class can't imagine what's going to happen next. The anticipation on their faces and their body language, as they move to the edges of their hard little seats, are the signs of students eager to see a demo that delivers.

Depending on the music you select, the students involved in the demo can be primed to juice-up the visual component that accompanies the music—their grand musical entrance. For example, if you're going to use *Rocky,* before or after the class prior to the demo, ask a few of the guys to wear hooded sweatshirts and tell them to put their hoods up and jog with their fists in the air when they get the cue. For Michael Jackson's "Bad," ask the students to dance, bounce, or moon walk. Some students are typically less inhibited and more willing to respond physically to the music than others. Encourage students to respond to the music as they see fit.

These added, impromptu visual effects contribute significantly to the parody and, consequently, to the humor effect. The laughter associated with any of these juiced-up entrances compared to having students simply walk to the front is noticeable. The students' exaggerated movements are simply funny. They're also not being performed at a party, where students wouldn't even take a second glance. The jogging, bouncing, or dancing is funny because it is totally out of context, *unexpected* in any college classroom. It piggybacks on the incongruity created by the music.

Further, the contrast between the visual images that pop into the students' brains when they first hear the music and the visual images of the men or women in class adds to the humor. The most dramatic example of this contrast occurs when the theme from *Rocky* is used. Visualizing Rocky running down the streets of Philadelphia or up the museum steps against a half a dozen guys in hooded sweatshirts running around the classroom is hilarious. It's even funnier when the guys are professors. When I demonstrate this strategy in my humor workshops for faculty, seeing "older" professors jog around the room to *Rocky* can be hilarious. In fact, that sight triggered hysteria in one female professor; she just couldn't stop laughing. I couldn't proceed until she stopped. When she did, I asked "What's so funny?" To which she responded, while looking at the male professors standing in front of the room, "They don't look like Rocky!" Everyone started laughing again. I responded, "No one does." That was the whole point of the exercise.

During a single semester, when half a dozen music-demos are sprinkled throughout all of the classes, the surprise element and the impact of the technique remain constant. The students have no clue when a demo is going to occur, what form it will take, who will participate in it, or the music that will introduce it. That's why it seems to be a consistently effective teaching strategy.

Seeing or walking through the demo.   When music is used to accompany the students' grand procession to the front of the classroom, the entire class is jolted into attention, fully engaged, laughing, and their minds are sharpened in preparation for the demonstration. Once the student-actors are standing before the entire class, you have to figure out what to do with them before they revolt. There are at least three content-based types of demonstrations that can be presented in any course: (1) process, (2) problem-solving, and (3) case study.

In order for the class to see a *process*, you need to direct and choreograph the students' movements through the process or use their characteristics to simulate elements in the process. For example, the concept of relationships between variables or quantities can be illustrated using obvious similarities and differences between pairs of students. Characteristics, such as gender, height, hair color, hair length, eyesight (glasses-no glasses), and clothes (pants-skirt or dress), can be identified as the bases for the comparisons. Engage the class by asking them specific content questions: Which pair of students has the most characteristics in common? Which pair has the least? Seeing those relationships metaphorically in the forms of their classmates gives new meaning to the statistical concept of *correlation*.

The problem-solving demo is similar to the process demo; it is just problem oriented. The focus of this demo is on how to solve a verbal or quantitative *problem*. For example, in my statistics classes I use students to represent data points, variables, and statistical quantities to "act out" distributions, equations, research designs, and statistical tests. The demo is a role-play simulation where students are assigned specific roles to illustrate concepts, principles, rules, and structured relationships (De Neve & Heppner, 1997). As the class solves the problem, they gain an understanding of the concepts and the process. They are thinking through the entire process to discover the solution. The exercise promotes creativity and often produces a Q & A exchange. The discussion that follows not only helps clarify elements in the problem-solving process, but often extends applications in different directions. Since the demonstration is generic, it can be used as the anchor for any application.

Another type of demonstration is the *case study*. Rather than just read about it and discuss it, act it out. In fact, two humorous spins can be put on a "real world" case study: (1) Create a humorous hypothetical case with all of the essential elements, or (2) in contrast to the case of "what is the correct action to take," create a humorous case of "what not to do" in a particular situation with a client or patient. These role playing exercises can be performed by faculty, students, or both. They can be structured or unstructured (Bonwell & Eison, 1991). The experiences of actually seeing the human encounter in the practice of business, medicine, nursing, law, or other case based professions can have a stronger impact on learning than trying to visualize it from a written description. The case demo will generate loads of questions and discussion.

Other types of demonstrations that are student-centered may include dramatizations of actual events, character studies, debates, and team processes. You may write, direct, and choreograph these demos or they may be created by small groups of students. As small group assignments, the demos may be performed in front of the entire class or for another small group. They challenge students to think, to analyze, and to discover. The greater visibility provides greater accountability and engagement by all of the students. Demonstrations are possible in every content area. They provide a highly visual, interactive, dynamic vehicle for learning. They are limited only by your (or your students') imagination.

Post-demo Q & A follow-up.   As the foregoing descriptions indicate, the demo can really stimulate thinking and generate very spirited in-class discussion. Capitalize on the enthusiasm and energy produced from the demo. When making subsequent verbal or quantitative applications of the material, anchor the explanations and discussion in the demo. Give the students an ample opportunity to ask questions and flush out their ideas in a follow-up Q & A session. However, you should also prepare questions to draw out the students' multiple intelligences to solve complex problems and other tasks requiring higher-order thinking skills. Ask them to critique the demo according to a prespecified set of rules or guidelines. For example, if you used a case study demo, solicit in written or oral form "what went right" and "what went wrong" in the physician-patient encounter.

Another follow-up to the demo might be to assign other problems to small groups as a role play activity (McKeachie, 1994), similar to what was presented in the class demo. First, the students see the activity modeled in class; then they do it. This strategy builds on the momentum of the demo; it may be performed in class as an active-learning exercise or out of class as a problem-solving application assignment.

All of these follow-up techniques continue to draw on the students' multiple intelligences in verbal, mathematical, interpersonal, and intrapersonal domains beyond those already tapped by the demo. The learning from the demo is, thus, reinforced and generalized to new applications.

Written Activity Interludes

Anytime students are requested to write something in class requiring 30 seconds to three minutes presents another opportunity for music. Consider what happens when students are writing answers to one or two questions you posed, writing a one-minute paper on the three most important points just covered, or solving a case or problem. What do you hear? NOTHING! Dead silence. Your students' brains are marinating. Certainly you don't want to disturb their concentration on the task you assigned, but it is possible to play music that isn't distracting and can even produce a chuckle or two or relax them.

The music you select is critical. If you want to produce laughter, pick music such as the theme from *Seinfeld* or *Jeopardy!* Other themes from popular TV shows or movies could also be used, but they may not be humorous. A couple of examples are "The Rainbow Connection" from *The Muppet Movie,* sung by our favorite muppet, Kermie, and the theme from *Cheers*. If soothing background music is appropriate, choose classical pieces, but not the *1812 Overture*. Trying to solve a problem while cannons are blasting in your classroom could be traumatic.

This musical interlude as a break from all of the other activities in class can be a welcome addition. It can create humor and a playful or restful mood within the context of the written assignment. The length of the music should also match the length of the activity. The timing for such music should be carefully planned with the writing activity. It should not be overused. As with all of the other music techniques described in this chapter, the element of surprise is essential to obtain the humorous effect.

Test Reviews

I've been using the *Jeopardy!* review format for my undergraduate and graduate statistics exams for more than 10 years. It has proven extremely effective. Not only can it be adapted to any content, but humor can be injected into the answers, and the theme music for *Final Jeopardy!* is recognizable to everyone. Despite the current game show fad with *Who Wants to Be a Millionaire, The Weakest Link,* etc., none seems to have the characteristics of *Jeopardy!,* especially the theme music which induces laughter by itself.

In fact, they have NO real music unless you call BOM BOM BOMM! or DUM DUM, DUM DUM, DUM DUM! music. Probably the best term to describe it is annoying or irritating.

The Weakest Link's recall drill format could be embarrassing to all except the best prepared students in your class, in other words, the majority of the weak links. The primary goal of the review is to build knowledge and confidence in the linkies, not to show off those few knowies. This format is too intimidating for most students.

Who Wants to . . . is in multiple-choice format, which could be identical to your exam format. Therefore, what type of content would you include in a multiple-choice review that's NOT on the exam? I think the idea is to review content that will be ON the exam, but not necessarily in the same question format. The multiple-choice format can also limit the review to recognition of information rather than recall, which is a notch higher on the learning chain. Also the redundancy of the *Millionaire* and the repetitiveness of expressions such as "Is that your final answer?" and of using "lifelines" are insulting to college students. Plus, one of those formats with all of the BOM BOM etc. and expressions is very time consuming.

The *Who Wants to Be a Millionaire* format can be used with one multiple-choice item for the whole class. The humor can be inserted into the item stem or choices (see Chapter 8). A step-by-step example is given in Appendix E at the end of the chapter.

The more flexible and efficient *Jeopardy!* format is described below:

Jeopardy! Review
  a. *Music:* Theme from *Final Jeopardy!*
  b. *Time:* Variable, dependent on amount of content to be covered
  c. *Preparation:* The most time-consuming aspect of using the *Jeopardy!* format is writing the review material and the humor. It's advisable to start with one category of content at a time and try out that first in one of your reviews. Then you can simply add *Jeopardy!* material, one category at a time, to subsequent reviews. Here is a suggested procedure for converting your serious content into a jocular *Jeopardy!* version:
    1. List the basic content you want to cover in your review. It may be facts and/or problem-solving situations. Higher-order thinking skills can be drilled by requiring students to make decisions when

presented with scenarios in your discipline. They can simulate the professional decisions of a physician, nurse, lawyer, teacher, accountant, economist, psychologist, geologist, researcher, serial killer, or drug kingpin/queenpin.

2. Convert the content into *Jeopardy!* format answers (see Trebek & Bersocchini, 1990; Trebek & Griffin, 1992; *http://www.nintendo.com/n64/jeopardy* for billions of examples).

3. After each answer, add a humorous cue. That cue is the key that triggers the laughter and makes the review FUN!!

4. Prepare all of the answers in *Jeopardy!* format blue boxes under category headings. Money values are optional. The trick is to cover all of the review material efficiently and hysterically so the students are thoroughly prepared for the exam. The actual game format is too time-consuming for the test review.

5. Write the *Final Jeopardy!* item. It should be a problem that is important and requires special attention because it may have been an item with which some students have experienced serious difficulty or confusion.

6. Develop an answer sheet with blanks that students can use to record their "questions."

d. *Transparencies:* You will need transparencies for the following;
   1. *Jeopardy!* Review
   2. Each category
   3. Each answer
   4. *Final Jeopardy!*
   5. Category
   6. Answer

Examples for formatting these transparencies are available in *Gone with the Wind* (Chapters 6 and 7) and on the *Jeopardy!* Web sites.

e. Execution:
   1. Distribute the *Jeopardy!* answer sheet to the students
   2. Place *Jeopardy!* Review trans on projector and say, "I think we're ready to begin our *Jeopardy!* Review."
   3. Turn on projector light
   4. Say, "For each category in the review, I will present specific answers. Write the content questions in the numbered blanks on your answer sheet. This will provide a self-assessment to diagnose what you know or don't know in preparation for the exam. After

we have completed a category, we will review each item and answer any questions you might have. I'm not sure where you are right now in test preparation; but, by the time this review is over, you should be able to pinpoint the specific areas you need to study for the test."

5. Place first category trans on projector and say, "The first category is HUMOR."

6. Place the 1st answer trans on projector and say, "The answer for number 1 is":

> **This is the number of elements in most forms of humor delivered orally and also the number of bears who mauled Goldilocks.**

Read each answer aloud as the students read it. Then pause a few seconds until it appears that most students have finished writing their question.

7. Place the second answer trans on the projector and just say "Number 2, . . ." (pause)

8. Repeat step 7 for every answer in the category

9. Go back to number 1 and say, "For the first answer, shout out your question." Provide clarification and explanations as necessary, and answer students' questions.

10. Repeat step 9 for all answers.

11. Repeat steps 5–10 for all categories.

12. Place *Final Jeopardy!* trans on projector and say, "It is now time for *Final Jeopardy!*

13. Place category trans on projector and say, "The category is _____."

14. Say, "You will have 30 seconds to write your question to the following answer."

15. Place answer trans on projector and read answer.

16. Say, "Good luck!"

17. Press button to begin music.

18. As music comes to an end, say, "How many of you need more time?" Usually a few could use more time. Let the tape continue to play a repeat of the *Jeopardy!* theme.

19. When the music ends, stop the tape

20. Say, "On the count of 3, I want you to shout out your question. Ready. 1, 2, 3."

Post-Review Send-Offs

After the test review, send the students out of class pumped up and motivated to do their best on the exam. A few choice words of encouragement should be followed by appropriate music as they leave to set a proper supportive tone and the feeling that you really care about their performance. Consider the following:

1. Say, "As you prepare for the exam, contemplate the thoughtful words to this song to motivate you to study extra hard."

2. Press the button to begin the music.

   "Hakuna Matata" (*Lion King*)

   or

   "We Will Rock You" (Queen)

   Prior to the final exam, I do the following:

1. Say, "I know you're going to ace the final. I have selected a theme song for you that reflects my respect for your abilities and confidence in you."

2. Press button to begin music

   "We Are the Champions" (Queen)

Post-Test Pick-Me-Ups

At the beginning of the first or second class after the exam when you comment on the students' performance or answer questions about the exam, use music to say something positive to those who didn't do as well as they expected. It is best to do this at the end of class as students get ready to leave. Simply do the following:

1. Say, "I know some of you didn't do as well on the exam as you expected. I look forward to working with you to make necessary first quarter adjustments. I know you'll perform significantly better on the next exam. Despite your disappointment, seriously think about the words to this song."

2. Press button to begin music

   Choose from the following:

   "Tomorrow" (*Annie*)

   "Don't Worry, Be Happy" (Bobby McFerrin) (Use singing fish, Billy Bass, if you have it.)

"What a Wonderful World" (Louis Armstrong)

"Happiness" (*You're a Good Man, Charlie Brown*)

"The Impossible Dream" (*Man of LaMancha*)

Holiday Frolic

As if the preceding seven techniques don't provide enough ideas on how to inject music into your course, I thought I would add just one more that's consistent with the spirit of those methods, but has no instructional value whatsoever. It's purely for fun.

When holidays roll around, consider appropriate music and a solo demo with costumes and props. But be careful with religious characters and music; your choice could be offensive. For example, dressing up like Moses in a sheet and Birkenstocks to deliver the Top 10 Commandments of (some content) or wearing a dreadlock wig and tam à la Rastafarian could be interpreted as making mock of religious figures. I suggest avoiding such characterizations.

Instead, consider costumes, props, and music if your class falls on Halloween. Stay away from evil, grotesque, and vulgar costumes. Choose relatively benign images with well-known music such as the following:

Costume	Music
Cookie Monster	Theme from *Sesame Street* (Stone, Hart, & Raposo)
Jaws	Theme from *Jaws* (John Williams)
Phantom of the Opera	Theme from *Phantom of the Opera* or "All I Ask of You" (Andrew Lloyd Webber)
James Bond	"James Bond Theme" from *Dr. No* (James Barry)
Barry White	"You're the First, the Last, My Everything"
Superman/woman	Theme from *Superman* (Leon Klatskin)
Gorilla (with cellular phone)	"Stayin' Alive"(Bee Gees) or "I Just Called to Say I Love You" (Stevie Wonder)
A Baby	"Born to Be Wild" (Steppenwolf)

Costume	Music
Spock/Captain Kirk	Theme from *Star Trek* (Alexander Courage)
Pumpkin with leather headband (Halloween version of Michael Flatley)	Finale from *Lord of the Dance* (or in this case, *Gourd of the Dance*)

This time you get to be the star. The trick is in your grand entrance into class. Identify a student who can assist in this production. Here are the steps I have used year after year:

1. Arrive early in the morning to hide all of your course materials for class in the lecturn or in bag somewhere in the room. If there is a class in the room immediately preceding yours, have your assistant carry your materials.

2. Change into your costume

3. Go to the classroom about 5 minutes late so that most of the students are there waiting.

4. Stay outside the classroom door as your student assistant goes into the room.

5. Student gets everyone's attention and announces, "Dr. _____ was delayed. He or she will be here momentarily. I'm going to go back out and check." This introduction furnishes the expected serious premise.

6. Give the student the sign, such as an orange poster with black lettering of the following:

GOURD
OF THE
DANCE

7. Student re-enters the room hiding the poster at his or her side, goes to the front of the room, and then holds up the poster.

8. Wait a moment, then run into the room; when you get to the front, press the tape player and put it on a desk.

9. You now have the spotlight. Do whatever the costume character moves you to do. But do something. This is the unexpected part. Dancing, jogging, or flying always seems to work. Only about 30 seconds of slapstick silliness is required to crack up your class.

10. Teach your entire class in costume. The students will love it. And don't forget, pass around a bucket of candy.

APPENDIX A

INVENTORY OF MUSIC, ARTIST(S), AND SOURCES

Music	Artist(s)	CD	Catalogue no.
First-Class Blockbusters			
1. *Star Wars*	John Williams	*By Request . . .*	420178-2
2. *Mission: Impossible*	Lalo Schifrin	*Television's Greatest Hits 50's & 60's*	TVT1100
3. *Home Improvement*	Dan Follart	*Television's Greatest Hits Cable Ready*	TVT1900-2
Class Openings/Topic Intros			
Generic			
1. *Psycho*	Danny Elfman	*Psycho*	GEFD-25313
2. *Star Trek*	Alexander Courage	*Television's Greatest Hits 50's & 60's*	TVT1100
3. *Mister Rogers' Neighborhood*	Fred Rogers	*Television's Greatest Hits Vol. II*	TVT1200-2
4. *60 Minutes*			
5. *Masterpiece Theatre*	Jean Joseph Mouret	*Television's Greatest Hits in Living Color*	TVT1700-2
6. *The Odd Couple*	Sammy Cahn & Neal Hefti	*Television's Greatest Hits Vol. II*	TV1200
7. *The Good, the Bad, and the Ugly*	Buono, Brutto, & Cattivo	*The Good, the Bad, and the Ugly*	CDP7484082
8. *"Don't Cry for Me Argentina"*	Tim Rice & Andrew LLoyd Webber	*The Best of Broadway*	R271885
Content-Specific			
1. *X-Files*	Mark Snow	*Music from the X-Files*	946279-2
2. *"YMCA"*	Village People	*The Best of the Village People*	314522039-2
3. *Sesame Street*	Stone, Hart, & Raposo	*Television's Greatest Hits 70's & 80's*	TVT1300

Demonstrations/Skits		
Women		
1. "I'm Every Woman"	Whitney Houston	*The Bodyguard*	07822-18699-2
2. "She's a Lady"	Tom Jones	*The Best of . . . Tom Jones*	42284 4823-2
3. "Survivor"	Destiny's Child	*Survivor*	CK61063
4. "I Will Survive"	Gloria Gaynor	*Gloria Gaynor—I Will Survive*	31455-7236-2
5. "What a Feeling"	Irene Cara	*Flashdance*	314-558682-2
6. "Wanabe"	Spice Girls	*Spice Girls*	72438421742G
7. "Bad Girls"	Donna Summer	*Endless Summer*	314526178-2
8. "She Works Hard for the Money"	Donna Summer	*Endless Summer*	314526178-2
9. "Friends"	Bette Midler	*Experience the Divine Bette Midler*	82497-2
10. "Simply Irresistible"	Robert Palmer	*The Very Best of Robert Palmer*	7243855531224
11. "Stayin' Alive"	Bee Gees	*Saturday Night Fever*	4228253892
Men		
1. "Gonna Fly Now"	Bill Conti & Carol Connors	*The Rocky Story*	5201-2-3B
2. "Bad Boys"	Inner Circle	*Bad Boys*	792261-2
3. "Bad"	Michael Jackson	*Bad*	EK40600

Continued

Music	Artist(s)	CD	Catalogue no.
Men (Cont.)			
4. "Do You Hear the People Sing"	Boubul Schönberg, & Kretzmer	*Les Misérables*	9-24151-2
5. "Olympic Fanfare"	Noel Leon Arnaud	*Television's Greatest Hits in Living Color*	TVT1700-2
6. "Born to Be Wild"	Steppenwolf	*This is Cult Fiction*	72438-47850-2-4
7. "Hawaii Five-O"	The Ventures	*Television's Greatest Hits 50's & 60's*	TVT1100
Test Reviews			
Jeopardy!	Merv Griffin	*Television's Greatest Hits Vol. II*	TVT1200
Post-Review Send-Offs			
1. "Hakuna Matata"	Elton John & Tim Rice	*The Lion King*	60802-7
2. "We Will Rock You"	Queen	*Queen Greatest Hits*	HR61265-2
3. "We Are the Champions"	Queen	*Queen Greatest Hits*	HR61265-2
Post-Test Pick-Me-Ups			
1. "Tomorrow"	Andrea McArdle	*The Best of Broadway*	R271885
2. "Don't Worry, Be Happy"	Bobby McFerrin	*The Best of Bobby McFerrin*	CDP72438533292O
3. "What a Wonderful World"	Louis Armstrong	*Louis Armstrong's All Time Greatest Hits*	MCAD-11032
4. "Happiness"	Clark Gesner	*You're a Good Man, Charlie Brown*	09026-63384-2
5. "The Impossible Dream"	Richard Kiley	*The Best of Broadway*	R271885

APPENDIX B

FIRST-CLASS BLOCKBUSTERS

Mission: Impossible
  a. *Music:* Theme from *Mission: Impossible*
  b. *Time:* 1.6 minutes (script & music)
  c. *Props:* 2 sparklers
      lighter (or matches)
      mini-flashlight
  d. *Preparation:* Sparklers and lighter should be covered
  e. *Transparency:*

MISSION: IMPROBABLE at $p<.000000001$

  f. *Taped Script with Music:*
     "Hey, Bucko! Your mission, should you choose to accept it, is to teach this course like an adult version of *Sesame Street*. Your students should be flocking from hither and yon in anticipation of the fun they're going to have learning statistics.
     As always, should you botch or fail to complete this mission, resulting in comatose students, I will disavow all knowledge of your mission.
     This message will not, I repeat, will not self-destruct in 5 seconds. Destroying a perfectly reusable tape is the dumbest idea I've ever heard. This tape will end unceremoniously. Bye Bye."
     Theme from *Mission: Impossible*.

g. *Execution:*
1. Test projector procedure
2. Turn off projector light
3. Place trans on projector
4. Blackout room (see *Star Wars* for rationale)
5. Use mini-flashlight to find sparklers and lighter
6. Press button to start tape
7. When *Mission: Impossible* theme begins, turn on projector light
8. Light sparklers under table
9. When lit, move to right or left of projection screen against black background
10. Hold sparklers high and horizontal to stimulate fuse burning; then start dancing with the sparklers (*Note:* Their burn time is almost identical to the time of the theme music. Try not to catch on fire or set off the sprinkler system.)
11. When sparklers burns out, turn off projector light
12. When music ends, turn it off
13. Turn on room lights

Home Improvement
a. *Music:* Theme from *Home Improvement*
b. *Time:* 1 minute
c. *Props:* chair

bag with tool belt

assortment of tools (2 large screwdrivers, hammer, large pliers, wrench, tape measure, drill)
d. *Preparation:* Before class, place a chair next to the projector table or lectern. The seat should face you, not the students. Use a backpack, canvas bag, or some other type of bag to conceal the belt and tools. Set the bag on the chair seat so it is easily accessible. The element of surprise in the transformation from suit and tie (regardless of gender) to the tool belt is significant to the success of this demo.
e. *Transparencies:* 2 are required, 1 containing "Tool Time" and a second identifying, "The Tool Man" or "The Tool Woman."

STATISTICAL "TOOL TIME"

RON "THE TOOL MAN" BERK

f. *Execution:*
1. Test projector procedure
2. Turn off projector light
3. Place first trans on projector
4. Say, "I think we're ready to begin."
5. Press button to begin music
6. Take off your jacket and hang it around the back of the chair
7. Pull tool belt out of the bag and put it on
8. Place heavier tools (kept at the bottom of bag), such as a hammer and drill, into their compartments or holsters
9. (*Optional:* Put on suspenders: I use bright yellow tape-measure design suspenders to keep the belt from falling to the floor with 300 lbs. of tools)
10. When music ends, stop the tape
11. Readjust lectern microphone or reattach the lavaliere to your suspenders, if necessary
12. Turn on projector light
13. Move into an aisle close to your students
14. Say, "What time is it?" The students will respond unevenly with "Tool Time" because they're not sure what to do. Say, "That was pathetic. I'm going to give you another chance. This time I want the (Dean, everyone in this building, etc) to hear what time it is. Are you ready? Okay. What time is it?" The response this time is thunderous. Your students have been transformed from spectators to participants.
15. Put second trans on projector
16. Say, "I'm Ron, The Tool Man, Berk, and I'd like to welcome you to this special edition of Tool Time. This (morning, afternoon, evening) I am going to be talking about tools, statistical tools. "We use a variety of tools to answer research questions. Sometimes we use a screwdriver. At other time we use a hammer. Each tool is intended for a specific purpose. Selecting the right tool for the job is critical. However, for some jobs these tools may not be adequate. We may need more POWER! (pause). In that case, may I suggest the new Binford® turbo-charged 50,000 RPM statistical drill. This puppy will answer any question lickety split."

APPENDIX C

CLASS OPENINGS/TOPIC INTRODUCTIONS (*GENERIC*)

Star Trek
  a. *Music:* Theme from *Star Trek*
  b. *Time:* 45 seconds
  c. *Props:* Spock ears (optional)
     mini-flashlight
  d. *Preparation:* Conceal ears in pocket or under something near projector
  e. *Transparency:*

> **STAT TREK**
> **Where No Statistician Has Gone Before!**

  f. *Script:*
     "STATISTICS"
     The Final Frontier.
     These are the voyages of *STAT TREK!*
     Its 15 week mission:
     To explore strange new statistics;
     To seek out new methods for conducting research;
     To boldly go where no statistician has gone before!"
  g. *Execution:*
     1. Test projector procedure
     2. Turn out projector light

3. Place trans on projector
4. Blackout room (see *Star Wars* for rationale)
5. Put on ears
6. Use mini-flashlight to find script and trans
7. Read script
8. As you read last line, turn on projector light
9. Press button to begin music
10. After 30 seconds, turn off music
11. Turn on room lights

Mister Rogers' Neighborhood

a. *Music:* Theme from *Mister Rogers' Neighborhood*
b. *Time:* 1.3 minutes
c. *Props:* chair
   sweater
   sneakers
d. *Preparation:* Place a chair in front of the room facing the class so it is visible to everyone. Hide a pair of tennis shoes under the chair and place a cardigan or zippered sweater rolled up in a ball on the seat. Cover both with paper, plastic, or canvas bags. No one usually anticipates what those props mean even when they see them.
e. *Transparency:*

**MISTER RONO'S
NEIGHBORHOOD**

---

f. *Execution:*
   1. Test projector procedure
   2. Turn off projector light
   3. Place trans on projector
   4. Say, "I think we're ready to begin."
   5. Press button to begin music
   6. Turn on projector light
   7. Take off your jacket and hang it around the back of the chair
   8. Put on the sweater while standing
   9. Sit down in the chair
   10. Remove one shoe and throw into the air (but not onto your students)

11. Reach under chair and put on the tennis shoe (preferably the right one)
12. Repeat 10 or 11 for all your other feet
13. Walk back to tape recorder
14. When the music ends, stop the tape
15. Turn off projector light
16. Readjust lectern microphone or reattach the lavaliere to your sweater, if necessary
17. Say, "Welcome to Mister Rono's Neighborhood. I'm Mister Rono. This (morning, afternoon, evening) I'd like to talk to you about (topic)."

60 Minutes

a. *Sound:* Stopwatch clicking from *60 minutes*
b. *Time:* 1 minute
c. *Preparation:* Record five sets of clicks from the TV program with a one second pause between each
d. *Transparencies:* 2 transparencies are needed, 1 that lists 3 purposes, topics, issues, or areas to be covered on the exam, 1 phrase or sentence each, and a second that has the number of minutes of the class, presentation, or exam.

There are 3 major issues we're going to cover:
1. . . .
2. . . .
3. . . .

90
MINUTES

e. *Execution:*
1. Test projector procedure
2. Turn off projector light
3. Place first trans on projector with cover paper
4. Turn on projector light
5. Reveal intro statement (There are 3 . . .) and read it
6. With tape recorder in other hand, press button to play first set of clicks

 7. Press pause button
 8. Reveal and read point 1
 9. Release pause button for second set of clicks
10. Repeat steps 8 and 9 for points 2 and 3 for fourth set of clicks
11. After point 3 is read, release pause button for fourth set of clicks
12. Press pause
13. Think of 4 popular persons' names to say in the following format:

"I'm Ricky Martin"

"I'm Denzel Washington"

"I'm Britney Spears"

"I'm totally nuts"

"Those stories and Mickey Rooney this (morning, afternoon, evening) on *90 minutes*"
14. As you say "*90 Minutes,*" place second trans on projector
15. Release pause button for fifth set of clicks
16. Press stop

Masterpiece Theatre

a. *Music:* Theme from *Masterpiece Theatre*
b. *Time:* 55 seconds
c. *Props:* smoking jacket
    calabash pipe
d. *Preparation:* Before class, place a chair next to the projector table or lectern. The seat should face you. Use a backpack or canvas bag to hide jacket and pipe. Set the bag on the chair set so the props are easily accessible.
e. *Transparency:* Create a title using a content topic that ends in *th* so it is impossible to say without lisping, such as *Math*terpiece, *Path*terpiece, etc.

```
MATHTERPIECE
THEATRE
```

f. *Execution:*
    1. Test project procedure
    2. Turn out projector light
    3. Place trans on projector
    4. Say, "I think we're ready to begin."
    5. Press button to begin music

6. Take off your jacket and hang it around the back of the chair
7. Pull smoking jacket out of bag and put it on
8. Take out pipe and put in your mouth or hold it
9. When music ends, stop the tape
10. Turn on projector light
11. Say, "Good (morning, afternoon, evening)! I'm Alistar Berko. On the count of 3, everyone say aloud the name of this program. 1, 2, 3. . . This (morning's, afternoon's, evening's) story is about a class that developed a speech impediment just trying to say the name of the program"

The Odd Couple

a. *Music:* Theme from *The Old Couple* movie or TV series
b. *Time:* 30 seconds
c. *Props:* baseball cap
large cigar
old sweatshirt
d. *Preparation:* This demo can be used in a team presentation on any topic or a professor and student presentation on "relationships." It should be used with "older" undergraduate and graduate students. Most Gen-Xers are not familiar with *The Odd Couple* music, TV series, or movies.
e. *Execution:*
Team Presentation
1. If two professors are going to present during class, one should be dressed impeccably (Felix) and the other, slovenly (Oscar), in a sweatshirt, sneakers, baseball cap (of course, worn backwards), cigar, etc. The Oscar look can also be created as a surprise by hiding the sweatshirt, cap, and cigar in a bag and putting them on when the music begins.
2. When class is ready to begin, say, "Since both of us are going to present today, we thought we needed some special theme music to commemorate the occasion"
3. Press button to begin music
4. Oscar character takes off suit jacket and tie and hangs over chair
5. Take sweatshirt out of bag and put it on
6. Put on baseball cap (backwards)
7. Stand next to each other
8. Pass out handouts, if appropriate
9. Stop the tape

Relationship Presentation

1. If the topic deals with the relationship between variables, people, groups, objects, etc., this demo may work

2. Prior to class, identify a student who physically contrasts with you in terms of height, hair length, and other characteristics, same or opposite gender; the more extreme the contrast the better. Gender doesn't matter in this demo. It's the contrast in appearance that counts. Two men, two women, or one of each will work. If either of the characters are female, just name her Felice or Oscarette.

3. Ask the student to dress up for the next class and sit in the back; it's better for you to play the Oscar character because it's unexpected. If you normally dress like Oscar, then switch roles with the student.

4. On the day of the presentation, tell the student, "I'm going to walk to the back of the room and stand by you now. When I nod, stand up and move out of the row next to me. Follow me down to the front of the class."

5. Introduce the topic. Say, "Today we're going to examine the relationships between variables. Wait. I have an idea."

6. Walk to the back of the room, hiding the tape recorder, hat, and cigar in your hand on your side away from the class

7. Nod to the student, and as you turn to walk to the front with him or her, press the button to start the music and put on the cap backwards and cigar in your mouth

8. As you walk, pull out your shirt, open your tie, and try to look like a slob

9. When you get to the front, stand next to each other and let the music play

10. After an appropriate point in the music or about 30 seconds, stop the tape

11. Say, "We are this school's version of the *Odd Couple*. This is Felix (or Felice) and I am Oscar (or Oscarette)." (These introductions are important so everyone knows the concept of an "odd couple" and can associate the music with the TV series or movie. A few students may not be familiar with the music from the TV series. Your intro brings those students up to speed.)

12. Say, "Now let's talk about our relationship. Take a moment and jot down on a piece of paper 2 or 3 characteristics we have in common and 2 or 3 characteristics that are different about us."

13. After about 3–5 minutes, say, "Share the characteristics you wrote down with the student to your right (or left or behind you)."
14. After a couple of minutes, say, "Okay, let's see what you came up with. First, let's list the characteristics we have in common (write students' answers on transparency or chalkboard)." Repeat for characteristics that are different. Use this exercise as a springboard for your presentation on relationships.

The Good, the Bad, and the Ugly

a. *Music:* Theme from *The Good, the Bad, and the Ugly*
b. *Time:* 30 seconds
c. *Props:* humongous Western big brim hat
    small cigar
    poncho (optional)
d. *Preparation:* This demo can be used to introduce any topic where you plan on presenting a comparison of good and bad, pluses and minuses, advantages and disadvantages, strengths and weaknesses, or similar lists. Place props in a bag under the projector table so they are easily accessible.
e. *Transparency:* 1 transparency is needed to create the hook for the topic and humorous spin on the Clint Eastwood image

EXPERIMENTAL DESIGN: **THE GOOD,** **THE BAD** **AND** **IT COULD GET UGLY!**

f. *Execution:*
1. Test projector procedure
2. Turn off projector light
3. Place trans on projector with cover paper
4. Say, "I think we're ready to begin."
5. Bend under table with recorder in hand
6. Put on hat and put cigar in your mouth
7. Press button to begin music while under table
8. Stand up
9. Turn on projector light
10. Move paper down slowly on trans to reveal 1 line at a time with the music

11. After the last line, stop the tape
12. Turn off projector light
13. Say, "This (morning, afternoon, evening) we're going to examine what's good and what's bad about (topic)."

Evita

a. *Music:* "Don't Cry for Me Argentina" from Broadway show or movie (instrumental part)
b. *Time:* 50 seconds
c. *Props:* blonde hair bun (you'll probably have to spray one blonde to look like Eva Peron or Madonna), vocal cords
d. *Preparation:* This demo can be used with any topic, concept, term, etc. It is integrated into the lyrics. Hide the bun under the projector.
e. *Transparencies:* 2 are needed: one with the topic and the second with the lyrics. To introduce students to the statistic chi square, I used the following transparencies

> **CHI**
> **SQUARE**

> **Don't cry for Chi,**
> **I'll be with you**
> **The truth is I never left you**
> **All through our classes**
> **My presentations**
> **I kept my promise**
> **If you stayed with me.**

f. *Execution:*
1. Test projector procedure
2. Turn off projector light
3. Place first trans on projector
4. Say, "We're now going to begin a new topic. The statistic is called chi square. I want to make sure you remember the term as we proceed with the analysis."
5. Turn on projector light
6. Say, "Shout each word with me several times." (Point to Chi.) "Chi! Chi! Chi! Chi!" (Point to Square.) "Square! Square! Square! Square!" (Although the students don't have a clue why you're doing this, it still works. It's a parody of Argentina shouting: "Peron! Peron! Peron! Peron!")

7. Remove trans and leave projector light on.
8. Bend down below projector and attach bun.
9. Press button to begin music while your down.
10. Once music starts, stand with your back to your class and the projector light on your back. Raise arms, cup hands, and walk toward the screen to create a full shadow of your upper body and arms. The light spotlights your bun and shadows you as you get ready to address Argentina. Stand there for about 10 seconds moving your heads slowly from left to right to acknowledge your cheering subjects.
11. After the intro music, turn around, walk up to the overhead, put lyrics trans on the projector and burst into song, keeping your arms raised throughout. (Since it's a parody, it doesn't matter whether you can sing. I can't!) "Just Do It!"
12. When you finish, stop the tape.
13. Turn off projector light.
14. Maybe, just maybe, you'll get thunderous applause.

APPENDIX D

CLASS OPENINGS/TOPIC
INTRODUCTIONS
(CONTENT-SPECIFIC)

YMCA

   a. *Music:* "YMCA" (Village People)

   b. *Time:* 1 minute

   c. *Props:* construction worker's hard hat or leather motorcycle jacket with lots of chains

   d. *Preparation:* Before class, place a chair next to the projector table or lectern. The seat should face you. Use a backpack or canvas bag to conceal the hat or jacket. Set the bag on the chair so it is easily accessible.

   e. *Transparency:* 1 containing a 4 or 5 letter term, concept, topic, acronym, abbreviation, or name, such as 5 letter abbreviation "ANOVA" for the statistical test called analysis of variance

A NO V A

or a 4 syllable word

Port Fo Li O

   f. *Execution:*

     1. Test projector procedure

     2. Turn off projector light

     3. Place first trans on projector

4. Say, "We're now going to begin a new topic. The statistical test is called analysis of variance, abbreviated ANOVA. I want to make sure you remember this abbreviation."
5. Turn on projector light
6. Say, "Say each letter with me." (Point to each letter as you say it.) "A NO V A. Again. A (pause) NO V A. Now let's try it to the music."
7. Press button to begin music.
8. Pull hat out of bag and put it on
   or
   Take off jacket and hang it on chair. Take out leather jacket and put it on and arrange chains.
9. Say, "Get ready. A NO V A. A NO V A. Wait it's coming up again. Ready. A NO V A. A NO V A. Excellent!"
10. Stop tape and rewind to the beginning
11. Say, "Guess what's next? Yup. Everyone stand up. Lets do the arm movements."
    (Demonstrate each letter shape with arms, one at a time, very slowly. Do the letters faster the second time through, saying the letter with each shape.)
12. Say, "Okay, now let's do it to the music. Ready. A NO V A. A NO V A. Wait. Ready. A NO V A. A NO V A."
13. Say, "I suspect you will never forget this topic. It will be permanently etched in your memory."

Sesame Street

a. *Music:* Theme from *Sesame Street*
b. *Time:* 15 seconds
c. *Execution*

1. Identify any piece of content where a particular letter or number can be the answer to a question. The answer to most any math problem can be used.
2. As you are describing certain content, stop and say, for example, "What do you think the name of this distribution is?" (Point to graph on chalkboard or overhead)
3. Say, "I'm going to give you a hint."
4. Press button to start music
5. After about 15 seconds, stop tape
6. Say, "Today's class is being brought to you by the number '8' and the letter (pause and point to shape on graph) 'U' " (*Note:* Students always say the letter after the cue.)

APPENDIX E

TEST REVIEWS

Who Wants to Be a Millionaire

a. *Music:* None

b. *Time:* Too long for 1 item

c. *Preparation:* Meet with 1 student in advance to explain the process, but NEVER, I repeat NEVER, speak to a student as I do in the next 19 steps:

1. Say, "Arnold, we're going to do a take-off on *Who Wants to Be a Millionaire.*" (Student interrupts: "Wait a minute. My name is Sophia.") "Oops! Sorry. Anyway, I'm going to present a multiple-choice item to the class and then ask those students who know the answer to raise their hands (isn't it actually arms?). Here's where I need your help. Make believe I'm Rege, dressed in the same color everything from head-to-toe because I have the color coordinating ability of a mongoose."

2. Say, "I'll call on you and say, 'Arnold, I mean Sophia, what's the answer?' "

3. You say, " 'D', you moron."

4. I say, "Whaaat? You freak of nature, are you sure?"

5. You say, "No."

6. I say, "Do you want to use one of your lifelines?"

7. You say, "Sure, why not."

8. I say, "Do you want to ask a friend or ask the class?"

9. You say, "I'll ask a friend because the class is a bunch of idiots."

10. "Go around to the other side of the class and chat with one of your buds."

11. I say, "What's your answer?"

12. You say, " 'C,' you knucklehead. I know what you're going to say next. If you ask that question, I'm going to vomit."

13. "Get a bag and let her fly because I say, 'Is that your final answer?' Ewww. That's disgusting."

14. You say after you clean up, "No. You're going to be smacked. Rege, I'd like to use my last lifeline before I kill you."

15. I say, "Okay, Arnold, let's poll the class." I poll the class on each choice and then ask you, "Do you want to go with the idiots' choice or yours?"

16. You say, "Mine. I pick 'D.'"

17. I say, "Final answer?"

18. You say, "I don't care anymore. This is the stupidest thing I've ever done."

19. I say, "After a long pointless pause, guess what? You're right! And you win NOTHING!"

d. *Transparency:* 1 multiple-choice item, such as the following:

> According to legendary comedian Red Buttons, which one of the following is a sign that you're OLD?
> A. Your friends compliment you on your new alligator shoes, and you're barefoot.
> B. Your doctor doesn't give you X-rays anymore; he just holds you up to the light.
> C. Your spouse says, "let's go upstairs and fool around," and you respond, "pick one, I can't do both!"
> D. Your children say your memory is so good that you remember when the Dead Sea was only sick.

e. *Execution:*
1. Place trans on projector and say, "I think we're ready to begin."
2. Turn on projector light
3. Say, "Read the following item."
4. Say, "If you know the correct answer, raise your hand."
5. Call on pre-selected student and say "Sophia, what's the answer?"
6. Student: "D."
7. You: "Are you sure?"

8. Student: "No."
9. You: "Do you want to use one of your lifelines?"
10. Student: "Yes."
11. You: "Do you want to ask a friend or ask the class?"
12. Student: "Ask a friend."
13. You: "Okay, go ask one of your friends."
14. After the students talk for about 30 seconds, say "What's your answer choice?"
15. Student: "C."
16. You: "Is that your final answer?"
17. Student: "No, I want to use my last lifeline."
18. You: "Okay, let's poll the class. How many of you think 'A' is the correct answer? How many would pick 'B'? How many 'C'? How many 'D'?"
19. You: "Sophia, do you want to go with the class or stick with your previous choice?"
20. Student: "I'll go with the class. I pick 'D.'"
21. You: "Final answer?"
22. Student: "Yup."
23. You: "Let's see. (pause) It's a good one!"

Note: This parody is a great gimmick to use *once* if you have the time. The class is engaged and the students will laugh. But it is an extremely inefficient use of course time and test content. Can you imagine repeating those 23 steps even two or three times? And there isn't even any music you can use.

www.hilariouscourse.yeahright

Disclaimer: This chapter will not cover the technical and artistic procedures for transforming course materials onto a Web site. That's because I don't know anything about that. You probably know what to do anyway or you can find someone who has the necessary skills. The more important issue here is writing something worthy of putting on your Web site. That "something" draws on *your* imagination and creativity, not the Web master's.

In recent years academia has witnessed the growth of course Web sites and distance-education programs. For a while, they were popping up everywhere. However, lately many of them have stopped popping. Universities who have created for-profit companies to sell distance-education courses have been forced to revamp their business models to adjust to the harsh realities of the distance-education marketplace (Blumenstyk, 2001). Administrators have been required to use a lot of quotes, such as

- "No one has yet found a way for online learning to be economically viable."

- "Someone who plunges into online course development and delivery to make money shouldn't be allowed to walk around with a sharp object."

- "Costs so far exceed revenues that I've had to consult with loansharks."

- "Who made me invest gazillions in a fiber-optic network, computers with built-in obsolescence instead of service agreements, and digital television systems without HBO or Showtime?"
- "I'm now willing to become a dot-com millionaire punk with eyebrow rings."
- "Do you think I'm a moron?"

Despite the financial woes of distance-education programs, Web sites used in conjunction with traditional courses are booming. Computer-savvy professors are developing their own Web-based courses or are working with instructional designers to convert their courses into an online format. At some campuses there is a distance-education division with a team of experts responsible for developing online courses. That team is headed by an instructional designer and often includes an instructional technologist, who helps with computer programming; a graphics designer, who "livens up" Web pages with images and animated artwork; a technical typist, who polishes the final copy; and a production specialist, who handles copyright approval and other documentation.

My review of online courses indicates that most professors are simply dumping many of their traditional, serious in-class materials onto their Web sites. These sites are boring.com. Certainly the sites afford instant communication with students to post assignments and notices to utilize the Internet, and even to converse using the chat room. Although the access to information is unlimited, the professor-student interpersonal connection is diminished. The chat room is actually a type room, where you type responses in tiny bites. If you're long winded, the chat room's not the appropriate vehicle for communication. Try a conference call. It's more fun. Real professor-student connections occur in the classroom or office in Web-based courses, but they are zippo in distance-education courses.

There is one ingredient missing in these online experiences that not only can stimulate interest and increase the fun quotient in learning, but actually facilitates performance in the course. That ingredient, of course, is: food. No. It's HUMOR. Playing on your PC can take on a new dimension when humor is systematically integrated into the materials that appear on your course Web site.

As noted in Chapter 1, there are five different instructional forms of humor. The third form is the subject of this chapter. The task is to identify humor that can take advantage of the unique characteristics of learning from a computer. Two categories of techniques are described: print and non-print.

Print Forms of Humor on the Web

Since nearly all of the instructional materials placed on course Web sites are in print form, we need to begin the transformation process by inserting humor into the printed content. As with all forms of humor described previously, prepare the serious text first. The messages and information to be transmitted online remain intact. The humor is inserted or added to the content that the student reads. There are 10 different techniques presented next with loads of examples: (1) course components; (2) course disclaimers; (3) announcements; (4) warnings or cautions; (5) lists; (6) word derivations; (7) foreign word expressions; (8) acronyms and emoticons; (9) locations of colleges/universities, institutes, agencies; and (10) serious-humor contrast table.

Web Course Components

The first opportunity to insert humor is in the list of the course components. After reviewing every distance-education course in the universe, I compiled an eclectic list of more components than you would normally find in any single course to demonstrate the options available. Those components in the following list with a (✔) already contain humor, based on the methods outlined in *Gone with the Wind* (Chapter 6):

- Syllabus
  - Professor's Name and Title (✔)
  - Course Description
  - Prerequisites (✔)
  - Office Hours (✔)
  - Objectives (or Outcomes)
  - Schedule (or Calendar)
  - Teaching Strategies (✔)
  - Assignments
  - Grading Criteria
  - Reading List (✔)
- Announcements
- Course Disclaimers
- Warnings and Cautions (✔)
- Lecture Notes

- Text Information
- Examples (✔)
- Links to Related Resources (Databases)
- Problem Sets (✔)
- Test Review (✔)
- Tests (✔)
- Discussion Forum/Chat Room
- Parties
- Movies
- Restaurants
- Cruises

Make believe you're a student in one of your classes and you click on this list for the first time. As you peruse the list, what component would you probably click first? WRONG! You're not thinking like a student. A real, normal, fun-loving student would pick one of the last four components. It's those components that make this list different from all other lists. The technique follows the basic incongruity formula by listing the *expected* (serious) components and then the *unexpected* (punchline) ones.

The unexpected components also provide the vehicle for additional humorous Web pages. When the student clicks one of those components, such as "Parties," the page may say

GOTCHA!

or

MADE YA LOOK,
MADE YA LOOK!

Even though these examples may appear stupid or infantile, they will, at least, elicit a smile. It is the playful spirit we're trying to release in our students. Their attitude toward learning from the Web site is probably as important as the substantive material.

You also have the option of creating a page with fictitious, but hilarious movies, restaurants, or cruise information. If you can write parodies, go for it. You may even find book or Internet joke material on those topics.

Course Disclaimers

Capitalizing on the legal requirements for disclaimers on almost all goods and services we purchase, I tried to create or adapt disclaimers seen elsewhere to a course Web site where they would be *unexpected* because they're out of context and ridiculous. Four examples are given below:

- No animals were harmed or mistreated during the development of this Web site, although I was watching "Shark Week" on the Discovery Channel as I entered this disclaimer.

- This course Web site is opposed to all animal testing. However, if any animals must be tested, their SAT, ACT, or GRE scores should be given less weight than their GPA, DNA, IRA, HDL, LDL, PSA, and other three letter characteristics.

- The student using this course Web site takes full responsibility for everything and anything that could and/or does go wrong resulting from leaky roof, broken glass, fallen rocks, mud slides, forest fire, or projectile, which can include, but is not limited to, arrows, buckshot, shrapnel, lasers, napalm, torpedoes, emissions of X-rays, Alpha, Beta, or Gamma rays, sticks and stones, will break my bones, etc.

- The warranty on this course Web site does not cover damage due to misuse, lightning, flood, tornado, volcanic eruption, earthquake, blasting by mine crews, jackhammering, or sonic boom vibrations.

Announcements

This page is checked regularly by students for any notices you may post. They expect to see important information on assignments, project due dates, exam dates and locations, etc. Their expectations provide the first element in the incongruity formula, which cries out for the second element, unexpectations. This is your opportunity to create some really unusual announcements.

Five types to consider are as follows: (1) joke of the day, (2) awards or honors bestowed on the Web site, (3) Web site user warranty, (4) funding support for assignment, and (5) sponsor for homework problems.

Joke of the day.   Although the other options in this section (2–5) are jokes, you can present your Top 10 List, multiple-choice joke, or other humor format delivered in class on this page. Students regularly request copies of the winners anyway, so they can simply download them off the Web site. Alternatively, offer *new* jokes the students haven't seen before. This may motivate some to check out the site to get their daily chuckle. A few Web site sources are listed below:

- *http://www.twistedhumor.com*
- *http://www.humor.org/jokeme.cgi/lists/school*
- *http://minot.com/~nansen/links/humor/humor.html*
- *http://netec.mcc.ac.uk/JokEc.html*
- *http://www.columbia.edu/~sss31/rainbow*
- *http://www.twinkiesproject.com*
- *http://www.rider.edu/users/grushow/humor.html*
- *http://www.rpu.com*

Awards or honors.   Here are three examples of ridiculous Web site honors:

- I am pleased to announce that this is the only Web course in the universe to receive the Pulitzer Prize in fiction, Tony Award for best musical, and Olympic Gold Medal in the shotput. Aren't you reeeallly glad you're in this course now?
- This is the only Web course that has been formally recognized by the AMA, ABA, NBA, NFL, ASPCA, and Comedy Central.
- I am EXCITED to inform you that this Web course has received one of the greatest honors one could bestow on a course—a service area on the New Jersey Turnpike was named after it, appropriately called, "This Is the Dumbest Course I've Ever Had to Take Service Area."

User warranty.   One example of a warranty is given below:

- The user of this Web-based course here and forever more, in sickness and in health, 'til death do us part. Oops! Wrong warranty. I meant to say: agrees to the terms of this warranty that nobody reads, as well as the Middle East Accord, UN weapons inspections, and promises not to remove the label from his or her mattress. If the user fails to abide by these conditions, real or imaginary, the college shall deem it necessary and appropriate to examine the user's underwear drawer by the dawn's early light and the rockets' red glare. We have no idea what this means, but, then again, we didn't expect you to read this far into the warranty.

Funding support.   Although funding support is "expected" for research, it's "unexpected" for assignments. Make them as outrageous as you can, such as the following:

- Today's assignment is being inadequately funded by partial support of
  - Helga's Tattoo & Taco Parlor
  - Bubba's Bar-B-Que & Bullwhip Shop

Sponsor for homework.   Similar to the above funding sources, bizarre sponsors can also be listed with any homework assignment. The next example might be appreciated in a business or management course Web site:

- Today's problem set is being sponsored by the world-renowned MISFORTUNE 500 company, Amalgamated Consolidated Coagulated Conglomerate of America

Warnings or Cautions

Using the same humor techniques as above, I wanted to develop a generic warning for using the Web site. Here it is:

Warning: Use of this Web site many cause insomnia, euphoria, lung flukes, tapeworms, and leprosy. Now listen carefully. In fact, put your best ear right on the screen. I'm only going to say this once. The preceding effects are not real. I made them up for your entertainment. However, if you get earwax on this screen, I'm going to poke you in the eye with my PDA stylus.

In addition, warnings or cautions are needed for the tons of print material posted for the course. The following warning could precede a literature review or research article:

Warning: Reading the following paragraphs, which contain a drillion killion research findings, could cause drowsiness, nose bleeds, bloating, hair loss, various mutations, and a substantial penalty for early withdrawal.

The next one could be placed before any written material:

Caution: This section is so boring that you might want to sneak up behind your-self, blow up a paper bag, and slam your fist into it to keep yourself awake as you read it.

This last one can be used before any highly technical material:

Caution: The next section (paragraph, example, etc.) contains reeeally complex technical terminology, such as on, off, play, reverse, stand up, sit down, fight team fight. Proceed at your own risk.

Lists

You present lists of content, examples, procedures, and assignments all the time. The next time you list "anything" on your Web site, consider adding a few humorous entries at the end of the list. You've seen this strategy applied throughout the book. Here's the basic formula:

FORMULA:
Serious Names, Terms, or *Topics* (at least 2 or 3) followed by *Ridiculous Names, Terms,* or *Topics*

Here are examples of lists for 14 different topics or subject areas:

- *Accounting*
  Allowable tax deductions: interest, charitable contributions, medical expenses, business-related travel, business-related yachts, losses from business-related gambling, and business-related money laundering

- *Antacids*
  Tagamet®, Pepto-Bismol®, Zantac®, Tictac®, Nicnac®, Paddywack®, Give the Dog a Bone®

- *Anthropology*
  Research on prehuman species: Jane Goodall's work with chimpanzees, Dian Fossey's work with gorillas, Steve Irwin's work with alligators, and Brian Billick's work with Baltimore Ravens

- *Archaeology*
  Greek ruins, such as the Acropolis, Parthenon, Decathalon, Baklava, Temple of Kojak, Arch of Dukakis, and Oracles of Delphi

- *Art*

  Nineteenth-century French impressionists: Monet, Renoir, Pissaro, Iglesius, and DiCaprio

  Names of off-white paint colors: Antique White, Oyster White, Cottage Cheese White, Pigeon Guano White, Tofu White, Mayonnaise White, and Cocaine White

- *Biology*

  Organs: heart, lungs, kidneys, spleen, liver, onions, chitterlings, endives, and leeks

- *Computer Systems*

  Hardware, software, middleware, outerwear, innerwear, underwear, CorningWare®, Tupperware®, somewhere, and nowhere

  Popular software: Word, Number, Powerpoint, Weakpoint, Excel, D-Cell, Access, Deny, Abscess, Excess, and Obsess

- *English*

  Parts of speech, including noun, verb, adjective, diphthong, refraction, premonition, conjunctive epithelium, and prosthetic infarction

- *Geography*

  Environmental issues: greenhouse effect, toxic waste, acid rain, ozone depletion, hideous tool shed effect, and Howard Stern

- *Gerontology*

  Anti-aging interventions: exercise, nutrition, antioxidants, Viagra, cosmetic surgery, and cryonics

- *History*

  Founding Fathers: George Washington, John Adams, Thomas Jefferson, Ronald Reagan, and Alan Greenspan

  Inventors: Benjamin Franklin, Thomas Edison, Henry Ford, Ron Popeil, George Foreman, and Jake Steinfeld

- *Meteorology*

  Atmospheric processes: jet stream, cyclones, tornadoes, fronts, backs, air masses, air bags, wind bags, and hair bags

- *Philosophy*

  Problems of ethics: Spinoza, Spumoni, Kant, Kan, Mill, Floss, Dewey, Don'ty, Moore, and Less

- *Sociology*

  Serious problems in American Society: drugs, smoking, teenage pregnancy, illiteracy, "reality TV," acne, Bare Naked Ladies, and Marilyn Manson

  Target population: boomers, Gen-Xers, 20-somethings, techies, Trekkies, suits, stay-at-home moms, bean counters, and eye candy

Word Derivations

Every discipline has loads of terminology and jargon known only to members of that respective discipline. Since students are just becoming immersed in that language, there is an opportunity to create a parody of that jargon. It may appear as an add-on to an assignment, a footnote, or an assembled list in glossary format on a separate Web page. Making mock of the terminology in your field provides a perspective students wouldn't normally see, plus it may help them remember some of the technical language. Given that the students already know the real meanings of the terms, this humorous insert is rather innocuous. The technique is simply to create Latin or Greek root words and meanings for each term with which the students can identify. This application of the incongruity formula and the appropriate grammatical structure are presented next.

FORMULA:
Real term, derived from two Latin (or Greek) words, *"1st half of word,"* meaning *"Serious meaning,"* and *"2nd half of word,"* meaning *"Ridiculous meaning"*

Several examples using a few statistics terms are shown below:

- *statistics,* derived from two Latin words, "stat," meaning "manipulation of numbers," and "istics," meaning "that will make your life miserable"
- *hypothesis,* derived from two Greek words, "hypo," meaning "guess," and "thesis," meaning "the outcome of the research although I know you're going to change it later so it is consistent with your results"
- *correlation,* derived from two Greek words, "co," meaning "two," and "rrelation," meaning "columns of numbers living together"
- *multivariate,* derived from two Greek words, "multi," meaning "many," and "variate," meaning "variables that will impress my thesis committee"

Foreign Word Expressions

Similar to the preceding, terminology or expressions that appear in any content the students encounter on your Web site provide another chance for jocularity. In this case, we're creating ridiculous meanings for foreign word expressions. Certainly many of these expressions are more appropriate for some subject fields than for others, but they can be inserted anywhere for a humorous effect. Here are alternative incongruity formulas for expressions and words.

FORMULA:

Real foreign expression, a Latin (or Greek or French) expression meaning (literally), *"Ridiculous meaning"*

or

Real foreign word (a Greek or Latin word meaning, *"Ridiculous meaning"*)

A few examples using fairly common expressions and words are as follows:

- *crème de la crème,* a French expression meaning literally, "There's Cool Whip® on your nose"
- *pièce de resistance,* a French expression meaning, "They're storming the Bastille, Pedro!"
- *carpe diem,* a Latin expression meaning literally, "Your carpet looks ugly"
- *Eureka!* (a Greek word meaning, "Gimme five!")
- *raison d'être,* a French expression meaning, "Cinnamon-raisin bagel with cream cheese"
- *escargot* ("phlegmwad in a shell")
- *mea culpa,* a Latin expression meaning, "In your dreams"

For practice, try writing hilarious definitions for these expressions:

- *quid pro quo,*
- *voilà,*
- *bon appétit,*
- *habeas corpus,*
- *fait accompli,*
- *modus operandi,*
- *sine qua non,*
- *joie de vivre,*

- *a capella,*
- *mano-à-mano,*

Acronyms and Emoticons

Our students are using Internet shorthand or *chatspeak* in their online yakking in chat rooms and e-mails. Why shouldn't we do the same in our communication with them? Plus it provides another vehicle for humor. There are two basic forms: acronyms and emoticons.

Acronyms or *netcronyms* appear everywhere in cyberspace. There's even a Web site (*http://www.chatdictionary.com*) that contains more than 1400 entries. So why not make up your own? They may be generic or content-specific. Insert them anywhere in your Web pages. All you need is a bunch of letters which stands for a bunch of words, such as *TAIDOSHH* (This Assignment Is Due On Sunday Ha Ha). Three incongruity formula humor spins on acronyms are presented below.

FORMULA 1:
Acronym (Humorous or *Popular Phrase* or *Expression)*

This format is similar to what currently appears on the Internet for serious abbreviations. A bakers dozen examples are given below:

- *LWOS* (Laughing With Occasional Snorts)
- *FGAI* (Fuhggedaboudit)
- *YWWANYA* (You Write With A Noo Yawk Accent)
- *TISO* (That Is So Over)
- *YHI* (You Have Issues)
- *BMM* (Byte My Mouse)
- *AYRAWHI* (Are You Really A White House Intern)
- *TABGOYS* (There's A Beaver Gnawing On Your Shins)
- *HHTSFEAAG* (He Has The Same Facial Expression As A Grouper)
- *WISMMDT* (Why Is She Making Me Do This)
- *YGTCWYSTE* (You're Going To Chuckle When You See This Exam)
- *YGTDITHL* (You've Got That Deer-In-The-Headlights Look)
- *EMBHYSMNPAHA* (Excuse Me But Have You Seen My Nobel Prize Around Here Anywhere)

FORMULA 2:
Real Acronym (which stands for *Completely Different Real Acronym*)

Here are a few examples:

- *CIA* (which stands for *KGB*)
- *AFL* (which stands for *CIO*)
- *CNN* (which stands for *MSNBC*)
- *RSVP* (which stands for *ASAP*)
- *GATT* (which stands for *NAFTA*)
- *AARP* (which stands for *Rx*)

FORMULA 3:

Real Acronym (which stands for *Ridiculous Definition* or *Terms*)

Check out the following examples:

- *UCLA* (which stands for *Harvard University*)
- *WHO* (which stands for *International Monetary Fund*)
- *HMO* (which stands for *Send Me All Your Money*)
- *DNA* (which stands for *Dioxyriboestablishmentarianism*)
- *CDC* (which stands for *Mayo Clinic*)
- *IRB* (which stands for *Immediate Research Blockade*)
- *24/7* (which stands for *Yourekillingyourself*)

Emoticons are simply standard punctuation marks used to express human emotions, such as happy :), sad : (, and laughing :-D. The punctuation combo is placed at the end of a statement to convey how the writer is feeling. For example, you may make the following flat, emotionless statement:

There's a squirrel on your head.

With an emoticon, it will look like this:

There's a squirrel on your head :-D.

Now you have a flat, emotionless statement with weird, unintelligible punctuation marks at the end.

Although there are barrels of emoticons already floating in cyberspace, you can create your own so your students will know exactly how you feel when you communicate with them. A few examples of emoticons with their meanings are given below:

: (*—C   (Student is unhappy because he or she can't decide which cell phone company to choose)

:)))A+   (Student is very happy to have gotten an A on the exam)

: ((((T*	(Student is very unhappy to have failed exam)
: ((..,	(Professor regrets that she failed student)
:> <V	(Professor finds head of giant squid on her desk)

Locations of Colleges/Universities, Research Institutions, or Government Agencies

As academicians we frequently cite the names of institutions as sources or references for information related to course content or research. Since the correct citations for these references are usually given elsewhere, the simple name of the institution can be used as a vehicle for humor. The incongruity formula in this application uses two punches. Hopefully at least one of them will work.

FORMULA:

Real Institution, which is located in *Wrong City, State,* also the home of *Wrong Similar Institution* or *Sports Team*

Here are three examples:

- Johns Hopkins University, which is located in San Francisco, CA, also the home of Princeton University
- UCLA's Higher Education Research Institute, which is located in Buffalo, NY, home of the Denver Broncos
- Stanford University, which is in Boston, also the home of the University of Alabama (or the New York Yankees)

Some of you are probably thinking, "That's not funny. Why not just make up names for the institutions as well?" Okay. A slightly different spin on the above formula can produce the following:

- Research was conducted at the world-renowned Heimlich Center in Geneva, Switzerland, also the home of the Vienna Boys Choir

Serious-Humor Contrast Table

One of the best strategies for learning the serious correct procedure or method to carry out a task is to present an incorrect alternative. Assuming you have described the correct steps or techniques in class with humorous examples, you can give a follow-up summary on your Web site by developing a humorous incorrect example. This can precede the assignment on the Web page.

If you can exaggerate the incorrect to the level of the absurd and ridiculous, the extreme contrast fits the *expected* (correct)—*unexpected* (incorrect) formula for the humor. First, list the correct serious "Recommended steps, procedure, behaviors, products, businesses, etc. Then, list the ridiculous "Not Recommended" alternatives. Table 4.1 presents this incongruity application for responses at a job interview.

A variation of this format is a serious true list of statements with a heading such as "When Your Professor Says . . .," and a humorous corresponding list translating those statements into "What He/She Really Means Is . . ." Always start with the serious list first. Sample headings might be:

- "When a Student Says . . ."
- "When Your Advisor Says . . ."
- "When Your Thesis Chairperson Says . . ."
- "When Your Dean Says . . ."
- "When Your Letter of Recommendation Says . . ."

TABLE 4.1   Recommended and unrecommended responses at a job interview.

Interview questions	Recommended responses	Unrecommended responses
1. Welcome! How are you?	Fine	Yo, Jobmeister!
2. Who referred you to this job?	Jeff Bezos	Madame Cleo, Psychic to the Stars
3. What previous jobs have you had?	Systems analyst, IBM V-P, Amazon.com	Elvis impersonator ("Thangkew, thangkew vera much")
4. Have you ever been convicted of a crime?	No	Yes, but my conviction is currently under appeal
5. Do you consider yourself to be a hard worker?	Yes	Kinda, but do you have regular coffee breaks?
6. Who is your role model?	Bill Gates	Joe Isuzu
7. Is the proposed work schedule acceptable?	Yes	No, I'd like to leave early each day to watch *The Jerry Springer Show*
8. Is the starting salary acceptable?	Yes, you're too generous	Yes, but can I have a month's advance now?
9. Do you consider our office policies fair?	Yes	No, I still don't understand why I can't bring my pot-bellied pig to work
10. Where do you hope to be 5 years from now?	CEO of Micro or Soft	In *your* job

Non-Print Forms of Humor on the Web

Once the print humor is in place, you now have the option of embellishing the content with visual and sound effects that can increase the impact and "fun" quotient. Remember, we're trying to recreate the *Sesame Street* experience online for college students.

Almost any non-print technique is possible given the current state of technology. Based on the research on humorous TV ads described in Chapter 3, the elements of music, visuals, and color scheme can be manipulated to increase the surprise and the humor. Consider adding (1) music to your syllabus, consistent with the prerequisite TV programs listed; (2) animals or cartoon icons to your class assignment; (3) sound effects with warnings or cautions; (4) graphics or animation to announcements; (5) humorous video snippets to accompany text information; and (6) animal voices (such as Babe) to present examples. Any combination of visual and sound effects can be added to any Web site component. Let your imagination fly.

Visual Effects

There are thousands of pieces of visual material available free on the Internet. The categories of material include the following:

- Pictures/photographs
- Graphics
- Animation
- Icons
- Letters, backgrounds, borders
- Slideshows
- Movies
- Commercials

Most popular sources.   Consider the following sources and repositories of visual effects for your Web site:

- *Barry's Clip Art Server—www.barrysclipart.com*—large collection of free clip art.
- *Go Graph—www.gograph.com*—provides searchable directory of icons, animated GIFs, photographs, and clip art.
- *Clip Art Connection, The—www.clipartconnection.com*—large collection of clip art, graphics, and other DTP/Web page development resources.

- *www.clip-art.com*—over 500 images, sorted by category.
- *Clip Art Universe*—*www.nzwwa.com/mirror/clipart*—many free backgrounds, icons, dividers, and animated GIFs.
- *Clipart Castle*—*www.clipartcastle.com*
- *Clip Art Searcher*—*www.webplaces.com/search*—customized search forms designed to locate graphics on the Web.
- *Free Clipart*—offers clip art images and Web elements.
- *AAAClipArt.com*—*www.AAAClipArt.com*—offers categorized images.
- *Bestclipart*—*http://bestclipart.com*—clip art for everyone; free images to download.

Video sources.   A list of sites for funny videos, clips, and pictures is provided below:

- *Video Clipart*—*http://www.videoclipart.com*
- *Cool Video Clips and Funny Videos*—*http://www.coolvideoclips.com*
- *Funny Pictures and Video Clips*—*http://video.www9.50megs.com*
- *Filmzone.com*—*http://www.filmzone.com*
- *Hollywood.com*—*http://www.hollywood.com/stories/multimedia*
- *Bali Video Clips*—*http://www.balivideoclips.com*
- *Movie Gallery.com*—*http://www.moviegallery.com/m*
- *Movies, etc.*—*http://pages.prodigy.com/coolie/movies.htm*
- *Free funny movie clips*—*http://www.laughmybuttoff.com/cgi-bin/movies.cgi*
- *Funny video clips of cats and kittens*—*http://www.stego.com/funny_cat/index.html*

Additional sources.   An inventory of additional sites is given below:

- *Best Collection of Webimages*—free backgrounds, animations, bullets, buttons, sets, borders, and holiday images.
- *A-Z Free Clipart Graphics*—provides categorized clip art images, including alphabet, holidays, people, and sports.
- *Absolutely Free Clipart*—offers alphabetically listed categories, including animals, cliches, holidays, lumberjacks, and theatre.
- *All Clipart Site*—offers animated GIFs, buttons, backgrounds, flags, and icons.

- *All Fish Graphics*—*http://www.myallfish.com*—directory of fish, animal, and insect clip art, and animated GIFs.
- *All Free Clipart*—free clip art graphics sorted by category.
- *All Free Icons*—categories include animals, cartoons, holidays, sports, and transportation.
- *All Season Clipart*—*http://www.allseasonclipart.com*—offers a variety of downloadable images, including holiday, special occasions, finance, entertainment, and sports.
- *Awesome Clip Art*—*http://www.freestuffcenter.com/awesome*
- *BannerBlast!*—*http://www.bannerblast.com/bannerblast.htm*—offers clip art, backgrounds, banners, animations, and video games.
- *Binaries.Org*
- *Bow Wow Meeow*—*http://www.rats2u.com*—offers cards and graphics with dog or cat theme.
- *Canadian Flag Clip Art Gallery*—*http://canflag.ptbcanadian.com*
- *Chinese Symbol Database*—*http://www.formosa-kingdom.com/chinese*—provides clip art for various events.
- *Clip Art Archive*—[*ftp.uni-stuttgat.de*]
- *Clip Art Center*—*http://www.freestuffcenter.com/clipart/sports*—a selection of free clip art, downloads online, sorted alphabetically, with a directory to similar sites.
- *Clipart Resource*—free clip art images browsable by category.
- *Clipart Theatre*—*http://www.baycomedy.com/clipart.htm*
- *Cowboy Clip Art*—*http://www.maroon.com/cowboyclipart*—country and western themed.
- *Customized License Plate*—*http://dewa.com/plate*—comes with alphabetics (A to Z) and numbers to cut and paste to spell anything.
- *Derek's ClipArToons*—*http://www.clipsahoy.com/index.htm*
- *Extreme Clipart*—*http://www.eclip-art.com/*—offers free clip art images, including animals, food, music, and sports.
- *Fairy Survana's 3-D Library*—*http://dewa.com/3D*—download free 3-D letters and 3-D graphics.
- *Fantasy Clip Art*
- *Funky Guys*—*http://www.niu.edu/~ca0pab1/funky_guys/fu_home.html*—humorous cartoons, inspired on primitive art and computers; site

includes illustrations and free graphics such as clip art, comics, animated GIFs, and greeting cards.

- *Graphics by PeeLee*

- *House Ravenscroft Scriptorium—http://www.geocities.com/SoHo/ Lofts/3374/index.html—*Celtic clip art.

- *Inki's Clipart—http://www.inki.com/clipart*

- *Karen Shader Designs Free Clip Art—*hand-painted watercolor backgrounds, buttons, and bars.

- *Lori's Craft Clip Art*

- *Magic Web Gift Tags—http://www.cpsweb.com/giftcng.htm—*for Mother's Day, Father's Day, Valentine's Day, Christmas, and birthdays.

- *Microsoft Clip Gallery   http://dgl.microsoft.com/default.asp* provides clip art.

- *Miss Jan's Graphics and Stuff—*holiday, flowers, teddy bears, and other clip art.

- *Neferchichi's Egypt Links & Clip Art—*includes Egyptian clip art, hieroglyphics and mummification lessons.

- *Noetic Art—*clip art created by the author, original and free for general use.

- *OhBother's Classic Pooh Gift Tags—http://members.tripod.com/ OhBotherPooh/index.html—*for Christmas, birthdays, and other special occasions.

- *Over the Rainbow—*thousands of beautiful free Web graphics— original clip art, icons, backgrounds, animations, transparent GIFs; plus tons of links to the best graphics sites.

- *Pam's Clip Art Page—http://web.mountain.net/~wayne—*collection of clip art, landscape, and nature pictures.

- *Police Clipart Library— http://lawenforcement.about.com/careers/lawenforcement/cs/clipart/ index.htm—*provides pictures of vehicles, badges, and more.

- *SimplyTheBest.com—*offers clip art including backgrounds, buttons, textures, wallpaper, animated GIFs, and dividers.

- *Speccy Icons—http://www.soft.net.uk/watkins/specicons/index.html—* a set of icons based on the Spectrum.

- *Strange Benedictions—*antique style images.

- *Weird Clipart Archives—http://www.weirdclipart.com/wcarcivs.html—* graphics and animated images.
- *Zena's Clipart Collection— http://www.hutchal.clara.net/zena/index.htm—*over 60 categories of full color clip art.
- *Zitelli by Design—*a smorgasbord of graphics and links; plus buttons, rules, bullets, animations.
- *Usenet—alt.binaries.clip-art*

Sound Effects

> **Note:** Before reading this section, you may want to survey your students' access to speakers on university computers and their own. If that access isn't universal, much of the effort expended to add clever sound effects will be wasted. Just a thought!

Although Napster and its latest offspring Aimster provide music files that you can copy at no cost, I suspect that by the time you read this page the music industry will have succeeded in blocking free access to the copyrighted songs. However, don't despair; there are tons of other free sources of sound clips for the following:

- Music (e.g., movie, TV, popular)
- Sounds/noises (e.g., screams, crashes, horns, applause, snoring)
- Voices (e.g., cartoon, animals, movie, TV)

When you select specific sound effects for your Web site, ask your Web master about the following options, which can add variety, surprise, and humor:

- Clickable Sound vs. Automatic Sound
- Customized Sound (e.g., using your voice)
- Streaming vs. Nonstreaming

Clip art review.   *Sound Clips (www.webplaces.com/html/sounds.htm)* furnishes a listing of a wide range of sound effects. Those categorized by topic or theme are given below:

- *Animals (Japan)—www.tamacc.chuo-u.ac.ip/sounds/tmp/animal—* almost 25 fairly lengthly animal sound clips; birds, domestic animals, wild animals, and bugs; .wav format.

- *Animals (Sunsite)—http://sunsite.sut.ac.jp/multimed/sounds/ sound_effects/animals*—about 45 animal noises, including rattlesnake, monster, wolf, tiger, hyena, gorilla, bat;.au format.
- *Bathroom—http://sunsite.sut.ac.jp/multimed/sounds/sound_effects/ animal*—a few sounds from La Salle De Bains; shower, flush; .au format.
- *Birds—http://sunsite.sut.ac.jp/multimed/sounds/birds*—about a dozen bird sounds; kookaburra, crow, bluejay, chickadee; .au format.
- *Cans—http://sunsite.sut.ac.jp/multimed/sounds/sound_effects/cans*—a few canned sound effects related to cans; garbage cans, spray cans, kick-the-can; .au format.
- *Cats—http://sunsite.sut.ac.jp/multimed/sounds/sound_effects/shorty*—about a dozen cat sounds, small files; .au format.
- *Classical Music Midi files—http://www.prs.net/midi.html*—a large, well-organized collection, including Bach, Beethoven, Brahms, Chopin, Debussy, Handel, Haydn, Liszt, Mendelssohn, Mozart, Scarlatti, and Schubert.
- *Clicks and Beeps—www.wavenet.com/~axgrinder/other/loops.htm*—very short sound files of various noises; also some longer musical loops.
- *Domestic—www.tamacc.chuo-u.ac.jp/sounds/tmp/domestic*—about 25 home and garden type noises; shower, phone, door, hammering, typing, sawing, cooking; .wav format.
- *Doors—http://sunsite.sut.ac.jp/multimed/sounds/sound_effects/doors*—creaky doors, door buzzers, door bell, door knock; sorry, no Jim Morrison; .au format.
- *Emotions—www.tamacc.chuo-u.ac.jp/sounds/tmp/emotion*—people expressing their feelings with voiced sounds such as yeah, wow, yuck, and boo; about 45 sounds; .wav format.
- *Glass—http://sunsite.sut.ac.jp/multimed/sounds/sound_effects/glass*—glasses, dishes, bottles, plates, and breaking glass; .au format.
- *Guns & Bombs—http://sunsite.sut.ac.jp/multimed/sounds/ sound_effects/gunsbomb*—machine guns, explosions, mortar, and more guns; .au format.
- *Greetings—http://www.tamacc.chuo-u.ac.jp/sounds/tmp/greeting*—about 40 voiced greetings, in English or Japanese; .wav format.
- *Japan Sounds—http://www.tamacc.chuo-u.ac.jp/sounds/tmp/j_sound*—about 30 medium-length sound clips, assorted themes, including music, combat, Japanese ceremonies, and sound effects; .wav format.

- *Kitchen—http://sunsite.sut.ac.jp/multimed/sounds/ sound_effects/kitchen*—a few kitchen noises; liquid pouring, cork popping, ice cubes; .au format.

- *Music: Joe's Original Wav Files—http://www.sky.net/~jdeshon/ joewav.html*—a nice assortment of unusual sound effects and musical interludes; lots of music-related sound bytes.

- *Nature—http://www.tamacc.chuo-u.ac.jp/sounds/tmp/nature*—about 15 lengthly nature sounds such as fire, typhoon, rain, earthquake, thunder; .wav format.

- *Paper—http://sunsite.sut.ac.jp/multimed/sounds/sound_effects/paper*— a few paper sounds, including crumple, tear, and cut; .au format.

- *People Noises—http://www.tamacc.chuo-u.ac.jp/sounds/tmp/people*— lengthy clips of snoring, clapping, drinking, laughing, walking, coughing, and the like; .wav format.

- *People Sounds—http://www.erols.com/imager/billyd/sounds*— expressions and sounds, from "groovy" to "bummer" to "back off man"; and some sound effects.

- *Sports—http://www.tamacc.chuo-u.ac.jp/sounds/tmp/sports*—about 20 sports sounds from bowling, golf, car racing, diving, Sumo wrestling, baseball; various lengths; .wav format.

- *Star Wars—http://www.cms.uncwil.edu/~rodrigu/starwars/ starwars.html*—sound effects and dialogue clips from the movie.

- *Street Sounds—http://www.tamacc.chuo-u.ac.jp/sounds/tmp/street*— about a dozen noises you might hear on a street (in Japan); lengthy files; .wav format.

- *TV Series Themes—http://sunsite.sut.ac.jp/multimed/sounds/series*— about 50 well-known TV themes from recent years and the past; .au format.

- *Vehicles—http://www.tamacc.chuo-u.ac.jp/sounds/tmp/vehicle*— ambulance, bicycle, car, bus, helicopter, ship, crashes; .wav format.

- *Whales—http://sunsite.sut.ac.jp/multimed/sounds/whales*—yes, whale sound clips; eerie sounding whale cries; .au format.

Assorted sites of sound clips include the following:

- *Artisto-Soft—http://www.aristosoft.com*—1,600 free sounds (as well as commercial products).

- *Japan: Sound Effects Index—http://www.tamac.chuo.u.ac.jp/sounds/ tmp*—index page for hundreds of sounds, many related to Japan, many with universal appeal.

- *Movie & TV—http://www.wavbazaar.com*—sound clips from well-known TV shows and movies.

- *Sunsite Sound Effects— http://sunsite.sut.ac.jp/multimed/sounds/sound_effects*—well over 100 sound effects, small files, many inanimate noises such as beeps, clicks, tones, as well as human sounds, clocks and more; .au format.

- *Wav Central: Effects—http://wavcentral.com/effects.htm*—a wide variety of short sound clips; about 75; includes such oddities as Tarzan yell, laser, antique car horn and more; .wav format.

There are other sites, such as *http://www.geek-girl.com/audioclips.*, that provide links to digitized sound archives for miscellaneous sounds, music collections, and voice repositories.

PART II

ASSESSMENT

Warning: How hilarious could this section possibly be even if Dave Barry or Art Buchwald wrote it? The topic is a verbal anesthetic. Reading it can induce a coma. Consistent with the preceding four chapters that dealt with techniques for infusing humor in your teaching, the next four focus on creative strategies for using humor to construct and administer assessment tools. At this point you're probably thinking: "ASSESSMENT? WHAT IN THE WORLD DOES ASSESS-MENT HAVE TO DO WITH TEACHING? MIS-TUH HU-MOR, HAVE YOU GONE NUTS, AGAAAIN?" Calm down. There's no reason to flip out in CAPS LOCK mode. Assessment is an integral part of teaching. At minimum, you have to assess whether your students learned anything from what and how you taught. You may even assess whether your humor methods were effective (see end of Chapters 1 & 8). The chapters in this section address different aspects of the assessment process with a primary emphasis on the tools themselves. Chapter 5 presents a consumer's guide for selecting and applying appropriate assessment methods and the general rules for developing them. Chapters 6 and 7 concentrate only on multiple-choice formats. Although attention is given to matching and completion, constructed-response and performance assessment formats are omitted. They're just not very funny, plus the objective, selection item formats are still the most prevalent in undergraduate and many graduate courses. All of the rules described in Chapters 5–7 are those on which there is a consensus by measurement experts regarding their importance in test development (Haladyna & Downing, 1989a) and 75 years of research (Haladyna & Downing, 1989b). These rules and guidelines are also consistent with the latest edition of the *Standards for Educational and Psychological Testing* (AERA, APA, & NCME Joint Committee on Standards, 1999). Of course, the twisted style of my descriptions and the nearly 100 bizarre examples presented would render those rules unrecognizable to those experts anyway. The final chapter in the book examines test anxiety and specific techniques to reduce it, especially methods for injecting humor into multiple-choice, matching, and constructed-response formats. You don't want to miss it.

5

ASSESSMENT IS LIKE A BOX
OF CHOCOLATES . . .

Reader Advisory: Despite this chapter title's reference to chocolates, this page should not be consumed. If you swallow or lodge it in your ear or nose, seek medical help immediately, maybe even Dr. Phil. My guess is that you might have issues, the least of which is grappling with the topic of this chapter.

Teaching and assessment are inescapably intertwined, like Will & Grace, Felix & Oscar, Kermit & Miss Piggy, Tokyo & Godzilla, Letterman & CBS, Roto and Rooter, bush and whack, Celine & Dion, and the list goes on. Teaching and assessment are inextricably interwoven through the tapestry of our curricular draperies. "Excuse me, but UGGGH! Those draperies are hideous. I much prefer miniblinds." They're not real! It's a metaphor. "Oh."

The primary reason for this link between teaching and assessment is so I can justify both topics between the covers of this book. Ha Ha. Actually, they're built on the same foundation—the course content and the learning outcomes. Further, teaching and assessment must be tailored to fit the characteristics of your students. Most important, however, is the potential for using humor systematically in both to reduce student anxiety, stress, and tension in order to improve learning and academic success.

The functions of teaching and assessment are complementary: *Teaching facilitates learning; assessment measures the extent to which learning has occurred.* Assessment provides information that is meaningful, dependable, and relevant so that teaching decisions can be made and the appropriateness of the outcomes, methods, and materials can be determined. "That's easy for you to say. But how do we do that?" I was just getting to that with my next heading. However, as we submerge ourselves in assessment, don't lose sight of our students' spin on this topic. They want to know:

"What test can I take to waive this course?"

or

"What hoops do I have to jump through in this course to get an 'A'?"

In other words, you hold the key to your students' *hoop dreams,* their hopes and aspirations on career paths that eventually one day will lead to an appearance on *Oprah.* Those "hoops," disguised with jargon like *test* and *assessment,* are examined next.

Four Types of Classroom Assessment

Pretentious Term Alert: Timeout! I am admittedly a stickler for accuracy. In fact, I own a stickle the size of a moose. So before I continue, I need to clarify the difference between two terms that are often used interchangeably, *test* and *assessment.* Their meanings are not the same.

> *Test* is a device, tool, or procedure to measure student performance on a specified domain of content.
> *Assessment* is a *process* that integrates test information with information from other sources to draw inferences and make decisions about students and programs.

Are we clear? "Crystal." This reminds me of Lt. Kaffee's (Tom Cruise) questioning of Col. Jessep (Jack Nicholson) in *A Few Good Men.* Anyway, back to the alert. Recently, *assessment method* has become a popular, more encompassing generic term than *test item* to include any paper-and-pencil test item, which may be a selection or constructed-response format, as well as a performance task, project, portfolio, or assessment center. The latter two, in fact, contain multiple assessment methods. To keep you awake during these *Snooze-O-Matic®* chapters, I will be using all of these terms.

The efficiency and effectiveness with which we execute our teaching methods are contingent on the information we employ to make instructional decisions. Consistent with the theme of "threes" popping up throughout this book, such as humor trifecta, three-prong model of humor research, and

Goldilocks and the Three Beavers, there are, you guessed it, four types of classroom assessment information that we can use to guide our teaching: (1) precourse, (2) beginning of course, (3) during course, and (4) end of course.

Precourse (Waiver/Placement Assessment)

Many of our students take "advanced placement tests" to waive college courses eons before they sneak into our classrooms. A placement test is designed to answer the following question:

> *To what extent have the students already achieved the learning outcomes for the course?*

If a student knows the bulk of the material covered in your course, it is a total waste of his or her time to have to sit through your classes. If your course can be waived, build a test that students can take, preferably during the preceding semester or as early as possible so course scheduling adjustments can be made. Administering such a test can be a very efficient strategy for streamlining a student's course selection to satisfy program requirements. Also, as one student after another passes your test and waives "Bye Bye!" (hence, the name "Bye Bye Test"), your class size shrinks. *Voila!* (French expression, literally meaning "You go, girl!") You now have a shrunken class that can receive more of your instructional attention. Everyone benefits.

Beginning of Course (Screening/Diagnostic Assessment)

Once students cross our classroom threshold for the first time, another tool could be developed to assess entry-level skills and answer:

> *To what extent do the students possess the prerequisite knowledge and skills needed to take this course?*

Despite the formal catalogue listing of course prerequisites, students tend to slip through prerequisite cracks. For example, one student may have received a "B" in a physiology course taken so long ago that the transcript consisted of a single letter chiseled in a stone tablet, plus only five human organs were known to the medical community: brain, heart, pancreas, hernia, and foot. Such a course is inadequate preparation to enter a pathophysiology course in the 21st century.

Although careful scrutiny of prerequisites in terms of the course syllabus, institution, grade, date, and letters of reference by the students' relatives can help level the course-entry playing field, a screening test of essential preknowledge content can provide valuable information to profile the students' incoming skills. That diagnostic profile can direct teaching methods toward specific student needs at the beginning of the course. Hence, neither the professor nor the student is blinded by a deficit in entry-level information.

During Course (Formative/Diagnostic Assessment)

As you proceed through your course, occasionally it would be a good idea to check the pulse of your class and answer:

Are students progressing satisfactorily?

If you remain connected to your students, they will usually communicate how they're doing through the questions they ask and comments they make. You just have to take the time to listen. However, sometimes we may be oblivious to student learning until the first major test. Formally monitoring the students' progress throughout the course at appropriate checkpoints via quizzes (*Remember:* These are tiny Sarah Hughes size tests), 1-minute paper summaries, and the like can identify their strengths and weaknesses on small segments of course content. This *formative* assessment pinpoints individual learning errors so that corrective action can be taken to prevent a disastrous test performance. Your prescription for your students serves as an *assessment prophylactic*.

The primary focus of formative assessments is to identify students' weaknesses and problem areas and to remediate them before it's too late. In many undergraduate courses, professors may administer several tests containing thousands of items. These tests are assigned increasing percentage grade weights to furnish both formative and summative information. For example, three tests may be given weights of 20%, 30%, and 50%. The two lower weight tests can supply *diagnostic* information on common sources of error encountered by students, as indicated by "most frequently missed items." A post-test review by you can identify these items and the related errors or misconceptions and you can immediately correct them. The students also receive letter grades on these tests, which is *summative* assessment. However, they know that once they make the necessary quarter-time or half-time adjustments based on the formative feedback, they have 80% and then 50% of their final grade remaining to still get an "A." It is this formative use of the test results that provides the motivating force for students to know: "I still have a chance to improve my grade if I can just remove these imaginary steel plates from my head!"

Unfortunately, the traditional midterm-final test format, even weighted 40%–60%, doesn't permit the same amount of recovery time and motivation possible with a graduated-weight system based on three or more tests.

End of Course (Summative Assessment)

By the end of the course, my students and I are so exhausted after beating on each other for 14 weeks (13 if students are married and filing a joint final exam), we all just want to go on a cruise, but not the same one. Almost all of the current has been drained from our mental batteries. However, before we pack, drawing on what miniscule amount of juice we have left,

I ask:	"To what extent have the students achieved the course outcomes?"
Students ask:	"Can I take the final early so I can go skiing (December) or go to the beach (May)?"
I answer:	"Yes, if you take me with you."
Students answer:	"Sure, if you give us an 'A.'"

From my students' perspective, *summative* assessment means, "What's my final grade?" That grade certifies the level of mastery or competence on the course outcomes. Their "hoop dreams" are over! Although this single decision occurs at the end of the course, it is usually cumulative. In fact, the grade may be accumulated by assessment bits and pieces throughout the course, including several tests, quizzes, project papers, class participation, and/or a portfolio containing 300 elements. Any combination of assessment methods may be used to evaluate the outcomes. Each can be weighted according to breadth, depth, instructional time, student time, and importance in arriving at a final grade.

Multiple forms of summative assessment have distinct advantages over the very restrictive paper-and-pencil, multiple-choice midterm-final exam structure. With the vast array of methods at our disposal, the job of picking the right ones to measure course outcomes gets confusing. It often becomes a balancing act as you consider the pluses and minuses of each method. That process is examined next with

A Consumer's Guide to Selecting Assessment Methods

The process of assessing our students' achievement is, in Forrest Gump's words, "like a box of chocolates." We do not know what we're going to find until we commit to untangling the web of assessment methods to measure our course outcomes. What complicates this task is the variety of methods available. One consolation, at least, is that the underlying structure of virtually all forms of assessment you could choose is based on the classic Pavlovian model:

Stimulus → Response

That's probably why dogs even with the intelligence of a tomato perform really well on standardized tests. [*Pop Quiz:* By the way, do you remember the name of Pavlov's dog? I think it was Igor (pronounced NUH ta´ sha).] Examples of how different assessment methods fit this model are shown below:

Method	S	→	R
Multiple-Choice	Question		Pick a Choice
Completion	Statement		Fill in the Blank
Short Answer	Question		Write a Tiny Answer
Essay	Question		Write a Humongous Answer
Experiment	Mix These Chemicals		Lab Blew Up
Project	Do It in the Library		I Need More Time
Portfolio	Put It Together		But It's Too Much Work

The starting point for building your assessment tools is the set of objectives or outcomes that guide your teaching. That blueprint of course outcomes is the driving force behind *what* we teach and assess and *how* we teach and assess whether anybody attained those outcomes. Once the outcomes are clearly and explicitly stated, you can determine the *what* and the *how*. Both teaching and assessment must be aligned with your outcomes. The degree of alignment is crucial to the validity of the scores from any assessment device. The expectations of what your students are expected to demonstrate after teaching direct the form and substance of your assessment.

What you teach is what you assess, give or take a ton of content. Obviously you can't assess everything. It is infeasible to measure the entire domain of content or skills that are taught. The assessment tool or test is simply a *representative sample of what is most important.* The form of assessment is dictated by the course outcomes and the advantages and disadvantages of each assessment method. You are charged with picking the most appropriate, effective, and efficient methods to measure the intended outcomes in your course. That's the only task I'm going to give you in this paragraph.

Suppose you wanted to go shopping for an assessment tool at THE ASSESSMENT DEPOT® (also see Berk, 1996a, 1999a). A consumer's guide would certainly help. Surprise! Surprise! Table 5.1 was designed expressly for that purpose. When deciding on the best method to buy (to measure a specific outcome), weigh the pluses and minuses of each one against the cost (practical constraints) of the specific testing situation. That analysis can certainly whittle down the number of choices. Balance the different factors to

TABLE 5.1   Ratings of advantages and disadvantages of several assessment methods.

Characteristic	(✓) *Best Buy* Multiple-choice	Completion	Essay	Performance assessment methods[1]
1. Cognitive Outcomes Measured				
a. Knowledge	++	++	++	++
b. Comprehension	++	++	++	++
c. Application	++	++	++	++
d. Analysis	+	+	++	++
e. Synthesis	—	—	++	++
f. Evaluation	–	+	++	++
2. Construction				
a. Difficulty	—	–	+	+
b. Efficiency	—	–	+	–
c. Cost	—	–	+	–
3. Content Coverage				
a. Scope (sampling)	++	+	—	—
b. Depth	++	+	++	++
4. Administration				
a. Difficulty	++	+	++	—
b. Efficiency	++	+	—	—
c. Cost	++	+	–	—
5. Scoring				
a. Difficulty	++	–	—	—
b. Efficiency	++	–	—	—
c. Cost	++	–	—	—
d. Guessing	+	+	+	+
e. Accuracy	++	+	+	+
f. Consistency	++	+	+	+

++ = Marked Advantage
+   = Advantage
–   = Disadvantage
— = Marked Disadvantage
[1]Includes constructed-response formats other than completion and essay, such as direct observation, simulations, oral discourse, portfolios, and assessment center.

produce a test with the greatest breadth and depth of content coverage possible. In selecting multiple methods, try to maximize their strengths and minimize their weaknesses.

The multiple-choice item is check-marked as a *"Best Buy"* because of the types of cognitive outcomes it can measure and its marked advantages in content coverage, administration, scoring, and reliability over the other methods. However, it is not the preferred choice at the highest levels of cognition. Outcomes requiring "synthesis" and "evaluation" can be measured more appropriately by methods that force examinees to construct their responses, such as essay and various performance assessment methods. However, because of their practical constraints and other disadvantages, these methods should be reserved for cognitively complex outcomes.

The basic message here is (*Reader Alert:* I don't want you to miss this point, so please read the upcoming bold italicized words very carefully. In fact, you might want to rinse your eyeballs, clean your lenses, or schedule cataract surgery ASAP. But hurry; I don't have all page.): ***Pick assessment methods for what they can measure BEST*** (a.k.a. Characteristic 1) ***balanced against their practical and technical strengths*** (a.k.a. Characteristics 2–5). Now how clear was that, huh? For example, although constructed-response methods can be used to assess knowledge level outcomes, that use doesn't take advantage of their measurement potential and assigned mission in life, which is to tap the highest cognitive outcomes. *DO NOT* test the lowest level of cognition with essay items. It's a waste of valuable testing time, plus your students will hate regurgitating all over the blue book and you will regret grading their cognitive barf. They also may think you have the brains of an eggplant for requiring them to do that. The multiple-choice item would be the superior format to measure a jillion willion knowledge outcomes in an efficient and cost-effective manner; that is, why bother to shop elsewhere, when multiple-choice will get the job done? (*Note:* Matching, which is another form of multiple-choice, has many of the same advantages.)

The variety of assessment methods rated in Table 5.1 should be viewed as a set of tools, each of which has a specific measurement purpose or contribution to make. Rarely can a collection of instructional outcomes be measured adequately with just a single tool, whether it is multiple-choice, essay, performance task, bull-dozer, soldering iron, or pruning sheers. Plus, there are few forms of medieval torture comparable to the excruciating pain of developing or taking a "100-item multiple-choice test." A combination of tools may be the more likely and appropriate choice to measure a wide range of cognitive outcomes.

Kinda Boring General Rules for Writing Items

At last count there were a bazillion general rules for writing any type of test item, one more boring than the other. In an effort to prevent you from conking out as you plod through this chapter, I have picked only 19. I bet you're thinking, "*What? Only 19? Are you crazy?*" Settle down. I know you're upset, but that's no reason to use italics.

The 19 rules are listed in Memory Jogger 5.1, so you can review them and then go to the specific rules in the chapter that excite you or go out to a sushi bar. But, be careful if you put "wasabi" on your sushi. It's like turbo-charged horseradish; two drops and your eyes will blow out of their sockets and/or your hair will burst into flames.

If you proceed with the rules, be prepared to rupture one or more internal organs from laughing at the examples. Each rule is explained and then illustrated with usually one or more ridiculous examples. Beware that all of these examples are in multiple-choice format. There are two reasons for that:

1. It took the better part of 20 minutes to write them.

2. It's too difficult to write funny essay questions and portfolios.

MEMORY JOGGER 5.1   General rules for writing items.

---

1. Generate each item from a specific instructional objective or outcome.
2. Focus on a single, clearly stated problem.
3. Measure higher-order thinking skills when possible.
4. Measure important information.
5. Avoid ambiguity, whatever.
6. Avoid offensive and stereotypic language and situations.
7. Assure the representational fairness of all persons.
8. Avoid irrelevant material that makes an item more difficult.
9. Avoid opinion questions.
10. Cite an authority in a judgment-type item.
11. Tap different information with each item.
12. Avoid using the answer to one item as a prerequisite for answering other items.
13. Avoid trickery in items.
14. Test the answers of context-dependent items.
15. Develop multiple items for context-dependent material.
16. Format items vertically.
17. Minimize examinees' reading time with terse wording of each item.
18. Write the item at the appropriate difficulty level.
19. Use the standard rules for grammar, punctuation, spelling, and abbreviation.

Of course, I'm just yanking your chain mail. Virtually all of the rules still apply to most paper-and-pencil as well as performance item formats. Are you ready? Okay, here we go anyway.

1. Generate Each Item from a Specific Instructional Objective or Outcome

The test should measure what is taught. Duuuh! Therefore, the outcomes that guide instruction should also guide the measurement. Every item should be written from specific outcomes in the content specifications. The acid test of the clarity of each outcome is whether it can be easily transformed into several different item formats. That transformation is illustrated below with the following outcome:

> The student will be able to identify when dietary aides deliver meals to hospital patients.

Item Format   *Sample Item*

True-False: Dietary aides deliver meals to hospital patients when they are using the bedpan.

Short Answer: When do dietary aides deliver meals to hospital patients?

Completion: Dietary aides deliver meals to hospital patients when they are _____.

Multiple-Choice:
The *BEST* time for dietary aides to deliver meals to hospital patients is when they are
  A. being taken to X-ray or surgery.
  B. sleeping and drooling on the pillow.
  C. using the bedpan.
  D. hurling the previous meal.

---

2. Focus on a Single, Clearly Stated Problem

Each item should measure only one idea, fact, concept, principle, decision, or element in a process. It should be clearly stated to direct the examinee toward the correct answer. The examinee should not have to squint to figure out what to do.

The following example has an ambiguous stem that does not tell the examinee the point of the item so he or she can pick out the correct answer:

When it's fall in Baltimore,
A. the garbage men begin wearing shirts again.
B. the squeegee kids on street corners who clean your windshield change over to anti-freeze.
C. the leaves change colors on the one and only tree in Harbor Place.
D. there's a dramatic increase in the number of murders being committed with rakes and leaf blowers.
E. lovely fall colors are used for chalk body outlines.

All of the item information is in the choices. Any one of the choices could be correct because the examinee has no clearly stated direction or qualifier to distinguish the correct answer from the distracters. A revised version with a clearly stated stem is shown below:

What is the most obvious sign that it's fall in Baltimore?
A. The garbage men are wearing shirts again.
B. The squeegee kids on street corners who clean your windshield have changed over to anti-freeze.
C. The leaves are changing colors on the one and only tree in Harbor Place.
D. There's a dramatic increase in the number of murders being committed with rakes and leaf blowers.
E. Lovely fall colors are now being used for chalk body outlines.

Now the examinee has a specific focus as he or she searches for the answer that is the "most obvious sign." I hope you got it right. Here's another item with a sharp focus on a single fact:

In the Shakespearean play, *You Know How You Like It,* what was the name of the nobleman?
*A. Fabio
 B. Gonzo
 C. Magnesia
 D. Prosciutto
 E. Velcro

3. Measure Higher-Order Thinking Skills When Possible

An item should assess fundamental concepts, purposes, causal relationships, applications to new problems, and complex cognitive processes, rather than only simple facts acquired by rote memory or cheating. Unless testing basic skills and low-level knowledge content is essential, each item should emphasize higher level thinking. If teaching covers a range of cognitive levels, the items should reflect the same range as closely as possible.

Going beyond the basic knowledge level material measured by the preceding item on a Shakespearean play, the following item requires the examinee to interpret a specific quotation:

In Shakespeare's *Julius Caesar,* Act III, Folio VI, Book II, Verse XIV, Line LCVIX, which takes place in the Roman Senate, Big Julie uttered his final three Latin words: *"Et tu, Brute."* What was the significance of these words?

A. They meant literally, "Where's the Romaine lettuce and croutons, you low-life anchovy?"

B. They signaled the go-ahead for PBS to begin broadcasting its award-winning series about ancient Rome: *This Old House.*

*C. They triggered the idea to commemorate Caesar's death by naming a salad after him: "The Waldorf."

D. They paved the way for Brutus' advancement to other government jobs, such as gum-wad remover, chariot-station bathroom attendant, and vice-president.

When context-dependent material precedes a set of multiple-choice items (a.k.a. testlet, or "baby test"), you better watch out, you better not cry . . . wait, what happened to the rest of this sentence? Oh, here it is . . . those items can provide an efficient and cost-effective approach for assessing higher-order thinking skills, such as understanding, critical thinking, reasoning, problem-solving, cooking, ice fishing, and country line dancing. The material presented may be in *verbal form,* such as a problem, scenario, vignette, or case study, or *visual/pictorial form,* such as a table, chart, graph, map, figure, diagram, picture, photograph, or cartoon.

The emphasis on cognitively complex learning and testing over the past decade has produced a resurgence of interest in the "vignette" (Haladyna, 1992). A vignette (derived from a French word meaning "oily salad dressing") describes a problem-solving situation to which examinees respond (in a set of multiple-choice items) with certain real-life actions or decisions. This form has established a significant 25-year track record in professional licensing and certification examinations in medicine (Swanson & Case, 1993), nursing, and other healthcare occupations, such as cryonics and taxidermy. The multiple-choice "simulations" of decision-making skills are viewed conceptually somewhere between the traditional multiple-choice items and the current performance-based methods (Swanson, Norman, & Linn, 1995). They may be arguably "the next best thing to being there" (Berk, 1996a).

The contents of the vignette and the types of questions that follow in the testlet differ according to the professional real-life application. An excellent manual for writing vignettes for basic and clinical science test items has been developed by Case and Swanson (1996). Three content prototypes are given next for medicine/nursing, educational administration, and research/evaluation. Although all of these prototypes are structured to provide objectively scored M-C items, it is also possible to pose the vignette as a constructed-response item with one or more questions a student is requested to address in open-ended format. Of course, the major disadvantages of the latter are the subjectivity of the scoring and the fewer number of items.

Medicine/Nursing

> Vignette
>
> Detailed clinical problem
>
> 1. Patient history
> 2. Physical findings
> 3. Laboratory results

M-C Item Set

1. Diagnosis

2. Prognosis

3. Next step(s) in care

One item example of this structure that was rejected by *both* the National Board of Medical Examiners and National League for Nursing for their licensure exams is shown below:

> A 36-year-old male presents to the ER with complaints of a sore throat and severe abdominal pain after ingesting a hubcap from a '57 Chevy.
>
> What is the MOST critical health history question to ask this patient?
> A. Where does it hurt the most?
> B. Does your family have any eating disorders?
> C. Have you tried a hubcap from a '60 Ford Mustang?
> D. Are you into heavy metal?
> E. Is heavy metal into you?
> F. When was your last oil change?

Educational Administration

Vignette
  A. Job-related material
     1. Memoranda
     2. Letters
     3. Notes
     4. Transcripts (telephone)
     5. Transcripts (face-to-face conversations)
     6. Board policies
     7. Referenda
     8. Laws
  B. Depict interactions or pose problems involving
     1. Students
     2. Parents
     3. Teachers
     4. Principals
     5. School board

M-C Item Set
1. Actions
2. Decisions

Research/Evaluation

Vignette
  A. Research/Evaluation Problem
     1. Problem/Question
     2. Description of Program/Intervention
        a. Structure
        b. Content
        c. Length
     3. Description of Participants
        a. Students
        b. Teachers
        c. Administrators
     4. Outcome Measures (Dependent Variables)
  B. Limitations
     1. Design (Pre-experimental, Experimental, Quasi-experimental)
     2. Sample Sizes
     3. Location

M-C Item Set

1. Design

2. Sample Sizes

3. Instruments (tests, scales, questionnaires)

4. Statistical Analysis

4. *Measure Important Information*

Avoid questions about unimportant and trivial information. The items should test reeeaally significant and meaningful outcomes of instruction. What you test should be at least 2200 times more important than a painting of "Dogs Playing Poker" and 3700 times more important than a velveteen Elvis. If the material isn't important, don't ask it on the test. For example, testing information in footnotes, which is usually trivial, made you angry when you took tests. DO NOT provoke your students. If you do, when you leave the classroom after the test, they may be lurking in the shadows waiting to ambush you. The next thing you know, you're getting beat senseless with chalk-filled erasers or being dangled from a helicopter by one leg like a stunt from *Fear Factor*. So whatever you measure, make sure it's important stuff.

The following items measure important facts about one clinical effect of coffee and the generic name for a brand name medication:

Which one of the following is a clinical sign that you're probably drinking too much caffeinated coffee?

   A. In your will, you bequeathed your entire estate to Starbucks®.

   B. When you're asked, "How are you?" you answer, "Good to the last drop."

*C. You haven't blinked since the last lunar eclipse.

   D. You introduce your significant other as "Coffeemate®."

   E. You named your kids Juan and Valdéz and they're girls.

"Ibuprofen®" is the generic name for which popular brand name?

*A. Advil®

   B. Black & Decker®

   C. Charmin®

   D. Exxon®

   E. Ty-D-Bol®

---

5. Avoid Ambiguity, Whatever

The correct or best answer should be clearly discernable by the knowledgeable examinee. Any ambiguity in the item that impedes that examinee's quick and easy determination of the answer should be eliminated. The examinee should not be forced to guess your intent as the item writer. The answer to the following question would be crystal clear to any student of philosophy:

Who was the first student of Socrates?
   A. Amnesia
   B. Antithesis
  *C. Hysteria
   D. Peristalsis
   E. Prosthesis

---

6. Avoid Offensive and Stereotypic Language and Situations

Any words in an item that can be interpreted as offensive to anyone based on their gender, race, ethnicity, age, sexual orientation, or physical or mental disability should be avoided. In particular, stereotypes that ascribe certain characteristics to all members of a group should never be used. For example, white males should not be consistently depicted in positions of power, such as dictator, Mafia hit-man, pimp, and captain of the starship *Enterprise*. Nor should females, racial and ethnic minorities, older people, and people with disabilities be presented only as individuals devoid of power. Instead, they should appear in roles such as attorney general, White House press secretary, Judge Judy, and host/hostess of *America's Most Wanted*.

7. Assure the Representational Fairness of All Persons

Items should present people in everyday situations and groups as fully integrated as part of the multicultural composition of American society, wherever appropriate. In particular, males and females should be depicted in nontraditional as well as traditional occupations and roles, such as those on the *Jenny Jones Show*. Women, racial and ethnic minorities, religious groups, older persons, and individuals with disabilities should be presented respectfully in a variety of settings, environments, and occupations, and in roles of diverse status and power. Those roles should include crocodile hunter, bodyguard, and Columbian drug lord. If proper names are used, strive for a broad balance of national origins and genders.

8. Avoid Irrelevant Material That Makes an Item More Difficult

Any source of difficulty in an item that is irrelevant to what the item is intended to measure could result in an examinee answering the item incorrectly for the wrong reason. Possible sources include vocabulary, professional jargon, abbreviations, technical terms or farm machinery that are unfamiliar to some examinees. Excess verbiage and "window dressing" in multiple-choice stems can also be distracting (see Rule 3 in Chapter 6). Even the use of humor in the item can be confusing, if it isn't done properly and with the students' prior knowledge (see Chapter 8 for details). The examinees could produce wrong answers on items not testing that material. For example, unusual abbreviations in a mathematics problem, such as "VISA" (which stands for Master Card), could confound an examinee's answer to the mathematics component. All elements in an item must be understood by all examinees so that the single purpose of the item is isolated as the only reason for answering the item correctly or incorrectly.

9. Avoid Opinion Questions

An opinion item is inherently ambiguous. It is not scorable as right or wrong because it measures how an examinee feels about something rather than what they know. Ordinarily, a test item requesting an opinion is inappropriate, but, nonetheless, fun to answer. For example, is there any correct answer to either of the following items?

What's the STUPIDEST word in the English language?
  A. cockamamie
  B. gobbledygook
  C. meshugenah
  D. rigamarole
  E. sphincter

What's the WORST invention of the last 2000 years?
  A. bagpipes
  B. chewing tobacco
  C. guillotine
  D. polyester clothes
  E. telemarketing

The determination of the stupidity or worth of anything is a judgment call or an opinion, not an absolutely right or wrong answer. Although opinions can be formally measured by scales and questionnaires, they are just not appropriate on a test that is designed to measure knowledge or skills. However, there is a strategy to assess knowledge of someone else's opinion, which leads us nicely into Rule

10. Cite an Authority in a Judgment-Type Item

The best strategy to measure "knowledge" of opinions or judgments is through an acknowledged source or authority, such as Alan Greenspan or Icarus, the ancient Greek god of motion sickness. The item evaluates the examinee's knowledge of a particular source's position, opinion, or value, not the examinee's opinion. Qualifying the item with a beginning phrase, such as "According to (name source)," prepares the examinee to consider information that is correct or incorrect from the stated source. For example, in the item below try to fathom how the source of the opinion makes it possible to select a correct answer:

According to Al Bundy, which movie would be considered *MOST* romantic?
A. *The Blair Witch Project*
B. *Halloween H20*
C. *The Haunting*
*D. *Lethal Weapon 4*
E. *Scream 3*

Yes, even Al can give this item a molecule of legitimacy. A more frightening thought is to consider what the rest of the items on that test measure.

11. Tap Different Information with Each Item

If each item is generated from a learning outcome, it should contain content not presented in any other item. That means that not only should each item measure an outcome different from the remaining items, but no material in any part of an item should appear anywhere else. For example, in multiple-choice items, content in the stem of one item that is repeated in another could clue the examinee to the correct answer by a process of elimination rather than knowing the correct answer. There should be no overlapping content anywhere throughout the items on a test. The knowledge or skill required to answer any item should be independent of that needed to answer any other item.

In the following pair of items, identify how the correct answer is clued:

What was Leonardo Da Vinci's greatest contribution?
A. Bowflex Fitness®
B. Cuisinart® food processor
C. George Foreman® grill
D. Renaissance Festival
*E. Semigloss latex paint

What brand of paint did Da Vinci use to paint his classic work, *Sal Monella Crossing the Delaware?*
A. Dutch Boy®
*B. Glidden®
C. Pittsburgh®
D. Sears®
E. Sherwin-Williams®

If the correct answer to the first item wasn't selected by the examinee, the stem of the second item is sure to clue the testwise examinee that "paint" has to be in the answer. The overlap of "paint" in the choice of the first item and stem of the second violates the assumption of item independence, plus it clues the correct answer to an item so that no knowledge is needed to answer it.

The following set of putrid items illustrates how repetition of choices can clue answers:

---

1. Who is the composer of the opera *Madame Mothballs?*
   A. Georges Bengay
   B. Don Corleone
   C. Richard Sauerkraut
   D. Guiseppe Weirdi
   *E. Giacomo Zucchini

---

2. Who is the composer of the opera *The Marriage of Orthogro?*
   A. Gioacchino Canelloni
   B. Pietro Mascara
   *C. W. Amadeus Mazeltov
   D. Engelbert Pumpernickel
   E. Guiseppe Weirdi

3. Who is the composer of the opera *Il Fettuccine?*
   A. Antonio Maraschino
   *B. Pietro Mascara
   C. W. Amadeus Mazeltov
   D. Englebert Pumpernickel
   E. Giacomo Zucchini

Once the correct answer is chosen to one item, it is no longer useful as a distracter in any other item. In the preceding three examples, if the examinee picks Zucchini and Mazeltov as the answers to the first two items, the third item has only three instead of the original five choices. Overlapping choices in items appearing anywhere on a test (*Note:* They do not have to be in sequence) prompt the testwise examinee to use "process of elimination" rather than "knowledge" to choose correct answers.

The rule is clear: *A content choice in a multiple-choice item can be used only once; it should NEVER EVER EVER appear again in a multiple-choice or any other type of item.* Should you violate this rule, we're talking about a sure-fire felony conviction with a minimum sentence of two years in the SAT item writing division of Educational Testing Service (formally called "We Write the Items Here Division"). In other words, don't even think about it.

Dilemma: You want to ask several questions, maybe 5 or 10, but there are only a few possible choices available and it's illegal to use them more than once. What's a test developer to do?

Possible Solution: Either use a matching format where choices may be used over and over again without cluing or use completion items where no choices are presented and, instead, the examinee supplies the answers. The matching format solution shown below is actually a series of multiple-choice items smushed together. Can you tell which column contains the stems and which one contains the choices?

Directions: Match the world famous *OPERAS* with the bunch of *COMPOSERS* below. Mark your answers (A–E) in spaces 11–22 of your answer sheet. Each choice of composer may be used once, more than once, or not at all.

OPERAS	COMPOSERS
_____ 11. *Rigatoni*	A. Georges Bengay
_____ 12. *La Boínggg*	B. Don Corleone
_____ 13. *Carmine*	C. W. Amadeus Mazeltov
_____ 14. *Madame Mothballs*	D. Guiseppe Weirdi
_____ 15. *Il Fettuccine*	E. Giacomo Zucchini
_____ 16. *Not Godunov*	
_____ 17. *Thu Cudilluc du Suvillu*	
_____ 18. *La Sagna*	
_____ 19. *The Magic Galoot*	
_____ 20. *Lucia di Hammerhead*	
_____ 21. *The Marriage of Orthogro*	
_____ 22. *Das Fahrvergnügen*	

Did you identify the multiple-choice components embedded in the matching structure? Way, to, go! The 12 operas are actually the stems and the composers are the choices. In this format, however, those choices may be used more than once and the answer to any one of the stems is not clued by the answers to the other stems. Notice the last line in the directions. That statement is critical to clearly communicate the rules of the matching game to the students. The matching structure condenses twelve 5-choice multiple-choice items into a very compact item bundle without any cluing violations. That's quite a testing bargain.

12. Avoid Using the Answer to One Item as a Prerequisite for Answering Other Items

Creating items where examinees must answer one item correctly in order to answer others is called "hinging." It violates the assumption of item independence described in the preceding rule and produces an unfair testing situation for the examinee who answers the prerequisite item incorrectly. That examinee could not possibly answer any subsequent hinged items correctly. The following pair of items illustrates this flaw:

---

1. If Janet Jackson boards a train at 5 P.M. in New York going west at 70 mph, how long will it be before one of her lackeys goes to the dining car and buys her a cup of coffee and a cookie for $9.00?
   A. 5 minutes
   *B. 15 minutes
   C. 1 hour
   D. 2 hours

---

2. From the time of the purchase, how long will it take Janet to arrive at Sony Picture Studios in California to be a contestant on *Celebrity Jeopardy?*
   *A. 18 hours
   B. 1 day
   C. 2.5 days
   D. She still hasn't arrived.

Obviously the answer to question 2 depends on the answer to question 1. As noted above, this "hinging" is not nice because an examinee who misses the first item will also miss the second. He or she is hit with a double whammy. The information required to answer one item should be independent of the information needed to answer any other item. A revised version of item 2 is shown below:

---

3. If the dining car is disconnected from the rest of the train and stranded on the tracks near Indianapolis, how long will it take for the FOX TV crew to arrive and film a segment for *World's Most Incredible Amazing Rescues of Dining Cars?*
   A. 10 minutes
   *B. 2 hours
   C. 6 hours
   D. 3 days

This is certainly an improvement over the previous item 2, plus this one will be televised. I hope my new shirt looks okay. Aren't you supposed to wear blue?

The subject matter where hinging most frequently occurs is mathematics. In the interest of testing time, an examinee may be asked to use the computed answer from one problem to solve another. Independent problems should be given or the answer to hinged items should be scored for process rather than just a computed answer.

Another example of a "hinged" set of items is given below:

---

1. Pick a number from 1 to 9;
2. Subtract 5;
3. Multiply by 3;
4. Square your answer;
5. Add the digits together until you get only one digit (e.g., 64 → 6 + 4 = 10 → 1 + 0 = 1);
6. If your number is less than 5, add 5 to it; otherwise, subtract 4 from your number;
7. Multiply your answer by 2;
8. Subtract 6;
9. Find the letter code for the number using the scale: 1 = A, 2 = B, 3 = C, 4 = D, 5 = E, etc.;
10. Pick a country that begins with that letter
11. Take the 2nd letter of the country and pick a mammal that begins with that letter;
12. What is the color of that mammal?

Answer: Grey elephant from Denmark.

This item set provides an examinee with 11 opportunities to make a mistake before reaching the final answer. This format should be avoided on tests that count for anything and only used in books like this where you can get away with any mistake and know one will know!

13. Avoid Trickery in Items

Trick questions may be intentional or unintentional. You should not attempt to deceive, confuse, or mislead examinees in the form or content of an item. Unintentional trickery occurs when item flaws go undetected, such as an ambiguity in the wording, excess verbiage, or more than one correct answer (for multiple-choice and matching items). Intentional trickery takes two common forms: (1) testing content that is trivial or unimportant, and (2) asking questions about content not taught or not covered in the text or course materials the students studied to prepare for the test. Trick questions can antagonize examinees. When they encounter one, their first collective thought is: "There's a water buffalo outside the door." No. That's their third thought.

There first is: "That item is not fair."

Their second thought is: "(Insert bad name for professor) needs to be whacked."

It is tough enough for most examinees to answer a question without the additional challenge or aggravation of trickery. That practice as a professor is sadistic and it will yield useless information from the item.

14. Test the Answers of Context-Dependent Items

Context-dependent items using paragraphs, illustrations (figures, pictures), vignettes, graphs, tables, or charts should be answerable only by comprehending or analyzing the context. When an examinee is requested to read material prior to answering one or more items, make sure that material is entertaining and *essential to answer the questions*. Sometimes factual information requested in items can be answered independent of the accompanying context. This is usually evident during the test when students start sticking number 2 pencils up those noses. Not a good sign. It should be impossible to answer any item without analyzing the contextual material.

15. Develop Multiple Items for Context-Dependent Material

Since considerable time is often necessary to process context-dependent material, several items should be developed to tap the examinee's knowledge on a variety of aspects of the material presented. Milk the material for all it's worth. This strategy makes efficient use of valuable testing time compared to the alternative of requiring an examinee to interpret a complex table of data or a case study and then ask only one question.

16. Format Items Vertically

Items with different parts, such as stem and choices, can be presented vertically or horizontally. Although the latter may conserve space and reduce reproduction costs, those advantages are offset by the increased reading time and potential confusion or difficulty in identifying the correct answer. Cramming bushels of items onto a single page can be intimidating and can produce unnecessary anxiety. The conventional vertical format is preferable for ease and speed of reading to pinpoint the best or correct answer. It is also appropriate for any length choice, from one word or number to several sentences. Choices with more than a couple of words would be unwieldy for the horizontal format. Which of the following is easier to read?

> Which one of the following is a protein factor in the blood?
> A. Albumin   B. Timbumin   C. Jillbumin   D. Wilsonbumin

or

> Which one of the following is a protein factor in the blood?
> *A. Albumin
> B. Timbumin
> C. Jillbumin
> D. Wilsonbumin

"Neither." Oh, you're just playing with my mind.

17. Minimize Examinees' Reading Time with Terse Wording of Each Item

Get to the point quickly. Items should be worded as precisely and efficiently as possible. Otherwise, valuable testing time may be wasted. Because the number of items asked affects both the validity and reliability of the test scores, minimize reading time by eliminating excess verbiage and shrubbery in the items. Prune those items to reserve time for more items that assess high-level cognitive processes. The following items illustrate this rule:

> Which description suggests your friend, relative, or enemy may NOT be as bright as you thought?
> A. A few ice cubes short of a tray
> *B. Has a full 6-pack, but lacks the plastic thingy to hold it together
> C. Not the sharpest quill on the porcupine
> D. Several drawers shy of a file cabinet
> E. Slipped into the gene pool when the lifeguard wasn't watching

> Which of the following instruments would be found in the brass section of an orchestra?
> A. baboon
> *B. basinette
> C. pickles
> D. strumpet
> E. tangerine

18. Write the Item at the Appropriate Difficulty Level

The item should be custom-tailored at the difficulty level appropriate for the outcome, ages and abilities of examinees, and decisions to be made with the test scores. If the item is too easy or too difficult for its intended purposes, then it may need to be revised or discarded. Actual results from the first administration will typically indicate the difficulty level and the direction for any modifications.

19. Use the Standard Rules for Grammar, Punctuation, Spelling, and Abbreviation

Precision in writing items is critical. Any error in an item that is unintended can be distracting, confusing, or misleading to an examinee. Care should be taken to adhere to all of the formal rules of English in the structure and content of items. Avoid lesser known unintelligible grammatical forms, such as subcutaneous debentures and carnivorous refractions.

Proofreading and meticulous editing of the items in the early stages of test development can usually catch and correct the most obvious mistakes. When examinees detect errors, it's too late. Corrections would then have to be made during the test administration. Depending on the type of error, the item may be salvaged or discarded.

The difficulty with editing our own test items as well as any other written product is that sometimes we simply can't see the errors; we're too familiar with the content. This is a temporary condition known as *editorial meopia.* You're probably thinking right now, "Meopia schmeopia. Big deal! That's not new." You're right. In fact, this problem dates back four million years to ancient Greece when test developers, such as Plato, Aristotle, Onassis, Stephanopoulos, Eucalyptus, and Androgynous experienced meopia when they edited their items.

You have two options: (1) persuade a colleague or your favorite teaching assistant (TA) to edit the test or (2) recruit a student of yesteryear to take on the task. So what's it going to be? Make a decision. "Okay, my TA." You seem confident. Is that your final answer? "No! Maybe I should use one of my life-lines, Rege." You don't have any lifelines and my name isn't Rege; it's Bucko. So what are you going to do? "Oooh, you're making me nervous. My TA!" Your final answer? "Yes, Bucko, and if you ask me that again, I'm going to smack you."

Since your TA will be editing the items, he or she needs to be familiar with the basic editorial symbols. A comprehensive list of the most common ones has been compiled in Figure 5.1. It includes operational, typographical, and punctuation symbols with their literal English translations. A few were adapted from Weller (1987, p. 74).

FIGURE 5.1 Operational, typographical, and punctuation editorial symbols.

Operational Symbols

Symbol	Meaning
ℒ	Take out
◠	Eat in
◡	Close up
◡→	Lock up and go home
⊏	Move to left
⊐	Move to right
⊓	Stand up
⊔	Sit down
(ff)	Fight team fight
(sp)	Spin around
=	Lie down
tr	Trash manuscript
#	Play Tic Tac Toe
⊄#	Insert horsey
/ \	Pencil broken
*?#@	Computer broken
∪	Editor in rocking chair
stet	Edit right now (Editorial version of STAT)

Typographical Symbols

Symbol	Meaning
cap	Take off cap
pac	Turn cap around
lc	Lower cap over face
bm	Byte me
✗	Bad letter
✗✗	Reeeally bad letter
✗✗✗	Send letter to bed without MTV
sf	Manuscript makes me barf
wf	Dog barking while editing

Punctuation Symbols

Symbol	Meaning
⁄ₙ	Author is a ninny
⁄ₘ	Get editor more M&Ms
:|	Eyeballs need alignment
;|	One eyeball crying
⊙	Insert belly button
∧	Campgrounds ahead
⌃̂	Comma on ceiling
❝ ❞	Quotation marks living together

6

DO-IT-YOURSELF
TEST CONSTRUCTION

> **CNN News Bulletin:** This is Christiane Amanpour standing here at the first paragraph of Chapter 6. And I'm wondering, Wolf, if the cameras can really give a sense of how unusual this chapter is. Feelings of magic and hilarity permeate this entire page. The air is filled with the scent of, wait, that's disinfectant. EWWW! I'm outta here. This is Christiane Amanpour running away from Chapter 6.

Question: What test item format (a) holds world records in the categories of Most Popular, Most Unpopular, Most Used, Most Misused, Most Loved, and Most Hated; (b) has its own wall space at the Test Item Hall of Fame in Princeton, New Jersey, which is in Texas; and (c) has been already named the Official Test Item Format of the 2006 Winter Olympic Games in Torina, Italy? *Answer:* Portfolio. Gotcha! Of course, it's multiple choice.

I bet you've always wondered, "Who invented the multiple-choice item? Actually it was Edward T. Standardized (abbreviated ACT). He has been named "Father of the Multiple-Choice Item." In fact, the first test was named after him: the Spelling Test. The next obvious question is: "Who's the mother? Huh? Huh?" Calm down. It's Scanny Bubble Answer-Sheet (*Note:* Her hyphenated last name means she's British or it's a typo) from the quaint English town of Gabardine-Upon-Woolite, which is only 20 millimeters outside of Orlando!

Hundreds of thousands of students in U.S. colleges and universities take nationally normed, standardized, multiple-choice tests each year. These tests are used for a variety of decisions, including diagnosis, placement, selection, awards, licensure, certification, course credit, grades, and employment. As academicians, we make some of those decisions and even administer some of those tests, rather well I might add. But, in addition, we must develop our own tests to measure our students' achievement of specific course outcomes or objectives.

The multiple-choice item is the most frequently chosen item format for these tests in undergraduate courses and even in many graduate courses in colleges and universities throughout the universe, including the new planets, *Micro* and *Soft*. Despite the increasing popularity of performance assessment methods during the 1990s (Arter, 1999; Berk, 1986), my previous evaluation of assessment methods in Table 5.1 indicates that multiple-choice still provides a *Best Buy* for content coverage, administration, ease and accuracy of scoring, and reliability, especially for large class sizes, which are those greater than 30 and less than the Mormon Tabernacle Choir.

Anatomy of a Multiple-Choice Item

There are more than a dozen variations of the multiple-choice item presented in the literature (Haladyna, 1999). Despite that number, only two models frequently appear in the tests that our students take: (1) the conventional "Camry" format and (2) luxurious "Lexus."

Conventional "Camry" Format

This basic totally equipped model consists of two parts:

1. Stem (a.k.a. question, problem, or incomplete sentence)

   and

2. Choices

   a. 1 Correct or BEST Answer

   b. 1–4 Wrong Answers (a.k.a. distracters, foils, incorrect alternatives)

The purpose of this structure is to determine whether an examinee can discriminate among the choices to recognize the answer. The "knowledgeable" examinee should be able to pick it out lickety split. The "less knowledgeable" or "unprepared" examinee who may be unsure of the answer should be *distracted* by the plausible wrong answers, *foiled* away from the correct answer, or *sent* home to go study some more. In other words, the wrong answers' sole function in life is to lure the examinee away from the correct answer because he or she wasted time watching *Friends* or *South Park* instead of studying and, therefore, deserves to get it wrong. An example of the "Camry" format is given below.

What is the name of the original version of the word processing software WordPerfect®?
A. WordVeryGood
B. WordAverage
C. BadWord
D. ReallyBadWord
*E. WurdWitoutSpelchek

Luxurious "Lexus" Format

The "Lexus" has one major luxury feature that raises the cognitive complexity of the item—a piece of material that must be read and interpreted before it can be driven (See Rules 3, 14, and 15, Chapter 5). The material may consist of a paragraph, passage, vignette, table, chart, graph, figure, photograph, volleyball, or battleship. Once this material is processed, then the stem and choices are introduced. Since the additional material takes several minutes to interpret, usually several "Camrys" follow to measure different aspects of the content. This baby test is called a *testlet,* like piglet, froglet, or tyrannosauruslet. It is essential that the multiple-choice questions in the testlet be answerable only by understanding the material presented (see Rule 14, Chapter 5). In other words, the questions must be dependent on the context of the material; hence, the term *context-dependent* items. An example of this structure where the examinee must interpret a graph before answering three questions is shown in Figure 6.1.

FIGURE 6.1 Bar height from 1995 to 2001.
Source: American Bar Association

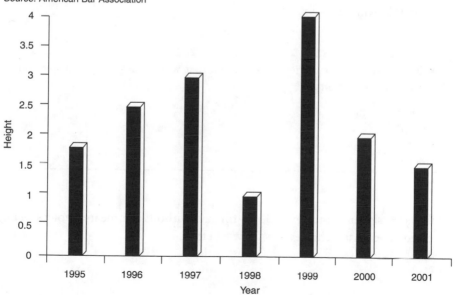

1. During which year was the highest bar produced?
   A. 1996
   B. 1997
   C. 1999
   D. 2000
2. Given the trend in bars since 1999, what is the predicted bar height in 2002?
   A. 1
   B. 1.5
   C. 2
   D. 2.5
3. During which year was the relative decline in bar height the greatest?
   A. 1995
   B. 1998
   C. 2001
   D. Cannot be determined from graph

Ancient Origin of the Multiple-Choice Format

Most of you are probably aware of the popularity of the multiple-choice item during the past millennium. What you may not know is that the basic multiple-choice structure dates back more than two millennia to ancient Rome. It was common practice at the Coliseum during half-time at a Detroit Lions—Jacksonville Jaguars game to hear the emperor ask one of the gladiators the following question:

Behind which door is the ferocious animal that will chew you up and spit you out for our entertainment?

Door A
Door B
Door C
Door D

This was a skeleton multiple-choice format without the meaty choices being revealed. The actual choices are shown below:

> Door A: A brand new 70 B.C. Toyota Chariot with Corinthian leather seats
> Door B: A ferocious animal with the head of a lion and the body of a yak
> Door C: The emperor's 85-year-old mother-in-law, Brunhilda
> Door D: A young maiden with a bottle of Maniochewitz wine and bowl of matzo
> ball soup

Interestingly, since picking the correct answer to the question meant a certain painful death-like experience, it was in the gladiator's best health interest to select a door that would NOT release the animal. This was the earliest example of a positive format item that was actually in a faulty negative format. Picking any of the "wrong" answers was to the gladiator's benefit, at least that's what he believed.

The problem of cluing the correct answer also occurred at about the same time because the gladiator could hear different sounds coming from behind the doors, particularly Brunhilda, complaining about her room. This was solved in subsequent testings by requiring total silence during the administration of all standardized multiple-choice tests.

A Brief and Fractured History of Multiple-Choice Item Writing Rules

The psychometric[1] literature on multiple-choice item-writing rules spans more than 75 years. In other words, some of those rules are older than dirt. The earliest research on specific rules dates back, hieroglyphically speaking, to two studies of the number of choices that should be used (Ruch & Charles, 1928; Ruch & Stoddard, 1925). That takes us up to the 1950s. I skipped over a few million years because most of the activities relevant to the topic of this paragraph, which is dirt, were really dull and boring. Now aren't you glad? Unfortunately, though, due to a scheduling mix-up, the '50s did not officially begin until April 1951 when, all of a sudden, the first prescriptive set of item-writing rules burst onto the measurement scene in the form of Ebel's (1951) chapter in the first edition of *Educational Measurement*. That contribution was followed by a 20-year hiatus that interrupted the trickle of scholarship on the topic.

---

[1]Derived from two Greek words, "psycho," meaning "crazy," and "metric," meaning "European measurement system that nobody in America, except lab rats and runners, wants to use."

Then, guess what happened? Yup! The Watergate Scandal, starring *The Washington Post* reporters, Robert Redford and Dustin Hoffman. Uuuh oh! These are the wrong notes. I meant to say Wesman's (1971) chapter in the second edition of *Educational Measurement* appeared. In the 1960s and 1970s, three monographs on writing multiple-choice items also were published in England by Brown (1966), MacIntosh and Morrison (1969), and Woods (1977).

During the 1980s the research trickle resumed. However, the decade ended with a flood when two researchers synthesized 43 item-writing rules into a taxonomy (Haladyna & Downing, 1989a) and then validated that taxonomy one page later in the same journal (Haladyna & Downing, 1989b).

The early 1990s witnessed attempts to drown the multiple-choice format. It met its most formidable challenge (a.k.a. "bashing") from the *performance* or so-called *authentic* assessment movement, which galvanized educators to "get real." This meant teach and measure higher-order thinking skills. The response by one segment of the measurement community was a constant stream of research that tested a variety of multiple-choice structures for measuring complex cognitive outcomes (Berk, 1996a; Case & Swanson, 1996; Haladyna, 1992) and compared multiple-choice to constructed-response formats (Bennett & Ward, 1993; Hakel, 1998; Haladyna, 1997).

These resources on multiple-choice item writing and research have been augmented by nearly 50 textbooks on educational and psychological measurement. These texts typically devote a section of one chapter, rarely more, to constructing multiple-choice items (e.g., Linn & Gronlund, 2000; Mehrens & Lehmann, 1991; Popham, 1999; Worthen, White, Fan, & Sudweeks, 1999). However, the most comprehensive and authoritative treatise on multiple-choice item development is Haladyna's (1999) volume.

A critical review of all that has been written on building multiple-choice tests leads to four inescapable conclusions: (1) regardless of which multiple-choice format one chooses to use, the basic structure of a stem with four or five choices has provided the foundation upon which all variations have been developed, (2) most format flaws occur within that basic structure rather than in the context-dependent material, (3) the rules for writing the items are derived primarily from experience and tradition rather than from theory and empirical research (Cronbach, 1970; Nitko, 1984), and (4) reading any of those rules for longer than 10 minutes can knock you out faster than the general anesthetic Isofluoraine®.

It is practically significant that today's test builders still follow the rules of their forefathers and mothers (or foreparents). "Why?" You ask. Because the rules were given to them by the previous generation and they were told, "Follow these rules, or else you'll be smacked with a broom." The tradition of passing down item-writing rules from one generation to the next can be traced to the seminal work of Zero Mostel, known as the "*Fiddler-on-the-Roof* Theory of Item Writing" (based on the popular Broadway musical, *Annie*). The **TRADITION** is so deeply entrenched that we're required to use capital boldfaced letters when referring to it. If you have any questions about the rules, they can't be answered because all of the foreparents are dead.

The one question *this* chapter will answer is: How do you write these items correctly? The remainder of the chapter is devoted to describing 10 boring rules for writing the stem and 7 more boring rules for writing the choices. But, hey, think how great your tests will be when you're finished. Your life will be changed forever. Hopefully, some of the weird examples will keep you awake.

Writing the Stem

Well, here they are. You might want to glance at the rules in Memory Jogger 6.1 to determine whether you already know this material, peruse the descriptions and items, or skip this chapter completely and watch *C.S.I.* or *60 Minutes*.

1. Present a Single Definite Problem or Idea

Only one concept, procedure, principle, or ATM machine should be tested. (*Note:* ATM stands for Federal Deposit Insurance Corporation). A complex problem can confuse the examinee. Further, if the examinee answers the

MEMORY JOGGER 6.1 Rules for writing the stem.

1. Present a single definite problem or idea.
2. State the problem as simply and clearly as possible.
3. Avoid excess verbiage, window dressing, and red herrings.
4. Use either the question or completion format.
5. If the stem is in completion form, place the blank at the end.
6. State the stem in positive form whenever possible.
7. Use the negative form only when it is consistent with the learning outcome.
8. If the negative form is used, *EMPHASIZE* the negative word.
9. State most of the information in the stem.
10. If the stem asks for the best or most appropriate answer, emphasize the words *BEST* or *MOST.*

question incorrectly, it would be impossible to infer which part of the problem the examinee didn't know. It is recommended that several single problems be asked rather than one complex problem. If a procedural problem is presented as separate questions, it will be easier to pinpoint which step in the procedure the examinee didn't understand. For example, several specific questions about a medication can pinpoint an examinee's knowledge of use, dosage, or other characteristics:

What "Directions for Use" are given for the children's antibiotic Amoxipenam-pecillinschmillin®?
  A. Take capsule while operating a bulldozer or other dangerous machinery.
 *B. Pour teaspoonful on top of Rocky Road ice cream.
  C. Chew tablets with alcohol to intensify the effect.
  D. Stick caplet in each ear for dramatic side effects.
  E. Dissolve in mouth with other medications for interesting interactions.

What is the correct dosage of Amoxipenampecillinschmillin® for chubby children 3–5 years of age who weigh less than a ton?
  A. 1 tablet before and after *Teletubbies*®.
  B. 2 caplets 2 times a day, except on Saturday between 9AM and 4PM.
  C. 3 tbsp. every 6 hrs. so *you* have to get up in the middle of the night.
 *D. 4 capsules hidden in a Wendy's® "Frosty."
  E. 5 lozenges per day until tongue turns green.

---

2. *State the Problem as Simply and Clearly as Possible*

The stem should be stated precisely using a simple sentence structure not like the sentences describing this rule. Avoid complex sentences and ambiguous terms, such as precisely, simple, and complex. When a knowledgeable examinee reads the question, the correct answer should pop out of his or her brain (EWWW! Gross!) and jump out of the list of choices into the numbered bubble on the answer sheet. Anything that interferes with this process can create confusion and even a cerebral hemorrhage, which may result in the best examinees answering the question incorrectly.

One way to check on the clarity of the stem is to cover the choices and try to answer the question. If you can't, the stem may be incomplete or confusing or you may be an idiot. For example, answer each of the following stems without looking at the choices:

> What was the MOST accurate predictor of admission to undergraduate college programs in 2002?
> A. Eenie
> B. Meenie
> *C. Meinie
> D. Moe

This stem can be answered without the choices, although I bet you peeked, but were really sorry after you did. Shame on you. Try the next item stem:

> Which one of the following items for sale was sold first when advertised?
> A. FOR SALE: Bull dog. Will eat anything. Loves children.
> B. FOR SALE: 9-volt smoke detector with silencer.
> C. FOR SALE: Decaffeinated coffee table.
> D. FOR SALE: Braille dictionary. Must see to appreciate.

This stem is impossible to answer without peeking. Made ya look. Made ya look. The content of this item does not lend itself to the above structure. However, the stem is still simple (whatever that means) and clear and the content choices are short, precise, and moderately amusing.

3. Avoid Excess Verbiage, Window Dressing, and Red Herrings

Get to the point quickly. That means do not clutter the stem with excess words (verbosity), irrelevant or extraneous material (window dressing), or information designed to mislead the examinee (red herrings or blackened catfish). Such clutter increases reading time, creates confusion, detracts or misleads even the knowledgeable examinees, and can make all of the others really mad. Consider how each of the following awful items can be revised:

Verbosity

> According to Hollingshead's classification system, which job category is predicted to have the highest number of employees by the year 2010?
> A. White collar
> *B. Blue collar
> C. No collar
> D. Ring around the collar

The adjective phrase at the beginning of the stem is unnecessary to answer the question. The stem can be simplified to the following:

> Which job category is predicted to have the highest number of employees by the year 2010?

Window Dressing

> Reading an Italian restaurant menu can be really confusing. There are a pazillion types of pasta with approximately a grillion of which taste exactly the same. Sometimes they even sound like people we know.
>
> Which one of the following is a type of pasta?
>   A. Lamborghini
>   B. Mancini
> *C. Manicotti
>   D. Maserati
>   E. Fonzarelli

The three sentences preceding the question are irrelevant. The question can be answered without any of that information. The simple question with the five choices is all that's needed to get the job done. Well, that's not totally true, especially for choice "E." To be familiar with "E" you would have to be either a boomer or watch *Happy Days* on the cable TV Land channel.

4. Use Either the Question or Completion Format

The question format is usually more direct, simpler, and easier to answer. It is the recommended choice, or rather stem. An example is shown below:

> What is the *BEST* time to deliver meals to hospital patients?
>   A. When they are being taken to X-ray or surgery.
>   B. When they are sleeping and drooling on the pillow.
>   C. When they are using the bedpan.
> *D. When they are hurling the previous meal.

Sometimes, however, the content presented in the stem may fit the completion form better. If the grammatical structure of the material lends itself more appropriately to the completion, then it should be used, particularly if the question form appears awkward. Also, in the preceding example, notice the repetition of the first three words in each choice which increases reading time. Those words can be placed in the stem of the completion form to shorten the choices.

In the completion form, the stem is the beginning of a sentence and the choices are the possible endings. Since each choice completes the sentence, the first word begins with a lowercase letter and the last word is followed by the appropriate punctuation, such as a period, question mark, ampersand, or calamari. The stem and each choice combined should be a grammatically correct complete sentence, or else! Read each combination aloud to make sure the structure is correct. Compare the completion form below to the preceding question form:

The *BEST* time to deliver meals to hospital patients is when they are
A. being taken to X-ray or surgery.
B. sleeping and drooling on the pillow.
C. using the bedpan.
*D. hurling the previous meal.

Isn't this item delightful? After seeing the question form of this item, I certainly hope you got this one correct. If not, you're probably going to need help on the items coming up next. Brace yourself; here they come.

5. If the Stem Is in Completion Form, Place the Blank at the End

When the completion is a word or phrase, it should always appear at the end. A blank at the beginning or in the middle is confusing to understand and it looks stupid. The examinee must read the complete stem and then go back to determine the answer that fits in the blank. This increased reading time and the potential confusion that can occur indicate that the internal blanks should be avoided. Consider the rotten stem below compared to the revised stem that follows:

_____ is the product of hemoglobin breakdown of red blood cells.
*A. Bilirubin
B. Bilibobrubin
C. Bilisuerubin
D. Peggysuerubin

(*Note:* "Bilirubin" is pronounced "Jon' ē Kash.")
A new and improved stem for this item is given below:

Hemoglobin breakdown of red blood cells produces _____.

6. State the Stem in Positive Form Whenever Possible

The objectives or outcomes of instruction and the methods by which most information is taught are positive. That is, what students should know or be able to perform is emphasized, not what they should NOT know or perform. It is the correct or best answer that counts. The stem format consistent with these characteristics is expressed positively. It asks the examinee to identify the correct or best answer out of a list of choices, the rest of which are all wrong answers, such as the following:

Which one of the following is the right answer to this stem?
A. Wrong
*B. Right
C. Wrong
D. Wrong

This form is also consistent with the way we think. An example is shown below:

Which of the following expressions by the airlines is an oxymoron?
A. Direct flight
B. Nonstop flight
*C. Airline food
D. Complete stop

In this item, you're hunting for an oxymoron. "Oxymoron" is actually derived from two Latin root words: "oxy," meaning "to combine," and "moron," meaning "two words that make a cute couple."

The negative form forces the examinee to search for a wrong choice that is the correct answer. The most frequently used negative terms in the stem are NOT, EXCEPT, and LEAST. The form is illustrated below:

Which one of the following is NOT the right answer?
A. Right
B. Right
*C. Wrong (correct answer)
D. Right

This is opposite of the way we are conditioned to think. Our minds have to be shifted from "drive" into "reverse," although some of you are still fooling around with "neutral" or "park." Two examples are given below:

Which one of the following expressions is *NOT* an oxymoron?
A. express mail
*B. first commencement
C. "girlie mon"
D. "Good Grief!"
E. legal brief

All of the following expressions are oxymorons *EXCEPT:*
*A. convention discount.
B. freezer burn.
C. jumbo shrimp.
D. newspaper facts.
E. tiny whale.

The negative form is often used for the wrong reason. With certain types of content, it may be much easier to construct one wrong and three right choices than the three wrong choices needed for the positive form.

7. Use the Negative Form Only When It Is Consistent with the Learning Outcome

There are legitimate conditions or circumstances for using the negative form, such as when the outcome being measured and instruction focus on rules, procedures, or practices to be avoided. Knowing what NOT to do in potentially dangerous situations should be assessed with the negative form. This could be a life-saving item. Two examples are shown below:

If your hand gets stuck in the cookie jar, what is *NOT* an appropriate method to release it?
*A. Amputate at the wrist.
B. Fill the jar with soap and cold water.
C. Pour extra-virgin olive oil on your skin.
D. Smash the jar.
E. You should be ashamed of yourself.

Valium is probably *LEAST* effective when
A. your hair is on fire.
B. you're being read your Miranda rights.
C. your significant other shows up at the front door in a straightjacket.
D. your picture appears on *America's Most Wanted.*
*E. you're looking in the mirror and do not see a reflection.

8. If the Negative Form Is Used, EMPHASIZE the Negative Word

The problem is that the examinee has been searching for the correct answer in previous items. He or she can easily miss the negative term when the item is read. This is why the term should be **boldface**, CAPITALIZED, underlined, *italicized,* or **_ALL OF THE ABOVE_**. This is to alert the examinee to shift gears. Even when the warning is given, the examinee may still forget or get confused. Another strategy to minimize such errors is to group the negative-form items into one section with directions explaining the change in format. For example:

DIRECTIONS: For each of the items in this section, pick out the choice that does *NOT* fit with the other choices or is the *EXCEPTION.*

Which piece of evidence suggests that your friend may *NOT* be as bright as you thought?
A. Scored 199 on the SAT
B. Couldn't find Waldo.
C. Thinks *20/20* are shoe sizes.
*D. Took 1½ hours to watch *60 Minutes.*

All of the following are redundant expressions *EXCEPT:*
A. end result.
B. real difference.
*C. romantic men.
D. totally valueless.
E. very unique.

> Which internship was rated *LEAST* desirable by college students last year?
> *A. Lifeguard at a sewage treatment plant
> B. Sensitivity trainer for the Montana Militia
> C. Projectile catcher at the bottom of the Washington Monument
> D. Hair stylist for the National Basketball Association

9. State Most of the Information in the Stem

For completion-form items, any word or phrase that is repeated at the beginning of all the choices should be cut and placed once at the end of the stem. This strategy streamlines the choices so they are easier and faster to read. The differences between the choices are also much clearer, such that the correct answer should pop out for the knowledgeable examinee. Identify the redundant words in the choices of the following atrocious item:

> If a person watched *Who Wants to Be a Millionaire* night after night,
> A. that would be evidence of an addiction.
> B. that would be evidence of a crush on Rege.
> C. that would be evidence of a pathetic, lonely existence.
> *D. that would be evidence of a need for a "Lifeline."
> E. that would be evidence of a compulsion to take multiple-choice tests.

I hope you picked the right words, because you haven't been doing too well up to this point. The redundant words are: "students wearing baseball caps backwards should" Oops! Wrong item. Sorry. The words "that would be evidence of a(an)" should be surgically removed from each choice and transplanted to the stem as shown below:

> If a person watched *Who Wants to Be a Millionaire* night after night, that would be evidence of a(an)
> A. addiction.
> B. compulsion to take multiple-choice tests.
> C. crush on Rege.
> *D. need for a "Lifeline."
> E. pathetic, lonely existence.

Notice the decrease in reading time and the clarity of the differences among the choices. They're also ordered alphabetically. Wow, am I glad I revised this item.

10. If the Stem Asks for the Best or Most Appropriate Answer, Emphasize the Words BEST or MOST

When the stem asks for the best answer or most appropriate answer, emphasize the words *BEST* or *MOST* to distinguish it from the correct-answer form, as illustrated in the following items:

What is the *BEST* method to produce an out-of-body experience?
  A. Touch an electric fence to see if it's turned on.
  B. Invite your friends over for a Super Bowl party when you don't own a TV.
  C. Go skydiving with a parachute you bought from a street vendor in New Orleans.
*D. Try holding a scalding cup of coffee between your legs as you drive into traffic.
  E. At your wedding, instead of saying, "I do," say, "I'll think about it."

What is the *MOST* popular course selected by varsity athletes at Penn & Teller State University?
  A. Criminal Law: Staying Above It
  B. English as a First Language
*C. Passing Drug Tests without Studying
  D. The Poetry of Charles Barkley
  E. Subtraction: Addition's Trick Pal

Since the best-answer form may require finer discrimination among the choices as opposed to right versus wrong, the examinee should be clearly informed of what is being requested. This is particularly important when correct- and best-answer forms are mixed in the test. Another method to caution the examinee of this difference is to separate the two forms in different sections of the test with directions that indicate what the examinee is to look for in the choices.

Writing the Choices

Now that you can write a terrific stem, as promised, this chapter presents 7 more really boring rules for writing the choices. The first 3 apply to all choices, the fourth focuses on how to devise incorrect choices, and the last 3 provide guidelines for the correct answer. Memory Jogger 6.2 summarizes this list of rules. Proceed at your own risk.

MEMORY JOGGER 6.2 Rules for writing choices.

1. State all choices as simply, clearly, and briefly as possible.
2. Order verbal choices logically and quantitative choices numerically from lowest to highest values.
3. Avoid or use sparingly "None of the above."

INCORRECT CHOICES
4. Use plausible distracters.
   a. Incorporate common misconceptions or errors of students.
   b. Use scientific or technical phrases.
   c. Use true but incorrect answers.

CORRECT ANSWER
5. Intended answer should be unequivocally correct or absolutely best.
6. Avoid stating the correct answer in textbook language or stereotyped phraseology.
7. The correct/best answer should appear about the same number of times in random positions throughout the entire test.

1. State All Choices as Simply, Clearly, and Briefly as Possible

The choices should be stated so crisply that the correct answer should pop out to the knowledgeable examinee and the differences between the distracters be clearly discernable to the less knowledgeable examinee.

2. Order Verbal Choices Logically and Quantitative Choices Numerically from Lowest to Highest Values

Ordering the choices makes it easier for the examinee to read and remember them as he or she searches for the correct answer. With certain verbal content there may be an implied or underlying order for the choices. The following item lists the choices illogically:

What cold remedy has been proven most effective in relieving cold-related symptoms?
*A. Triahers®
 B. Triatheirs®
 C. Triamine®
 D. Triahis®

The appropriate pronoun order of choices would be:

   A. Triamine®
   B. Triahis®
 *C. Triahers®
   D. Triatheirs®

There are many cases, of course, where there is no logical order of verbal content choices. If that occurs, simply alphabetize them.

In the following math problem, the unordered choices may be confusing:

Doofus (*Note:* His real name is Dweebus) gets $400 for stealing a Mercedes, $200 for a SUV 4 × 4, and $50 for a Ford. So far, he has stolen 1 Mercedes and 3 SUVs. How many Fords will Doofus have to steal to make $1200 so his kneecaps won't be broken?

 *A. 4
  B. 8
  C. 2
  D. 6

A better set of choices ordered numerically would be:

  A. 2
 *B. 4
  C. 6
  D. 8
  E. Who do we appreciate?

---

3. Avoid or Use Sparingly "None of the Above"

Picking "none of the above" means the correct or best answer to the stem isn't included in the choices. It tests the examinee's ability to identify incorrect answers. Therefore, it is not possible to infer that an examinee would know the correct answer to the question even if it smacked him or her in the face like a bug splattering on your windshield. EWWW! In other words, when "none of the above" is the correct answer, YOU PROBABLY HAVEN'T TESTED ANYTHING! The outcome has not been measured. The item is a waste of space on the test. This rule indicates: "none of the above" is **not** an appropriate choice to measure performance. For example, consider the following item:

When traveling by train overnight on the European railways, which type of sleeping quarters providers the BEST CHANCE for a good night's sleep?
  A. PLAIN OL' SEAT: 2 sets of 3 seats facing each other are pushed down flat so 6 people can lie across them with each head resting between 2 pairs of rancid feet
  B. COUCHETTE: a slab of plywood hanging from a wall, 6 per train compartment to accommodate the entire von Trapp family who always has a great time eating, singing, eating, shouting, eating, smacking each other, and, did I say, eating?
  C. PRIVATE CHAMBER: an extremely expensive couchette reserved for royalty, which we'll never see in our lifetime
 *D. None of the above

There is *one exception* to the above inappropriate use of "none of the above": it is frequently used in computational problems because it forces the examinee to actually compute the answer. It may be justified if the math problems must be in multiple-choice format for machine-scoring high-volume administrations. Otherwise, a supply or constructed-response format would be preferable to require the production of the answer. A typical math item of this type is shown below:

Bunky, Cosmo, and Rufus are linebackers in the National Football League, weighing 290 lbs., 325 kgs., and 250 lits., respectively.

What is their combined weight expressed in motor vehicles?
  A. 2 Volvos with ski racks
  B. 3 Isuzu Rodeos that tip over
  C. 4 Brinks armored trucks recently robbed
  D. 5 Mazda Miatas without roofs
 *E. None of the above

This item forces the examinee to:

1. convert Cosmo's and Rufus' weights to pounds,

2. add their combined weights to Bunky's weight,

3. transform the total to tons,

4. find each car's and truck's weight in the April issue of *Consumer Reports*, except Brinks, who has to be called,

5. call the Brinks Company only to be put on hold forever listening to country music until the person who finally answers wants to know, "when the truck is empty?"

6. compute the final answer, and

7. discover it's "none of the above."

Simple. That's why "none of the above" is so appropriate for computational problems.

INCORRECT CHOICES
4. *Use Plausible Distracters*

If a distracter doesn't distract or foil the less knowledgeable examinee away from the correct answer, then it's not doing its job. Remember, its *raison d'être* (a French expression meaning "je ne sais quoi") is to snare a few examinees into thinking it's the correct answer. Therefore, plausibility is the criterion for an effective distracter. If at least 5% of the examinees do not pick each distracter, then the nonfunctional distracter(s) needs to get another job. It should be revised so it's more attractive or discarded and replaced with a better one. Ugly or dysfunctional distracters clutter the item and serve no measurement purpose (a.k.a. "window dressing"). For example, if no one selects one distracter among 4 choices, the item is demoted to a 3-choice item with a guessing factor of 33% rather than the originally assumed 25%. It is simply a less effective item.

The problem seems clear: How do you build plausible distracters? I'm glad you asked. In addition to many of the preceding suggestions on choice construction which contribute to plausibility, there are a few other tried-and-true techniques:

a. Incorporate common misconceptions or errors of students. This is probably the best source for distracters. The mistakes students make or confusing concepts can be very appealing distracters. You may be thinking, "Where am I supposed to come up with these errors?" Excellent question. The most effective technique I have used is to pilot test (means to fly the test passed a few examinees) the items first in a completion or fill-in-the-blank format. In other words, just present the stem in question form with a blank, or reword the stem with a blank near the end (see Rule 3 under Stems). The most frequent wrong answers students supply will provide a pool of plausible distracters. At least you will be certain that several students actually believed those responses to be correct. The greater the frequency of a particular wrong answer, the more effective it will probably be as a distracter in the multiple-choice version.

b. Use scientific or technical phrases.   Technically phrased wrong answers can be attractive to examinees who are unsure of the correct answer. Distracters that sound impressive may be plausible.

c. Use true but incorrect answers.   Statements that are true but irrelevant and are clearly wrong answers can also be plausible to the less knowledgeable examinee.

CORRECT ANSWER

5. *Intended Answer Should Be Unequivocally Correct or Absolutely Best*

There should be no doubt by reputable—and a few disreputable—content experts which answer is correct or best. In other words, the answer should not be correct only in your classroom. Also make sure that none of the distracters could possibly be considered as a correct or best answer. For example, is the answer to this question clear?

What is the politically correct term for "ex-spouse"?
 A. cerebrally challenged
*B. insignificant other
 C. motivationally deficient
 D. processed tree carcass
 E. socially misaligned
 F. all of the above

I don't think so. Although the intended answer is "B," very persuasive arguments have been presented by ex-spouses that the best answer is "F." These choices create ambiguity so that if at least two seem correct, "F" might be selected. There should be no question regarding the choice of the answer. Alternatively, if the examinee knows that at least one of the distracters is incorrect, then "F" can be ruled out. A different collection of distracters is needed to revise this item, such as the following:

A. charm-free
B. cosmetically different
C. living impaired
*D. insignificant other
E. parasitically oppressed

6. Avoid Stating the Correct Answer in Textbook Language or Stereotyped Phraseology

It promotes rote learning of text material instead of higher-order thinking skills. Such language is often easier for examinees to recall than application of the concepts. Even less knowledgeable students may vaguely remember a frequently repeated expression or phrase, such as "get out of my house" or "no drugs in the dorm," and not have a clue what it means.

7. The Correct/Best Answer Should Appear About the Same Number of Times in Random Positions Throughout the Entire Test

The correct answer should be evenly balanced among the choices and across all items. That is, the correct answer for a 4-choice item should appear in each position (A, B, C, or D) 25% of the time. So that for a 40-item test, the correct answer would be located 10 times at each position randomly scattered throughout the test. There should be no discernible pattern of answers to clue the examinee. Typically more knowledgeable or testwise examinees benefit most because when they detect a pattern, they may guess several right answers which inflate their total scores. Consider the following answer patterns:

Pattern 1	Pattern 2	Pattern 3
A	B	D
B	B	D
C	B	D
A	C	D
B	C	D
C	C	D
A	A	D
•	•	•
•	•	•
•	•	•

In pattern 1, an examinee might say to him/herself, "Self, whoa, it's probably time for Mister B again." In pattern 2, it would be "Ms. A." In pattern 3, I'll give you a wild guess as to the examinee's response. "B" of course!

It cannot be assumed that ordering verbal choices logically or alphabetically and quantitative choices numerically will avoid answer patterns. If any patterns do emerge, adjust the choices within items and/or rearrange the order of the items. Although random guessing should not be a major concern with tests of more than 10 multiple-choice items, answer patterns should be avoided simply because some examinees may get answers right for the wrong reason.

7

DETECTING FLAWS
IN THIS OLD TEST

> **Caution:** As you begin your flaw detection journey through this chapter, you should try to avoid eating items with "runny" frosting, fillings, icings, or cheese, and pre-buttered goodies. When these substances melt, they may cause a sticky-icky build-up on these pages. You might as well just Superglue® the pages together.

So far in the previous two chapters combined, you've had to endure 36 item-writing rules; that's assuming of course, you didn't just skip to this chapter. That little smirk tells me you did. Gotcha! Anyway, suppose you've constructed your test according to those rules. I bet you feel proud. Well, don't get too puffed up just yet. There are errors that can occur within the internal structure of an item that not only mean it's flawed, but they can be used by testwise students to clue the correct answer. That leads us to the key question answered by this chapter which is:

Why Eliminate Item Flaws?

The first and most important reason is because I said so. After the six chapters you've known me, have I ever given you bad advice? Okay, well except for that one time? Then listen carefully. In fact, put your best ear right on this sentence. I'm only going to say this once: *An item containing a flaw that directs any examinee to the correct answer who otherwise would NOT know the answer is INVALID*. Yup! That's what I said. If an item is answered correctly, but for the wrong reason, then it is not measuring the outcome it was intended to measure. Similarly, a knowledgeable student should not be mislead into picking the incorrect choice. Several flawed items can also decrease the reliability of the test scores and restrict the inferences drawn from those scores (Sarnacki, 1979). Finally, flawed items create an unlevel, wobbly playing field that gives testwise students a clear advantage over not-so-testwise students. Expressed from a positive perspective, this means that tests that are free of item flaws will produce scores with higher degrees of validity and reliability than those containing flaws. Eliminating item flaws also levels the test-taking playing field for all students, regardless of their previous testing experiences. Test performance will be based more precisely on the students' knowledge, skills, and abilities related to the instructional outcomes. Students should answer an item correctly or incorrectly for the right reason.

The purpose of this chapter is to train your mind and eyeballs to detect even the most subtle format flaws in your test items. It provides an up-to-date, succinct, and moderately amusing description of 10 multiple-choice item flaws that, unlike 35 of the preceding 36 item writing rules, testwise students can use as correct answer clues to inflate their test scores. (*Note:* The one exception is violating Rule 11 in Chapter 5 where the correct answer to an item can be clued from repetitive content in the stem or choices of other items on the test.) Your sensitivity to these flaws should ultimately improve your current course tests as well as future draft picks to be named later. Pertinent research on the effects of these flaws on item characteristics and student performance will be cited, where applicable. But don't get your hopes up. There isn't a lot of empirical work on the topic. Fewer than a 100 studies have been published on all of the rules combined (Haladyna & Downing, 1989b).

Before proceeding with my top 10 list, it seems appropriate to test your testwiseness in detecting the most common item flaws. This is the "active learning" part of the chapter. Although we're not going to do Think-Pair-Share, I am requiring you to *Think*; you can Pair-Share Else-Where. If you can answer all of the items correctly and identify their flaws, then you can skip this chapter, pass GO, and collect 937 Euros, which is about $8.69. That should make you hemorrhage with joy. (*Note:* The answers are provided and explained at the end of the chapter in the Appendix, but only for the odd-numbered items. Kidding.)

Test of Testwiseness

Directions: Each of the following items contains at least one flaw. Use this flaw to choose the correct answer. You will be able to answer each item without any or only partial content knowledge. (Is that a dream come true, or what?) Circle the letter of your answer choice and write the type(s) of flaw(s) or answer clue(s) in the space(s) to the left. The number of blanks to the left of each number indicate the number of flaws in the item.

Item Flaw/Clue

1. Which synthetic fabric, chemically known as "polyacrylonitryl," was discontinued by DuPont?
   A. Acrylon
   B. Dacron
   C. Pylon
   D. Rayon
   E. Who cares?

2. Which of the following is an "onomatopoeia"?
   A. fizz
   B. hiss
   C. kerplop
   D. kerplunk
   E. all of the above

3. Which country in Eastern Europe has a chronic shortage of vowels?
   A. Bolivia
   B. Nambia
   C. Saskatchewan
   D. South Dakota
   E. Trskmykczstkygistan

4. A group of *frogs* is called an
   A. army.
   B. flick.
   C. gaggle.
   D. mob.
   E. pod.

5. In the TV series, *The Incredible Hulk,* when someone enraged Dr. David Banner, what did he say?
   A. "De plane! De plane!"
   B. "What 'choo talking' 'bout, Dudley?"
   C. "I've got dandruff older than you!"
   D. "Don't make me angry. You wouldn't like me when I'm angry."
   E. "Y'all come back now, ya hear?"

Continued

6. Who were the first two "founding fathers" to sign the *Declaration of Independence?*
   A. Thomas Jefferson and John Hancock
   B. Charles Thomson and Tony Bennett
   C. Ronald Reagan and John Hancock
   D. Charles Thomson and John Hancock
   E. Oscar Madison and Charles Thomson

7. Who was the only "Angel" to appear on the entire run of *Charlie's Angels?*
   A. Jennifer Aniston
   B. Drew Barrymore
   C. Halle Berry
   D. Roma Downey
   E. Jaclyn Smith

8. Which of the following is a sign that you're NOT young anymore?
   A. You choose your cereal for the fiber, not the toy.
   B. You play connect the dots on your liver spots.
   C. Getting the mail is one of the highlights of your day.
   D. You sprinkle tenderizer on your applesauce.
   E. You look both ways before crossing a room.

9. What is one of only two Disney cartoon movies in which both human parents are present and don't die?
   A. *A Beautiful Mind*
   B. *The Lion King*
   C. *The Lord of the Rings*
   D. *Peter Pan*
   E. *Titanic*

10. In a typical European city, there are
    A. always one big ole famous cathedral near the center.
    B. exactly six blocks of ritzy, overpriced "boutiques."
    C. only one famous bridge that's supposed to be romantic.
    D. one hill with a breathtaking view, always closed for repairs.
    E. two square miles of quaint, ancient, cobblestone roads, called the "Old City."

Top 10 Item Flaws

1. Incorrect Stem-Choice Grammatical Structure

In an effectively written multiple-choice item, the wording of the completion-format stem should adjust for the grammatical structure of the choices. If it does not, the ending of the stem can clue the correct answer, which makes the item easier (Board & Whitney, 1972; Carter, 1986; Dunn & Goldstein, 1959; Evans, 1984; Jones & Kaufman, 1975; McMorris, Brown, Snyder, & Pruzek, 1972; Plake & Huntley, 1984). This clue was, in fact, mentioned in Millman, Bishop, and Ebel's (1965) taxonomy of test-wiseness principles. It is essential to verify the consistency of the choices in grammatical form, tense, font, girth, weight, and blood pressure. The form of the article ("a" or "an") and tense of the verb (singular or plural) at the end of the stem are the most common clues. For example, note how the correct answer is clued in the following vocabulary item that did not make the final cut on the SAT:

A "SCHMO" is an
A. dog with a smashed in nose.
B. individual like Kramer on *Seinfeld* who just bursts into a room without knocking.
C. person with the attention span of a muffin.
D. teenager whose bedroom door cannot open because of what's on the floor.
E. Sumo wrestler who sets an Olympic high jump record of 3.76 inches.

Because all of the distracters above begin with a consonant, they are grammatically incorrect when preceded by "an." Like Duuuuuh! Choice "B" has to be the correct answer by a process of elimination and its grammatical consistency with the stem.

If more than one article or tense is required for the item choices, either reword the beginning of the choices or put both possible articles or tenses in the stem. For example, use "a (an)" or "is (are)." The stem for the above "SCHMO" item should be rewritten as follows:

A "SCHMO" is a(an)

Even if the stem does not end with an article or verb, other grammatical errors can clue testwise students. The best strategy to detect these errors is to test all of the choices by reading each stem-choice combination aloud, preferably when you're in a *X-Files*-type, dimly lit, foggy, secluded, spooky place, like your office. Each choice must *sound* grammatically consistent when read. When you hear an inconsistency, you're going to smack yourself in the forehead and say, "Hey, this is more fun than anything currently being funded by the National Endowment for the Arts." Any choice that sounds inappropriate, off key, or really weird would probably be eliminated by the testwise examinee as an implausible choice. Consider the following item:

According to pet psychologists, a dog's IQ is most similar to
  A. banana.
  B. brick.
  C. door knob.
  D. coleslaw.
  E. radish.

All of the choices except "D" are grammatically inconsistent with the stem; "D" has to be the correct answer. For all choices to be consistent, only the article "a" needs to be added to the stem and "D" changed to "gnat." Wait a minute. I know what you're thinking right now: "Are you sure that's how you spell *gnat?*" Gyes! A corrected version of this item is shown below:

According to pet psychologists, a dog's IQ is most similar to a
  A. banana.
  B. brick.
  C. door knob.
*D. gnat.
  E. radish.

---

2. *Verbal Association in the Stem and Choices*

In another type of item flaw, the actual content in the stem could clue the correct answer. This type of flaw is more subtle and, in fact, down right sneakier than the preceding grammatical clues because it is embedded in the content of the stem. Specific key words in the stem that direct the examinee to the choices must be inclusive of all choices. If they're not, it may provide a verbal clue. The clue usually appears at the beginning of the stem before reaching the main point of the question. Identify the verbal clue in the following item:

Which one of the following kitchen appliances is larger than a weasel?
  A. can opener
  B. jackhammer
  C. microwave oven
  D. Oprah
  E. Stealth bomber

The verbal clue is *kitchen appliances* in the stem. Only two of the choices, "A" and "C," qualify. Distinguishing which choices are kitchen appliances has nothing to do with the purpose of the item, which is to see whether the word *weasel* will make you laugh. Did it? Oh well, let's get back to the issue: Which appliance is larger than a weasel? Although choices "B," "D," and "E" are all considerably larger than a weasel, they would be automatically eliminated by the testwise student due to the verbal clue and their implausibility as distracters. Thus, this item contains only two plausible choices. To revise the item, three kitchen appliances need to replace the three faulty choices, for example, "toaster," "blender," and "trampoline." Oops! Sorry, I made the same error again. I'm just not concentrating.

3. Clang Association in the Stem and Correct Answer

A clang association is a word or phrase in the stem that is repeated in the correct answer. (*Note:* the word *clung* is derived from the Latin word, *clangus,* meaning "Ding dong the witch is dead.") This repetition should be avoided in the answer because it can provide an obvious clue. In fact, the repetition doesn't have to be verbatim; any similarity between a word in the stem and correct answer can clue the examinee (Diamond & Evans, 1972; Sarnacki, 1979; Slakter, Koehler, & Hampton, 1970). Identify the clang in the following item:

What is the name of the sea monster seen in Loch Ness, Scotland?
A. Lessie
B. Nessie
C. Bessie
D. Wussie
E. Arnold

The word *Ness* in the stem appears in choice "B." One way to revise this stem is to use "Northern" in place of "Loch Ness" or substitute a monster with a different name, such as "Skippy."

Try to pick out the clang in this item:

Sir Isaac Newton was sitting under a tree one day reading the *Wall Street Journal* when suddenly an apple fell on his head. This led to the discovery of
*A. apple strudel.
B. Dow Jones Industrial averages.
C. concussions.
D. protective head gear.
E. NO-FAT fig "you know what."

Did you find it? No, it's not *tree*. The clue is the word "apple." Probably the easiest way to revise this item is to change "apple" in the stem to another fruit, such as "kumquat." Or, perhaps, you could replace choice "A" with "prune danish."

The next example has a reverse clang association:

Which one of the following is Miss Piggy's favorite artist?
A. Piggleangelo
B. Pigmalion
C. Boarishnikov
D. Piggarotti
E. Pigcasso

In this case, the root word *pig* in the stem also appears in every incorrect choice. Choice "C" stands out as the correct answer because it the only choice without a *pig*.

4. Unequal Length and Complexity of Choices

If one test item choice is longer and more complex than the other choices, it tends to be considered the correct answer by the examinee because of the assumed need for more qualifying information. In other words, its presence can clue the examinee that the most detailed, comprehensive choice must be the correct or best answer (Millman et al., 1965). This flaw has been found frequently in item files of psychology textbooks (Mentzer, 1982). The research on this option-length clue indicates it makes the item easier to answer (Chase, 1964; Dunn & Goldstein, 1959; Evans, 1984; McMorris et al., 1972; Strang, 1977). You should strive to attain parallel lengths so that no choice draws the examinee's attention. If there is any choice that stands out for its length, make sure it is a distracter. For example, in the item below, the longer correct answer, "D," stands out among the five choices:

In *The Silence of the Lambs*, what were Dr. Hannibal Lecter's final words to FBI Agent Clarice Starling?
A. "Th-Th-Thaaattt's All Folks!"
B. "Let's kick it up a knotch."
C. "Liar, liar, pants on fire!"
D. "I have to go now; I'm having an old friend for dinner."
E. "You look mah-velous."

The most effective choices should be equal in length and complexity so that all choices will be considered as possible correct answers to the less knowledgeable examinee. The following item is such an example:

> BMW stands for
> A. "Brakes Might Work."
> B. "Break My Windmill."
> C. "Braid My Whiskers."
> D. "Broil My Whopper."
> *E. "Be My Walentine."

5. Nonparallel or Inconsistent Grammatical Structure of Choices

Choices that have the same grammatical structure, whether nouns, prepositional phrases, diphthongs, or conjunctive carbuncles, are easier to read and differentiate than mixed structures. In fact, the latter can be very confusing. Not adhering to a parallel structure can also clue test takers to the correct answer, especially when its structure is different from that of the distracters. Identify the inconsistent grammatical structure in the following item:

> Never ring a bell when Pavlov's dog is
> A. in your lap.
> B. on your new white carpet.
> C. on your dinner table.
> D. driving your car.

Obviously, the correct choice, "D," is not a prepositional phrase like the other choices; it's an invective marsupial. This item can be improved by recasting choice "D" in the parallel form of a prepositional phrase, such as "in your driver's seat."

An acceptable item with grammatically parallel choices (all in question form) is shown below:

> Based on a survey of recent college graduates, what on-the-job question is MOST frequently asked by liberal arts majors?
> A. Why does that work?
> B. How does that work?
> C. How much does that cost?
> *D. Do you want fries with that?

6. *"All of the Above" as a Correct Answer Clue*

"All of the above" should not be used as an answer choice because examinees can answer the item correctly based on partial information. If they recognize only two of the choices as correct, then they know "all of the above" is the correct answer. Conversely, if examinees detect just one of the choices as incorrect, then they can automatically eliminate "all of the above" as the correct answer. Using "all of the above" increases item easiness and lowers item discrimination (Dudycha & Carpenter, 1973; Mueller, 1975).

Pretend you're a testwise professor (no offense!) and apply the partial information strategy to the choices in the item below to determine the correct answer:

In completing a job application, which of the following should *NOT* be listed under "Previous Jobs"?

A. Organ donor
B. Recreation director for the Taliban prisoners at Camp X-Ray
C. Iceberg spotter on the *Titanic*
D. Alien on *The X-Files*
E. Guest on *The Jerry Springer Show*
F. The Weakest Link
G. All of the above

How did you do? Terrific! No, I've never been to Camp X-Ray. By the way, how do you like these one-way conversations? You say, "Isn't that an oxymoron?" Now that you mention it, it probably is. I think it's time to get back to the choices. Choices "C" and "E," at least, would clue an examinee that "all of the above" must be the correct answer. Also, if you didn't pick "B" or "D" as a clue to "G," you should probably seek counseling immediately before even applying for a job or reading the next item flaw.

7. *Absolute Terms in Distracters*

Absolute terms, such as *always, never, all, completely, absolutely, only, none,* and *croaked* should be avoided in the wording of distracters. [*Note:* These are in contrast to nonabsolute, vague, ambiguous, warm and fuzzy terms, such as *whenever, maybe, sometimes, usually, frequently, like sure, chill,* and *da bomb,* which should also be avoided according to a study by Case (1994)]. These terms are so extreme as qualifiers that they are viewed with suspicion by examinees and, as such, tend to make the distracters containing them implausible and ineffective. Because choices with those terms are commonly associated with false statements, examinees will eliminate them as possible answers.

This elimination will increase their chances of guessing the correct answer when, in fact, they don't know the material. Consider how the absolute terms in the item below render the distracters implausible:

In preparation for diagnostic tests at "Heaven Forbid You Should Have to Go to This Hospital," patients are
A. *always* required to fast for 40 days and 48 nights.
*B. so dehydrated that they are forced to lick condensation off the windows.
C. *only* required to swallow a disgusting solution that resembles liquefied tile grout.
D. *completely* abandoned in deserted hallways for several days at a time.
E. *always* informed that the results of such tests can *never* be conclusive and, therefore, must be repeated forever.

All of the distracters use absolute terms (in italics) that prescribe extreme or unrealistic conditions for conducting diagnostic tests. Those terms can clue examinees that, by a process of elimination, *only* choice "B" could be correct. The distracters can be revised easily just by cutting off the absolute terms at the beginning and replacing "can never" in the last choice with "may not" and "must be repeated forever" with "may need to be repeated."

Here is another example, but with multiple determiners in specific distracters:

What's the most common complaint by students about riding the infamous "yellow school bus"?
A. *All* of the shock absorbers are *completely* shot so that the ride makes you feel like a Piña Colada.
B. The windows are *always* stuck so that the *only* air in the bus is mixed with concentrated gas fumes.
C. The vinyl seats look like they've been ripped to smithereens by a rabid rodent.
D. The *only* place to sit is directly on the coiled springs, which impale your posterior at *every* bump.

Again, the determiners in distracters "A," "B," and "D" render those complaints as unrealistic for most students. Using less extreme qualifiers would make them more plausible, but make sure they're not in the preceding "warm and fuzzy" list.

The *only* condition under which determiners may be justified is when they are included in the correct answer as well as the distracters, but the choices must still be plausible.

8. Overlapping Choices That Include One or More Other Choices

Choices that contain content that appears in other choices are usually incorrect. They can clue the examinee to use the process of elimination of wrong answers to guess the correct answer. There are three forms of overlapping choices: (a) overlapping quantitative content, (b) overlapping verbal content, and (c) overlapping choice combinations, such as "A and B", "B and D," "C, D, and E on weekends only." These flaws can create cluing, ambiguity, and confusion. In addition, it cannot be determined for certain that the examinee really knows the correct answer.

Overlapping quantitative content. An example of overlapping quantitative content is shown in the item below:

What is the age range during which males most frequently download dirty pictures from the Internet?
A. 6–9
B. 10–15
C. 13–16
D. 16–21
E. 13–90

The overlapping ranges for choices "B–E" create confusion when the examinee attempts to select just one age range. The correct answer, "C," contains ages that overlap with choices "B," "D," and "E," making the choices somewhat ambiguous. To correct this flaw, simply write nonoverlapping ranges with equal intervals. A better set of choices for the preceding item with four-year intervals would be:

A. 5–8
B. 9–12
*C. 13–16
D. 17–20
E. 21–24

Overlapping verbal content. The following item contains overlapping verbal content:

Among Snow White's seven dwarfs, which two should have sought medical help for narcolepsy and personality disorder?

  A. Happy and Doc
  B. Sneezy and Sleepy
  C. Dopey and Grumpy
*D. Sleepy and Bashful
  E. Doc and Bashful

When part of the correct answer overlaps with other choices, it triggers the process-of-elimination strategy in the testwise student's brain. If the examinee knows one part of the answer, such as "Sleepy" or "Bashful," he or she will be drawn automatically to only choices "B," "D," and "E"; thereby eliminating "A" and "C." The overlapping content allows the student to whittle down the number of plausible choices to three and directs him or her toward the correct answer.

Another variation of overlapping verbal choices is shown in the example below:

Among Snow White's seven dwarfs, which two should have sought medical help for narcolepsy and personality disorder?

  A. Sleepy and Dopey
  B. Sneezy and Sleepy
  C. Bashful and Grumpy
*D. Sleepy and Bashful
  E. Doc and Bashful

In this case, notice how many times "Sleepy" and "Bashful" appear in the choices. They occur more frequently than any of the other dwarfs in the five choices. In fact, their frequency provides a sense of convergence toward the correct answer. It leads the testwise examinee to pick choice "D," because it includes the two elements most in common with the four distracters.

The underlying problem for test item writers illustrated by both "Snow White" examples is having to resort to overlapping choices because there simply aren't 10 different dwarfs available to create five nonoverlapping choices. Since there are only 7 dwarfs, a little integral calculus tells us there are only 3.5 pairs of "real" make-believe dwarfs. This problem would also occur, for example, if you attempted to write a five-choice item about Santa and his reindeer or Britney and her Spears. It is a stumbling block that most item writers encounter sometimes sooner, but usually later, in constructing three or four nonoverlapping distracters: *There may not be enough plausible content or a sufficient number of choices*. It is an intractable limitation of the multiple-choice format.

The easiest solution to this problem is to teach a different course that has enough content to create buckets of choices. Another suggestion is to switch to an alternative item format, such as completion, short answer, or alternate response. In the "Snow White" item, for example, only a question-type stem would be presented, to which the examinees would respond by supplying the names of the two dwarfs. Unfortunately, that solution would mean an end to our "Snow White" example and I don't think either of us want that to happen. So, for our entertainment, suppose we assume that some of the examinees were not exposed to all of the dwarfs during their dysfunctional childhoods. Then we could get away with a few, plausible, "unreal" make-believe dwarfs in the choices. In fact, if the stem were expressed in politically correct language, the question might be more believable. Consider the following revised item:

Among Snow White's many many many vertically challenged associates, which two should have checked into the Betty Ford Center?
A. Happy and Depressed
B. Sneezy and Weezie
*C. Dopey and Strung-Out
D. Sleepy and Bashful
E. Grumpy and Nasty

Overlapping choice combinations. Another form of overlapping choices is shown by the choice combinations in the following item:

What is the most famous quotation by Shakespeare's *Omelette, Prince of Thieves?*
A. "To be?"
B. "Or not to be?"
C. "To be a little of the time, and not to be at other times?"
D. "To be some of the time, and to be left alone at other times?"
E. "To be most of the time, and not to be the rest of the time?"
F. "To always be, so there is no time not to be?"
*G. A to B?
H. C, D, and E all of the time?
I. B and F whenever?

The overlapping choices in "G," "H," and "I" make the item unnecessarily complex, confusing, and less amusing; plus they can frustrate and anger examinees to a point that after the test they may tie you to a chair with duct tape and pierce parts of your body you don't want pierced. Instead of using this format to obtain multiple answers and (risking extra holes in your anatomy), ask multiple questions, each with only one content answer. The research on similar choice-combination formats, such as Complex Multiple Choice (CMC) and Type K by Albanese (1993), indicates a long list of disadvantages related to cluing by the overlapping choices. A well-constructed set of four- or five-choice standard format items with effective content distracters is superior to any choice-combination format.

9. Synonym and Antonym Choice Pairs

Two choices with either similar or opposite meanings can jump out of the list of options and draw an examinee's attention like being poked in both eyeballs by Moe of "The Three Stooges." Nyuk, Nyuk, Nyuk. If there is only one correct answer, then either choice in that pair is an unlikely candidate. That clue reduces the four-choice item to a 50-50 guess. Pick out the dynamic synonym duo in the following vocabulary item:

GEEK
A. airhead
B. bimbo
C. dweeb
D. studmuffin

The duo is: "pimple" and "zit." Oops, wrong item. Sorry, it's the synonyms "airhead" and "bimbo," which examinees automatically can eliminate as answers. This reduces the multiple choices to two choices. "Dweeb" and "studmuffin" may be considered antonyms, only one of which clearly means "loser." The discrimination power of the choices can be improved by eliminating the synonym and antonym pairs. A better set of choices would be:

A. bimbo
*B. dweeb
C. spazz
D. weenie

10. *Heterogeneous Content Choices*

Homogeneous content makes the choices easier to read and challenges the examinee's ability to pick the correct answer from among the distracters. If the content in the choices is heterogeneous or mixed, it may be confusing and more difficult to isolate the differences among the choices (Green, 1984). A mixed list of choices frequently occurs when the stem is worded ambiguously. If the stem lacks focus on a single problem, it is likely that the choices will lack focus on a single content category. There are two types of item-writing flaws that can yield heterogeneous choices: (a) one relates to the content category of the correct answer, and (b) the other involves the time period of the answer.

Content category.   To ensure choice homogeneity, the distracters should fall into the same content category as the correct answer. For example, if the answer to a question about political parties is "Federalists," possible distracters in the *party* category might be Republicans, Democrats, Charlatans, Brownnosers, and Anal Retentives. If a single choice contains material unlike the other choices, it may direct examinees to select it as the correct answer. Which choice in the following item differs in content category from the other four choices?

Which brand of chocolate candy is manufactured in New Jersey?
A. Lindt®
B. M&M/Mars®
C. Toblerone®
D. Droste®
E. Katarina Witt

Obviously choice "B" pops out as the correct answer because all of the distracters are imported from different countries. To test whether the examinee knows which one is made in New Jersey, the land of the free and home of the Washington Wizards, all five choices should be U.S. brands. The four distracters need to be replaced with brands such as "Hershey®," "Nestlé®," "Tootsie Roll®," and "Willy Wonka®."

The stem in the previous item was clear and direct. However, if that stem was ambiguous, greater confusion would occur in picking out the correct answer. Consider the following evil stem with the same candy choices:

Which of these choices does *NOT* belong with the others?

I don't have a clue. "Ohhh, Bucko! Didn't you read Rules 6 and 7 in Chapter 6 about using *NOT* in a stem? Get with the program." I'm ashamed of myself. Thanks for your gentle correction.

Time period.   Another factor in choice homogeneity is the time period during which the choices have occurred. It should be the same for all choices; otherwise, the examinee can eliminate choices without discriminating among the content differences. Consider the distracters in the following item:

Detective Mick Belker, who popularized such colorful expressions as "dirtbag," "slimeball," "move it or lose it," and "I'm gonna reach down your throat and rip out your spleen," appeared in what TV police drama?
*A. *Hill Street Blues*
 B. *Law & Order: SVU*
 C. *The District*
 D. *NYPD Blue*
 E. *Third Watch*

All of the distracters are 1990s programs, whereas "A" was broadcast in the 1980s during the Furillo-Davenportolithic Era. Plausible distracters that would be homogeneous with the TV time period of the correct answer might include these 1980s shows: *Magnum, P.I., 21 Jump Street, Hunter, Spencer: For Hire, Miami Vice,* or *Mister Rogers' Neighborhood.*

Summary

Probably the best way to summarize this chapter is in the form of a "Top 10 List." What a surprise! Are you ready? Okay, heeerrre we go.

From the home office at Johns Hopkins University, located in Buffalo, New York, home of the Chicago Bears, here are the Top 10 Item Flaws:

10. Heterogeneous content choices

 9. Synonym and antonym choice pairs

 8. Overlapping choices that include one or more other choices

 7. Absolute terms in distracters

 6. "All of the above" as a correct answer clue

 5. Nonparallel or inconsistent grammatical structure of choices

4. Unequal length and complexity of choices

3. Clang association in the stem and correct answer

2. Verbal association in the stem and choices

And the Number One Flaw (drum roll):

1. Incorrect stem-choice grammatical structure

APPENDIX

KEY TO TEST
OF TESTWISENESS

Item	Correct answer	Flaw explanation
1.	A	Clang association between poly*acrylon*itryl in the stem and choice "A"
2.	E	Any two correct answers, such as "A" and "B" or "C" and "D," clue *all of the above*
3.	E	First verbal association between *country* and "C" and "D" Second verbal association between *country in Eastern Europe* and "A" and "B"
4.	A	Grammatical clue "an" matches only the correct answer
5.	D	Longest choice Clang association between *enraged* in the stem and *angry* in the answer
6.	D	Overlapping choices converge on two most frequent names in the distracters Heterogeneous time period of Bennett, Reagan, and Madison Verbal association with *founding fathers* eliminates choices containing Bennett, Reagan, and Madison
7.	E	Heterogeneous time period between four contemporary actresses and the older one, which is the correct answer Verbal association with "Angel" eliminates "A" and "C"

Item	Correct answer	Flaw explanation
8.	C	Grammatical structure of "C" is nonparallel with the other four choices
9.	D	First verbal association between *cartoon* and three of the distracters reduces item to two choices, "B" and "D"
		Second verbal association between *human* and *The Lion King* eliminates "B"
10.	E	Longest choice
		Grammatical clue "are" eliminates choices "A," "C," and "D"
		Clang association between *city* in stem and in answer
		Absolute terms at the beginning of choices "A," "B," and "C"

8

INJECTING JEST
INTO YOUR TEST

Final Warning: Congrats! You've made it to the last chapter. You definitely deserve a medal. However, if you *hop* over the first section on research evidence, *skip* to the specific humor techniques, and *jump* over the descriptions to get the illustrative items, you could experience serious bodily injury from convulsive laughter. I suggest the following precautions: (1) wear a welding helmet at all times, (2) read the joke items sitting upright, not lying on your stomach or back, and (3) wear clothing without strings or dangling material which may get entangled when you roll on the floor. Anyway, have a great time. See you at the end of the book.

A significant problem in Biostatistics class is students conking out cold. I mean serious tremor-type snoring. Fifteen students who passed out regularly were identified by Professor Excitement using the "interocular perusal technique" (eye-balling). Those students were randomly assigned to 3 treatments: No-Doz®, Caffeinated Coffee, and Smack-in-the-Head (SMITH). The recommended dose of No-Doz® and one large cup of Coffee were administered 30 minutes prior to class and SMITH was given with a 2 × 4 by the closest student whenever the treatment student started nodding. Effectiveness was measured in length of time awake (minutes) after the first half hour of class. Which treatment was most effective?

NO-DOZ®	CAFFEINATED COFFEE	SMITH
10	7	15
16	13	21
8	5	18
11	9	17
14	8	21

a. Research hypothesis:
b. Null hypothesis:
c. Statistical test:
d. Significance level:
e. Sampling distribution:
f. Computation of statistic:
g. Conclusion:

Are your tests really funny? That's what I thought. But have you ever asked yourself the following questions?

• Should the preceding type of item be included on course tests?
• Do humorous items reduce the students' test anxiety and improve their performance?
• How in the world do you even use humor appropriately in tests without decreasing the validity and reliability of the scores?
• Will students even notice the humor?
• If they do notice it, will they find it distracting?
• Are some tests funnier than others?

This chapter begins where Chapter 6 in *Gone with the Wind* stopped. The tenth "humor in the classroom" strategy was *Humorous Material on Exams*.

The purpose of this chapter is fourfold: (1) to define the problem of test anxiety, (2) to suggest pre-testing techniques to reduce anxiety, (3) to provide an up-to-date summary of the research evidence related to humor in testing, and (4) to describe specific step-by-step techniques for injecting humor into a variety of test item formats, including multiple-choice, matching, and constructed-response.

Test Anxiety

Everyone has taken tests. So what's the problem? Why is anxiety such a big deal? What control do we have over our students' test anxiety? "Wait. Time out! Are you on some interrogative binge? You've asked more questions on this page than you have in the entire book. How about slipping in a good 'ole declarative statement occasionally? Huh?" Okay, just for you. Here it comes. Don't miss it. This section will define the scope of the test anxiety problem and suggest a few test administration and preparation techniques that can reduce anxiety before students even walk into class to take the test.

What's the Problem?

When I announce a test in my class, there is a chain reaction of responses that occurs in my typical student's mind and body:

I say:	"Next week we're going to have a test."
Student's mental image:	Shower scene from *Psycho*.
Student's thought:	"Why not just kill me now? Why must you drag out my pain and suffering by making me take this test?"
Student's physical responses:	Sweating, trembling, headaches, stomach ache, nausea, vomiting, dizziness, fainting, paralysis, swelling, ulcer, rash, hair loss, bloating, nose bleeds, chapped lips, dysentery, PMS, BPH, and grandmother dies.
Student's psychological responses:	Anxiety, stress, tension, anger, frustration, helplessness, depression, memory loss, dementia, hysteria, agoraphobia, and necrophilia.

To suggest that the word *test* produces a negative response by students is an understatement akin to saying "the Taliban was rude to women." *TEST* can terrorize students. It evokes a visceral reaction that seems to be universal. No one is immune. It strikes without regard to age, gender, ethnicity, nationality, or medication. And I'm only referring to the word, not how students feel on the day of the test, when they walk in to take it, or actually begin to answer the questions.

So what can we do to change the bad rep that tests have and to reduce the potential effects listed previously? A student who becomes mentally arthritic at the thought of taking a test will probably produce a score that does not provide a true picture of his or her performance. After all, a test is designed to obtain a person's best or true level of performance, not the worst.

Reducing Anxiety Before the Test

Although using humor in the test itself can have a positive impact on the test-taking experience, there are four preliminary techniques that can decrease anxiety before the test: (1) test scheduling, (2) test length/administration time, (3) test preparation, and (4) test format. Each of these techniques is examined next:

1. *Have students determine the best day to schedule the test.* About two weeks before the students are ready for the test, I present three or four class date options. I ask them "What's the best date when you have no other competing exams or projects due?" Frequently, one of the dates is a killer for them with one or two major tests already scheduled. The students vote on each date. Majority rules. I do this for each test in my undergraduate and graduate courses. This strategy not only gives the students a feeling of empowerment, but it also reduces anxiety over my exam and puts the burden of performance on the students. They have no excuse for performing poorly, such as two other exams on the same day. However, they may create other excuses later. You're probably wondering, "What about your scheduled class topics?" Whaaateverrrr! Actually, I don't lose a single step in content coverage. Once the test date is set, I proceed with new material in the classes before the test plus a test review. My students' test schedules are far more important than my topic schedule. The advantages above far outweigh any minor adjustments I have to make.

2. *Allow adequate time for all students to complete the test.* Unless speed is a criterion for performance, then the test should be at an appropriate length so that all students can finish in the allotted time. Of course, there are always some students whose hands will have to be pried from the test booklet and answer sheet with a crowbar when the time has

expired. Students should be told this test timeframe in advance, as part of test preparation. For example, when you describe the test structure, you could say: "The test is designed so that all of you should have adequate time to complete it; so don't rush and make careless mistakes. Pace yourselves accordingly, but you have to finish on time because I have to leave to have my dog neutered. Ouch!" This announcement may not change how the students study for the test, but it may reduce some stress by relieving some of the anticipated time pressure felt when taking the test.

3. *Prepare the students for the test.* Part of the students' fear of tests is simply the unknown, not knowing what to expect. Providing them with basic information on the test structure, item formats, and an outline of topics for which they are responsible can reduce that fear. Even simple practice items or guidelines/suggestions on "how to prepare" would really be appreciated. If time permits, a formal test review of critical content, areas of confusion and ambiguity, and careless errors or misconceptions can help alleviate anxiety and boost confidence. Try the *Jeopardy!* review format or other game structures described in Chapter 3. You have to decide, in the role of their coach, how to prepare them for "The BIG GAME." When they enter the room, will they be loaded for bear or squirrel? "Wait. That's hunting *game* you moron, not sports! You're mixing your metaphors." Oh. Sorry. I think I'm metaphorically challenged. Anyway, the more students know about what to expect and what is expected, the lower will be their anticipatory anxiety.

4. *Use open-everything or take-home test formats to tap higher-order thinking skills.* Unless you are measuring the lowest level of cognition, knowledge, memorization is unnecessary. Having access to notes, the text, or other materials will not help students perform better on application, analysis, or higher-level items, nor will they have much time during the test to consult those sources. However, research evidence indicates that *access alone decreases anxiety significantly* during the test (Berk, 1996b). Alternatively, a take-home exam or portion of an exam can also reduce anxiety. "Real-life" decision making is not conducted under artificial, closed-book, test-taking conditions. If you are trying to assess applications of content to practical settings, simulations and hypothetical scenarios, vignettes, or case studies can easily fit into either of the above formats.

The preceding strategies can have a profound effect on the students' perception of the tests in your course and, ultimately, on their performance. But they must be consistent with the outcomes being assessed by your test. The validity of what your test measures should not be compromised by any of these test preparation or administration techniques.

Does Humor Reduce Anxiety and Improve Performance?

Once your students enter your classroom on test-taking day, their *anticipatory anxiety* skyrockets. Is there any research evidence available on using humor in the test itself to reduce anxiety? There are two research domains in which evidence has been collected to determine the value of humor in course tests: (1) the psychological and physiological effects of humor and (2) the effects of humor in testing. Brief reviews of these domains follow.

Psychophysiological Evidence

Among the numerous psychological/physiological effects of humor previously reviewed in Chapter 2, the three most pertinent to the conditions of testing in a college classroom are the reduction of anxiety, tension, and stress. There is probably no other time throughout an entire semester when those negative emotions are at their peak as when the students walk into a class to take a test. Those emotions may even shoot off the chart when they see the test.

The primary psychological function of humor as an adaptive coping mechanism is applicable to the testing situation. If there is an optimal time for that mechanism to kick in, this is it. The humor produces a cognitive shift in perspective that allows students to distance or detach themselves from the immediate threat—the *TEST*. The humor can reduce the negative feelings that would normally occur. It also promotes a sense of objectivity and empowerment over the testing situation.

When humor permits students to deal more effectively with an aversive experience such as test taking, the physical response may be a giggle, possibly a chortle or cackle, but rarely rolling in the aisles. This response translates into physiological effects throughout the entire body, particularly stress reduction and improved mental functioning and performance (see Chapter 2).

Humor in Testing Evidence

The empirical research on the effects of humor in testing has been critically reviewed by McMorris, Boothroyd, and Pietrangelo (1997). It's not a pretty picture. They found only nine measly investigations of humor in college testing. All were conducted with students in undergraduate psychology classes. Seven used humor in multiple-choice items (one of those also included short-answer items), one used anagrams with cartoons, and another incorporated humor in written dialogue between therapist and client. McMorris et al.

(1997) concluded that, for the criterion of test performance, these studies provide insufficient and inconsistent evidence for using humor in tests to reduce anxiety and stress and improve performance, despite students' self-reported clear preferences for humor. Only the research by Smith, Ascough, Ettinger, and Nelson (1971) and Hedl, Hedl, and Weaver (1981) reported positive effects of humor on anxiety and stress reduction, respectively. Even a more recent, well-designed study by Bennett and Turner (2001) found no significant effect on performance. Considering the limitations of many of the investigations and the complexity of measuring interactions between humor in tests and other variables, McMorris et al. (1997) rendered the following verdict:

> Our own personal view at this juncture is to encourage the use of humor in tests, especially if instruction has included use of humor, the test has either no time limit or a very generous one, the humor is positive and constructive, the humor is appropriate for the group, test takers come from the same culture as the item writer, and the test developer feels comfortable in using humor. (p. 295)

What do students perceive?   Given the paucity of evidence on the effects of humor in tests and the limited focus and conditions of previous studies (i.e., primarily multiple-choice items with content-irrelevant humor in undergraduate psychology classes), I designed a totally different study of humor (for details, see Berk, 2000c) to target: (1) constructed-response item formats, but also include multiple-choice and matching formats; (2) content-relevant humor which is an integral part of "what" an item is measuring; (3) undergraduate and graduate level courses in statistics; (4) day and evening graduate courses; (5) students' perceptions of the extent to which humor is effective in reducing their test anxiety and improving their performance; and (6) the reliability of these perceptions with multiple cross-validation samples of different students over six years.

Based on the responses of 695 students enrolled in six undergraduate and eleven graduate introductory statistics courses, it was found that the median class ratings of students' perceptions of effectiveness ranged from *Moderately Effective* to *Extremely Effective* for "reducing test anxiety" and "performing your best." For "reducing test anxiety," the highest effectiveness rating, *Extremely Effective*, was found for the majority of undergraduate and graduate classes. These findings are consistent with the voluminous psychological research evidence reviewed in Chapter 2 on the anxiety-reduction effects of humor as well as the results of the Ascough et al. (1971) and Hedl et al. (1981) studies.

Despite the limitations of nonexperimental research based on self-report data, the evidence from this study is significant for four reasons: (1) it indicates that most students perceive that the humor reduces their anxiety levels and improves test performance, (2) this effect was demonstrated with three item formats measuring "real-life" higher-order thinking skills, (3) the effect was consistent over time (six years) for 17 different samples, and (4) the effect is generalizable across undergraduate courses, day and evening graduate courses, and a range of class sizes, students, and exams.

Injecting Humor into the Beginning and End of Your Test

The research described in the preceding sections defines the types and forms of humor investigated, some with illustrative items. Unfortunately, for professors who wish to include humor in their tests, there is only one article (Berk, 2000c) and no chapter or measurement book that provides step-by-step guidelines on how to use humor appropriately. In many cases, professors have incorporated humor inappropriately by default, which unfortunately has resulted in a few college departments banning the use of humor in tests.

Although inappropriate use may not be intentional, it can have a negative impact on the students and on the psychometric properties of the test. Instead of obtaining the sought after positive effects of reducing anxiety and stress and improving performance, inappropriate use can be offensive, distracting, and anxiety producing, which can decrease test performance. It can also adversely affect the validity of the items and the reliability of the scores.

In an effort to maximize the potential benefits of using humor, the next two sections present a variety of strategies I have tested over the past 16 years in my classes and in my humor research described previously.

This section examines three techniques for injecting humor into the beginning and end of your test: (1) incongruous descriptors under the title of the test, (2) jocular inserts in the directions, and (3) humorous note on the last page. Although these methods were described briefly and illustrated in *Gone with the Wind*, they will be repeated here for convenience and because I need some filler. The section that follows will cover strategies for injecting humor into the test items themselves.

Incongruous Descriptors Under the Title

The cover page provides the first opportunity to use humor. The humor on this page can have the most significant impact on the students' psychological state before they even see the first test question. The descriptors recommended previously in *Gone with the Wind* for syllabi and other handouts should appear under the title of each test. Choose totally incongruous descriptors from the list provided. For example, "BAKED WITH PRIDE" for the midterm and "DOLPHIN SAFE" for the final can be effective.

Jocular Inserts in the Directions

Similar to the above, encountering jocular directions on the first or second page is an unexpected twist that can really release tension. Suppose you read the following directions on your midterm:

GENERAL DIRECTIONS

The purpose of this test is to find out whether you know anything. Place the ANSWER SHEET somewhere in front of you. Using the little pencil you kept from your last miniature golf game, print your name, social security number, complete family history, including all diseases and hospitalizations since you were born, and test booklet number in the upper right corner so we can track you down. Read the directions for marking your answers. You may write your computations in the test booklet or on a separate worksheet, because if I said, "DO NOT MARK IN THE BOOKLET," I bet you would probably do it anyway.

Answer all questions as best as you can. There will be no penalty for guessing, so have a blast. You will have the entire class period to complete the test.

DO NOT begin the test until you are told to do so or you can be hurt by Jerry Springer's bodyguard sitting in the back of the room.

For the final try something totally different:

GENERAL DIRECTIONS

Sit down and make believe you're at the beach.

Place the ANSWER SHEET somewhere in front of you but NOT in the sand. Print your name, social security number, current blood pressure and pulse rate, cholesterol level (HDL & LDL), triglicerides, and test booklet number in the upper right corner. Read the directions for marking your answers.

Answer all questions as best as you can. There will be no penalty for guessing, so guess away. You will have the entire class period to complete the test, which means you have 1.25 minutes per question. Pace yourself accordingly.

DO NOT begin the test until you are told to do. I'm going to let you sit here and sweat in the sun for about 30 minutes before letting you start the test. You are allowed to breathe; but nothing else. Watch out! Here comes a wave!

Humorous Note on the Last Page

Finally, a humorous note on the last page of the test can end the grueling test-taking experience with a smile. It's a kind of cooling down jocular exercise or mirthful debriefing. Here are a couple of notes you can use on different tests:

NOTE: This was only a TEST. If this had been an actual emergency, you wouldn't be sitting here suffering through this stuff. You may now resume your regularly scheduled activities.

or

NOTE: This test was made possible by a grant from the Society for the Prevention of Cruelty to Statisticians (or any other group). Watch for our annual fund-raising drive featuring "Vladimir Putin Does *Riverdance.*"

Injecting Humor into the Test Items

Eight strategies for infusing humor into test items are covered next. They fall into two categories: (1) content-irrelevant and (2) content-relevant. The first set of techniques is the simplest to develop and apply because the humor is added to the existing test; the second involves incorporating humor into the content of the items.

Content-Irrelevant Strategies

The content-irrelevant strategies are most appropriate for multiple-choice format items. The first step is to construct your completely serious, cadaverous test. Suppose it consists of 50 four-choice items. The humor that can be inserted is an add-on to the "nonhumorous" test. That is, the humor will not affect the structural integrity, validity, or reliability of any item or of the total score. Regardless of what humor is used, the original 50-item test is preserved intact. The humor is irrelevant to the content of the test and the outcomes being measured. There are three strategies you can use: (1) add humorous distracters to several items, (2) add humorous items throughout the test, and (3) add humorous distracters and items, stir vigorously, shake for two minutes, and whala! You have an hilarious test.

Add humorous distracters to several items. If there are four content choices for each item, tack on a humorous choice "E" that is irrelevant to what the item is measuring. That choice should be:

1. rip-roaring funny;
2. irrelevant to the content being tested;
3. familiar to all students;
4. so ridiculous and outrageous that no student could possibly consider it as the correct answer;

5. consistent with the grammatical format and content of the other choices; and

6. the only *implausible* distracter in the item.

An example of this choice "E" technique is shown below:

Who wrote *The Love Song of J. Alfred Prufrock?*
*A. T. S. Eliot
 B. A. E.. Housman
 C. C. S. Lewis
 D. J. D. Salinger
 E. L. L. Bean

"L. L. Bean" satisfies the six criteria above; well, maybe it's not rip-roaring, but it's certainly within chuckle range. When writing your choice "E," make sure to address criterion 3. If the choice is not familiar to your students, it will fail to meet all of the other criteria, and "E" may be seen as plausible. For example, a choice such as "J. R. Ewing" would be meaningless to most under-graduates. "LL Cool J" (*Note:* His real name is "MM Cool K") may be more effective.

In addition to humorous content choices, for some items you might want to consider a generic choice "E." It's an expression to which students can relate, because it may be exactly what they're thinking. A few generic choices that are sure to elicit at least a smile are the following:

- "Who cares!"
- "I don't have a clue!"
- "Do I really need to know this?"
- "This is the only question I can't answer."
- "The answer temporarily escapes me."
- "I can't believe you asked this."
- "I know I should have studied this."

The humorous fifth choice should be added to several items throughout the test to help reduce anxiety and motivate students to plow through the items looking for those comic-relief items. If those humorous distracters are placed in items at *uneven* item intervals throughout the test, they provide a type of intermittent reinforcement. That is, as the students are suffering through the pain of the nonhumorous items, they know there's a prize waiting somewhere up ahead, but they don't know exactly when it's coming. The humorous distracters serve as motivators to keep the students alert and focused on their testing journey. Some of the students will even search for the humorous items. These distracters help them endure the torture of a very long test and to perform their best along the way. One particular advantage of this strategy is that the added distracters require no significant increase in reading time. In other words, it can be used in both speed and power tests. If students are pressed for time to finish the test, the humor in the distracters should not be a factor.

A preview in the test directions announcing the appearance of these items is advisable to convey there is actually something positive about the test-taking experience and to warn those few super-serious students with the sense of humor of varnish that choice "E" is just a joke and not to be chosen as a correct answer. The statement may take the following form:

Warning: This test consists of 50 multiple-choice items. Most of the items have four choices (A, B, C, or D); however, there are several items sprinkled throughout the test with a humorous choice "E" which is intended solely for your entertainment. Any other use, such as for the correct answer, is strictly prohibited without the prior written and notarized consent of next of kin.

If you use optical scanner answer sheets by Scantron, NCS, or TELEform, select or design a form with only *four* answer bubbles or boxes per item. Then choice "E" would not even be an option for the students to choose accidentally.

Add humorous items throughout the test. Instead of tinkering with the internal structure of the items by adding humorous distracters, you can just add a few humorous, content-irrelevant items to all of the nonhumorous ones. Since this strategy requires additional reading time, it should only be considered for tests where students have more than adequate time to complete all of the items. If speed of response is important and some students are rushed to finish the test, no other items should be added. Humorous items function most effectively in nonspeeded, power tests where what a student knows or can demonstrate is more critical than how fast he or she can answer. These tests are often called criterion-referenced, standards-referenced, mastery, or competency-based. Suppose five humorous items were inserted in a 50-item test. Each one might appear after every 10 serious items or at uneven item intervals, as suggested previously. These five would not be counted in the total score so that the validity and reliability of the original test scores remain intact. The humorous items may be written on any topic irrelevant to the specific content of the test. In fact, they may be opinion items or other items with no "real" correct answer. One such item is given below:

Which "oxymoron" actually makes sense?
  A. act naturally
  B. passive aggressive
  C. pretty ugly
  D. resident alien
  E. soft rock

It has also been argued that "humor in academia" is an oxymoron (Berk 1998b). The reasons for scattering the humorous items throughout the test are the same as for the items with humorous distracters. It is also recommended that a statement in the directions be written similar to the preceding, for example:

Caution: There are several humorous items sprinkled throughout the test which are intended solely for your entertainment. Any other use, such as for food, shelter, or wedding invitations, is strictly prohibited without the prior written permission of Moi. These items will not be counted in your final score. Therefore, it is your decision whether to answer them or not.

Add humorous distracters and items. One can use a combination of the two preceding strategies. A variety of humorous multiple-choice item examples can be found in Chapters 5–7 and in Berk (1998a, 1998c). However, **DON'T OVERDO IT.** Too much humor can be distracting. Power tests afford greater latitude in the use of humor than speeded tests. Ask your students to evaluate the effectiveness of the humorous distracters and/or items to determine which form they prefer. Evaluation techniques are described at the end of Chapter 1 and this one.

Content-Relevant Strategies

Content-relevant strategies involve injecting humor into the actual item content. It is not an add-on to be dismissed by the student. The humor is an integral part of the item. This form of humor can appear in constructed-response as well as multiple-choice and matching items. Five strategies are described next for inserting humor into: (1) the stem of a multiple-choice item, (2) the choices of a multiple-choice item, (3) the stems of a matching item set, (4) context-dependent material, and (5) constructed-response stimuli.

Insert humor into the stem of a multiple-choice item.   If knowledge or application of a concept is being tested, the example in the stem may be expressed humorously while all of the content choices are serious. This technique involves putting a humorous spin on a simple content statement or question. Consider the following item:

The Artist formerly known as MS-DOS® is:
  A. Linux®.
  B. Mac OS®.
  C. Unix®.
*D. Windows®.
  E. X Window®.

Here's an item measuring knowledge of figurative language with an amusing stem and choice "E":

If your urologist says, "You have a kidney stone the size of the Epcot golf ball," that is an example of a(an)
  A. analogy.
*B. hyperbole.
  C. metaphor.
  D. simile.
  E. rather unsettling thought.

Insert humor into the choices of a multiple-choice item.   The previous strategy can be reversed by placing serious content in the stem and writing humorous, but plausible, choices:

> Which of the following Cleveland billboard messages did God actually say?
> A. "Don't make me come down there."
> B. "Have you read my #1 best seller? There will be a test."
> C. "If you keep using my name in vain, I'll make rush hour longer."
> *D. "What part of 'Thou Shalt Not . . .' didn't you understand?"
> E. "You think it's hot here?"

Insert humor into the stems of a matching item set. Since a matching set is just a collection of multiple-choice items smushed together, the first column stems may be humorous, while the second column choices are serious. This strategy can be used with the two popular types of matching: (1) one with four or five choices that can be selected more than once and (2) the other with a long list of choices (3 or 4 more than the number of stems), each of which can be selected only once. The use of humor in these two types of matching are shown below. The first type is a compressed version of ten 4-choice multiple-choice items; the second consists of ten multiple-choice items with from 13 down to 4 choices.

Type I

> **Directions:** For each of the *VARIABLES* or questionnaire items below, select the highest, appropriate *LEVEL OF MEASUREMENT.* Mark your answers (A,B,C, or D) in spaces 1–10 of your answer sheet. Each response may be used once or more than once.
>
> | VARIABLES | LEVEL OF MEASUREMENT |
> |---|---|
> | _____ 1. Wait time to see your doctor | A. nominal |
> | 10 minutes or less | B. ordinal |
> | More than 10 but less than 30 minutes | C. interval |
> | Between 30 minutes and an hour | D. ratio |
> | More than an hour and less than a day | |
> | I'm still waiting | |
> | _____ 2. Years of experiences as a stand-up comic | |
> | _____ 3. Native language | |
> | English | |
> | Spanish | |
> | Latin | |
> | Greek | |
> | Psychobabble | |
> | Other | |

Continued

4. Degree of frustration
   Totally Give Up
   Might Give Up
   Thinking About Giving Up
   Refuse to Give Up
   Don't Know Meaning of "Give Up"
_____ 5. Scores on the "Where's Waldo" Final Exam (0–100)
_____ 6. Symptoms of exposure to statistics
   Vertigo
   Fainting
   Vomiting
   Tingling
   Ticks
_____ 7. Length of your big toe
_____ 8. Ratings on the Lack of Quality Inn Scale (0–60)
_____ 9. Health status leaving Johns Hopkins Hospital (dead or alive)
_____ 10. Quantity of blood consumed by Dracula per night

Type 2

Directions: Match the famous classical *MUSIC COMPOSITIONS* with the *GUYS* who probably wrote that kinda stuff. Mark your answers (A–M) in spaces 1–10 of your answer sheet. Each choice may be used once or not at all.

MUSIC COMPOSITIONS

_____ 1. *Les Quaaludes*
_____ 2. *Pictures of an Exhibitionist*
_____ 3. *Marche Slob*
_____ 4. *Orpheus in His Underwear*
_____ 5. *Le Coq Au Vin*
_____ 6. *Pathetic*
_____ 7. *The Firefly*
_____ 8. *Peter and the Moose*
_____ 9. *Capriccio Escargot*
_____ 10. *A Midsummer Night on Elm Street*

GUYS

A. Beethoven
B. Chopin
C. Debussy
D. Liszt
E. Mendelssohn
F. Mussorgsky
G. Offenbach
H. Orff
I. Prokofiev
J. Rachmaninoff
K. Rimsky-Korsakov
L. Stravinsky
M. Tchaikovsky

Insert humor into context-dependent material. When a student is presented with verbal or visual/pictorial stimuli to interpret before answering a set of multiple-choice items (a.k.a. testlet), that material provides an opportunity for humor. The verbal material may be a hypothetical humorous observation in a problem, scenario, vignette, or case study. The visual/pictorial material can take the form of a cartoon, humorous picture or photograph, humorous variables or data in a table, chart, or graph, or funny map, figure, or diagram. These forms of humor require more imagination than any of the preceding, but they can be just as effective as nonhumorous material in measuring higher-order thinking skills. One example of a vignette in medicine/nursing was presented in Chapter 5. Another example with a statistical problem is shown below:

One group of patients with flu-like symptoms was randomly split into 2 samples. Sample one received lozenge megadoses of *Cold-Wheeze*® (CW) and the other received comparable doses of *Zincy-Winky*® (ZW) (1 lozenge has so much zinc, you couldn't get through the airport metal detector). After one week, the patients rated the effectiveness of these two medications in reducing their symptoms. These ratings ranged from 0 (I still feel like a crudball) to 25 (I'm flying high like Rocky!). Determine whether CW was superior to ZW.

1. What is the most appropriate research hypothesis?
   A. *Cold-Wheeze*® patients will rate their medication as significantly more effective than will the *Zincy-Winky*® patients.
   B. *Zincy-Winky*® patients will rate their flu-lozenge as more effective than will the *Cold-Wheeze*® patients.
   C. There will be a significant difference in the effectiveness of *Cold-Wheeze*® and *Zincy-Winky*® in reducing flu-like symptoms.
   D. There will be no difference in *Cold-Wheeze*® and *Zincy-Winky's*® effectiveness in reducing flu-like symptoms.
2. What statistical test should be used?
   A. *t-test* (pooled variance)
   B. *t-test* (separate variance)
   C. *t-test* (repeated measures)
   D. *Chi-square test of independence*

Insert humor into constructed-response stimuli. The humor strategy for constructed-response format items is virtually identical to the preceding strategy. The difference between the items is the form of the student's response. Instead of providing answers to a testlet, the student constructs his or her own answer to an open-ended question(s) about the material presented. The following item is a statistics simulation problem unlike those found in most textbooks:

One group of 25 students volunteered to participate in a study about the quality of TV programs. Each student was asked, "Yo, student! Have you ever watched *The Practice, E.R.,* or *The West Wing?*" The typical response was: "Are you nuts? We're students. Heellooo! We don't have a life!" Anyway, 18 students had never seen any of those programs. Those 18 were randomly divided into 3 samples of 6 students each and then randomly assigned to watch 3 episodes of one of those programs. Each student then rated the overall writing quality of the episodes on a 15-point scale (0 = trite, dull, insulting to 15 = imaginative, powerful, super-creative). The ratings by group are shown below. Determine which show should receive an Emmy for creative writing.

THE PRACTICE	E.R.	THE WEST WING
2	1	11
4	3	12
6	5	13
8	7	14
10	9	14
12	11	15

a. Research hypothesis:
b. Null hypothesis:
c. Statistical test:
d. Significance level:
e. Sampling distribution:
f. Computation of statistic:
g. Conclusion:

Evaluating the Effectiveness of Your Humor

The criterion of whether the humor on the test is effective can be measured easily by just asking your students. Make every effort to solicit their reactions to the humor after the first test, so there is time to make adjustments on subsequent tests. The end of Chapter 1 described a formal rating scale approach. However, there's an even simpler strategy. The easiest and least time-consuming assessment method is to distribute one or two 3 × 5 index cards to each student and ask your class to answer any or all of the following yes-no questions:

- Did you like the humorous items on the test?
- Were they too distracting?
- Did they reduce your test anxiety?
- Did they help you perform your best on the test?
- Should humorous items be included on the next test?

Also ask for comments or humor suggestions. Assure the students anonymity by telling them not to write their names or other identifying information on the cards. This assurance is absolutely essential to obtain truthful feedback. And yes, you will get feedback; probably more than you ever expected. Their responses may run the gamut from "knock off the humor" to "keep it up; the more the better." The majority or median opinion should guide your use of humor in the next test. Your credibility is at stake. Report back to them the results of their index card evaluation and your justification for using or not using humor on subsequent course tests.

Conclusions

After reviewing the available research evidence and strategies for injecting humor into test items, here are six conclusions about the use of humor in course tests: (1) there is psychological and physiological research evidence that humor reduces anxiety, tension, and stress; (2) no one has documented the frequency, duration, and level of laughter (e.g., giggle, chortle, convulsive hysteria) that occurs during testing, although students do agree that some tests are funnier than others; (3) the few studies conducted on the use of humor in testing yield insufficient and inconsistent results; (4) the findings of the six-year study reported in this chapter indicate that undergraduate and graduate students feel humor is effective in reducing their anxiety and making it possible to perform their best on exams; (5) there are four major techniques for using humor in tests, only one of which involves the items; and (6) there are at least three content-irrelevant and five content-relevant strategies that can be selected to infuse humor into traditional multiple-choice, context-dependent multiple-choice, matching, and constructed-response item formats.

REFERENCES

Adams, E. R., & McGuire, F. A. (1986). Is laughter the best medicine? A study of the effects of humor on perceived pain and affect. *Activities, Adaptation, and Aging, 8*, 157–175.

Adams, P. (with Mylander, M). (1998). *Gesundheit! Bringing good health to you, the medical system, and society through physician service, complementary therapies, humor, and joy.* Rochester, VT: Healing Arts Press.

Adler, C. M., & Hillhouse, J. J. (1996). Stress, health, and immunity: A review of the literature. In T. W. Miller (Ed.), *Theory and assessment of stressful life events* (pp. 109–138). Madison, WI: International Universities Press.

AERA (American Educational Research Association), APA (American Psychological Association), & NCME (National Council on Measurement in Education) Joint Committee on Standards. (1999). *Standards for educational and psychological testing.* Washington, DC: AERA.

Aiello, J. R., Thompson, D., & Brodzinsky, D. M. (1983). How funny is crowding anyway? Effects of room size, group size, and the introduction of humor. *Basic and Applied Psychology, 4*(2), 193–207.

Albanese, M. A. (1993). Type K and other complex multiple choice items: An analysis of research and item properties. *Educational Measurement: Issues and Practice, 12*(1), 28–33.

Alden, D. L., Mukherjee, A., & Hoyer, W. D. (2000). Extending a contrast resolution model of humor in television advertising: The role of surprise. *HUMOR: International Journal of Humor Research, 13*, 193–217.

Allen, S. (with Wollman, J.). (1998). *How to be funny: Discovering the comic you.* Amherst, NY: Prometheus Books.

Allport, G. W. (1950). *The individual and his religion.* New York: Macmillan.

Anderson, C. A., & Arnoult, L. H. (1989). An examination of perceived control, humor, irrational beliefs, and positive stress as moderators of the relation between negative stress and health. *Basic and Applied Social Psychology, 10*, 101–117.

Arter, J. A. (1999). Teaching about performance assessment. *Educational Measurement: Issues and Practices, 18*(2), 30–44.

Astin, A. (1985). *Achieving educational excellence*. San Francisco: Jossey-Bass.

Attardo, S., & Raskin, V. (1991). Script theory revis(it)ed: Joke similarity and joke representation model. *HUMOR: International Journal of Humor Research, 4*, 293–347.

Barreca, R. (1991). *They used to call me Snow White . . . but I drifted: Women's strategic use of humor*. New York: Penguin.

Barry, D. (2000). *Dave Barry is not taking this sitting down!* New York: Ballantine.

Belanger, H. G., Kirkpatrick, L. A., & Derks, P. L. (1998). The effects of humor on verbal and imaginable problem solving. *HUMOR: International Journal of Humor Research, 11*, 21–31.

Bellert, J. L. (1989). Humor: A therapeutic approach in oncology nursing. *Cancer Nursing, 12*(2), 65–70.

Bennett, D. J., & Turner, G. F. W. (2001, July). *The use of humorous alternatives in multiple-choice tests: No pain, no gain?* Paper presented at the annual meeting of the International Society of Humor Studies, College Park, MD.

Bennett, M. P., Zeller, J. M., Rosenberg, L., & McCann, J. (in press). The effect of mirthful laughter on stress and natural killer cell activity. *Alternative Therapies in Health and Medicine*.

Bennett, R. E., & Ward, W. C. (Eds.). (1993). *Construction versus choice in cognitive measurement: Issues in constructed-response, performance testing, and portfolio assessment*. Hillsdale, NJ: Lawrence Erlbaum Associates.

Berk, L. S., Felton, D., Tan, S. A., Bittman, B., & Westengard, J. (2001). Modulation of neuroimmune parameters during the eustress of humor-associated mirthful laughter. *Alternative Therapies in Health and Medicine, 7*(2), 62–72, 74–76.

Berk, L. S., & Tan, S. A. (1996). A positive emotion, the eustress of mirthful laughter, modulates the immune system lymphokine interferon-Gamma (Research Perspectives in Psychoneuroimmunology). *Psychoneuroimmunology Research Society Program Abstracts*, June.

Berk, L. S., Tan, S. A., Eby, W. C., Carmona, M., & Vorce, D. (1984). Modulation of human natural killer cells by catecholamines. *Clinical Research, 32*, 38A.

Berk, L. S., Tan, S. A., & Fry, W. F., Jr. (1993). Eustress of humor associated laughter modulates specific immune system components. *Annals of Behavioral Medicine, 15*, Supplement, S111.

Berk, L. S., Tan, S. A., Fry, W. F., Jr., Napier, B. J., Lee, J. W., Hubbard, R. W., & Lewis, J. E. (1989a). Neuroendocrine and stress hormone changes during mirthful laughter. *American Journal of the Medical Sciences, 298* (December), 390–396.

Berk, L. S., Tan, S. A., Napier, B. J., & Eby, W. C. (1989b). Eustress of mirthful laughter modifies natural killer cell activity. *Clinical Research, 37*, 115A.

Berk, L. S., Tan, S. A., Nehlsen-Cannarella, S., Napier, B. J., Lee, J. W., Lewis, J. E., Hubbard, R. W., Eby, W. C., & Fry, W. F., Jr. (1988a). Mirth modulates adrenocortico-medullary activity: Suppression of cortisol and epinephrine. *Clinical Research, 36,* 121A.

Berk, L. S., Tan, S. A., Nehlsen-Cannarella, S., Napier, B. J., Lewis, J. E., Lee, J. W., & Eby, W. C. (1988b). Humor associated laughter decreases cortisol and increases spontaneous lymphocyte blastogenesis. *Clinical Research, 36,* 435A.

Berk, R. A. (Ed.). (1986). *Performance assessment: Methods and applications.* Baltimore: Johns Hopkins University Press.

Berk, R. A. (1996a). A consumer's guide to multiple-choice item formats that measure complex cognitive outcomes. In National Evaluation Systems, *From policy to practice* (pp. 101–127). Amherst, MA: Author.

Berk, R. A. (1996b). Student ratings of 10 strategies for using humor in college teaching. *Journal on Excellence in College Teaching, 7*(3), 71–92.

Berk, R. A. (1997). Top ten strategies for using humor as an effective teaching tool. In J. A. Chambers (Ed.), *Selected papers and awards from the Eighth National Conference on College Teaching and Learning* (pp. 9–27). Jacksonville, FL: Florida Community College and Jacksonville Foundation.

Berk, R. A. (1998a). A humorous account of 10 multiple-choice item flaws that clue testwise students. *Journal on Excellence in College Teaching, 9*(2), 93–117.

Berk, R. A. (1998b). Is humor in academia an oxymoron? *Quality in Higher Education, 7*(1), 1–2.

Berk, R. A. (1998c). *Professors are from Mars, Students are from Snickers: How to write and deliver humor in the classroom and in professional presentations.* Madison, WI: Magna Publications.

Berk, R. A. (1999a). Assessment for measuring professional performance. In D. P. Ely, L. E. Odenthal, & T. J. Plomp (Eds.), *Educational science and technology: Perspectives for the future* (pp. 29–48). Enschede, The Netherlands: Twente University Press.

Berk, R. A. (1999b). Laughter therapy. *The Johns Hopkins Health Insider, 2*(4), 1, 8.

Berk, R. A. (2000a). Does humor in course tests reduce anxiety and improve performance? *College Teaching, 48,* 151–158.

Berk, R. A. (2000b). LAUGH-O-FLEX®: The total body workout. *MedWorldNEWS, 1*(6). (www.medcareers.com)

Berk, R. A. (2001a). The active ingredients in humor: Psychophysiological benefits/risks for older adults. *Educational Gerontology: An International Journal, 27,* 323–339.

Berk, R. A. (2001b). Using music with demonstrations to trigger laughter and facilitate learning in multiple intelligences. *Journal on Excellence in College Teaching, 12*(1), 87–107.

Berk, R. A., Is, M. E., Nuts, S. C. Z., & Sick, W. E. (2002a). Opening the sardine-can theory of laughter. *Field & Stream of Consciousness Quarterly, 8,* 4621–4963.

Berk, R. A., Made, I. T., That, Y., & Up, W. H. U. S. (2002b). Estimating the aerobic value of laughter from thin air. In I. M. Right (Ed.), *Psychoclinical aberrations of laughter from extraterrestrials* (pp. 14–9621). Rambling, ON: Ironing Board Press.

Berk, R. A., & Nanda, J. P. (1998). Effects of jocular instructional methods on attitudes, anxiety, and achievement in statistics courses. *HUMOR: International Journal of Humor Research, 11,* 383–409.

Berk, R. A., Needs, H. E., & Help, S. K. (2002c). Unexpected, undocumented, nonempirical evidence-free effects of laughter. *Journal of Really Dumb Articles, 6,* 849,726–849,727.

Bihrle, A., Brownell, H. H., & Powelson, J. A. (1986). Comprehension of humorous and non-humorous material by left and right brain-damaged patients. *Brain and Cognition, 5,* 399–411.

Bizi, S., Keinan, G., & Beit-Hallahmi, B. (1988). Humor and coping with stress: A test under real-life conditions. *Personality and Individual Differences, 9,* 951–956.

Blumenstyk, G. (2001). Temple U. shuts down for-profit distance-education company. *The Chronicle of Higher Education,* July 20, A29–30.

Board, C., & Whitney, D. R. (1972). The effect of selected poor item-writing practices on test difficulty, reliability, and validity. *Journal of Educational Measurement, 9,* 225–233.

Bogaers, I. E. W. M. (1993). Gender in job interviews: Some implications of verbal interactions of women and men. *Working Papers in Language, Gender and Sexism, 3*(1), 53–82.

Bonwell, C. C., & Eison, J. A. (1991). *Active learning: Creating excitement in the classroom* (ASHE-ERIC Higher Education Report No. 1). Washington, DC: The George Washington University, School of Education and Human Development.

Bower, G. (1972). Mental imagery and associative learning. In L. Gregg (Ed.), *Cognition in learning and memory* (pp. 51–88). New York: Wiley.

Brill, A. A. (1940). The mechanism of wit and humor in normal and psychopathic states. *Psychiatric Quarterly, 14,* 731–749.

Brodzinsky, D. M., Barnet, K., & Aiello, J. R. (1981). Sex subject and gender identity as factors in humor appreciation. *Sex Roles, 7,* 561–573.

Brown, B., & Kulik, J. (1977). Flashbulb memories. *Cognition, 5,* 73–99.

Brown, J. (1966). *Objective tests: Their construction and analysis: A practical handbook for teachers.* London: Longmans.

Brownell, H. H., & Gardner, H. (1989). Neuropsychological insights into humor. In J. Durant & J. Miller (Eds.), *Laughing matters* (pp. 17–34). New York: Wiley.

Brownell, H. H., Michel, D., Powelson, J. A., & Gardner, H. (1983). Surprise but not coherence: Sensitivity to verbal humor in right hemispheric patients. *Brain and Language, 18,* 20–27.

Burns, D. M. (1998). *University students' responses to and preferences for various types of humor.* Unpublished doctoral dissertation, State University of New York, Albany.

Cann, A., Holt, K., & Calhoun, L. G. (1999). The roles of humor and sense of humor in responses to stressors. *HUMOR: International Journal of Humor Research, 12,* 177–193.

Cantor, J. R. (1970). What is funny to whom? The role of gender. *Journal of Communication, 26,* 166–174.

Carter, K. (1986). Test-wiseness for teachers and students. *Educational Measurement: Issues and Practices, 5*(4), 20–23.

Case, S. M. (1994). The use of imprecise terms in examination questions: How frequent is frequently? *Academic Medicine, 69,* (suppl.), 54–56.

Case, S. M., & Swanson, D. B. (1996). *Constructing written test questions for the basic and clinical sciences.* Philadelphia: National Board of Medical Examiners.

Chapman, A. J. (1973). Social facilitation of laughter in children. *Journal of Experimental Social Psychology, 9,* 528–541.

Chapman, A. J. (1975). Eye contact, physical proximity and laughter: A re-examination of the equilibrium model of social intimacy. *Social Behavior and Personality, 15,* 143–155.

Chase, C. I. (1964). Relative length of option and response set in multiple choice items. *Educational and Psychological Measurement, 24,* 861–866.

Clay, R. A. (1997). Researchers harness the power of humor. *APA Monitor, 28*(9), 1.

Cogan, R., Cogan, D., Waltz, W., & McCue, M. (1987). Effects of laughter and relaxation on discomfort thresholds. *Journal of Behavioral Medicine, 10*(2), 139–144.

Cohen, S., Frank, E., Doyle, W. J., Skoner, D. P., Rabin, B. S., & Gwaltney, J. M. (1998). Types of stressors that increase susceptibility to the common cold in healthy adults. *Health Psychology, 17,* 214–223.

Cohen, S., & Williamson, G. M. (1991). Stress and infectious disease in humans. *Psychological Bulletin, 109,* 5–24.

Cousins, N. (1976). Anatomy of an illness (as perceived by the patient). *New England Journal of Medicine, 295,* 1458–1463.

Cousins, N. (1979). *Anatomy of an illness as perceived by the patient.* New York: W. W. Norton.

Cronbach, L. J. (1970). Review of *On the theory of achievement test items* by J. R. Bormuth. *Psychometrika, 35,* 509–511.

Cushner, F. D., & Friedman, R. J. (1989). Humor and the physician. *Southern Medical Journal, 82,* 51–52.

Danzer, A., Dale, J., & Klions, H. L. (1990). Effects of exposure to humorous stimuli on induced depression. *Psychological Reports, 66,* 1027–1036.

Deaner, S. L., & McConatha, J. T. (1993). The relationship of humor to depression and personality. *Psychological Reports, 72,* 755–763.

Deckers, L., & Winters, J. A. (1986). Surprise and humor in response to discrepantly short and/or heavy stimuli in a psychological task. *Journal of General Psychology, 113,* 57–63.

DeNeve, K. M., & Heppner, M. J. (1997, Spring). Role play simulations: The assessment of an active learning technique and comparisons with traditional lectures. *Innovative Higher Education, 21*(3), 231–246.

Derks, P. L. (1987). Humor production: An examination of three models of creativity. *Journal of Creative Behavior, 21,* 325–326.

Derks, P. L., Bogart, E., & Gillikin, L. (1991). *Neuroelectrical activity and humor.* Address presented at the annual International Conference on Humour and Laughter, Brock University, St. Catherines, Canada.

DeSpelder, L., & Strickland, A. (1983). The last dance: Encountering death and dying. *Death Studies, 9,* 201–216.

Dewitte, S., & Verguts, T. (2001). Being funny: A selectionist account of humor production. *HUMOR: International Journal of Humor Research, 14,* 37–53.

Diamond, J. J., & Evans, W. J. (1972). An investigation of the cognitive correlates of test-wiseness. *Journal of Educational Measurement, 9,* 145–150.

Díaz-Lefebvre, R. (1999). *Coloring outside the lines: Applying multiple intelligences and creativity in learning.* New York: Wiley.

Dillon, K., Minchoff, B., & Baker, K. (1985). Positive emotional states and the enhancement of the immune system. *International Journal of Psychiatry in Medicine, 15,* 13–17.

Dillon, K. M., & Totten, M. C. (1989). Psychological factors, immunocompetence, and health of breast-feeding mothers and their infants. *Journal of Genetic Psychology, 150,* 155–162.

Ding, G. F., & Jersild, A. T. (1932). A study of the laughing and smiling of preschool children. *Journal of Genetic Psychology, 40,* 452–472.

Dixon, N. F. (1976). *On the psychology of military incompetence.* London: Cape.

Dixon, N. F. (1980). Humor: A cognitive alternative to stress? In I. G. Sarason & C. D. Speilberger (Eds.), *Stress and anxiety* (Vol. 7, pp. 281–289). Washington, DC: Hemisphere.

Doris, J., & Fierman, E. (1956). Humor and anxiety. *Journal of Abnormal and Social Psychology, 53,* 59–62.

Dowling, J. S. (2001, July). *How does a sense of humor help children cope with the stressors of cancer?* Paper presented at the annual meeting of the International Society of Humor Studies, College Park, MD.

Dreher, W. (1982). *Gesprächsanalyse: Macht als kategorie männlichen interacktionsverhältens.* Sprecherwechsel und Lachen Master's thesis, Berlin, Germany.

Dudycha, A. L., & Carpenter, J. B. (1973). Effects of item formats on item discrimination and difficulty. *Journal of Applied Psychology, 58,* 116–121.

Dundes, A. (1987a). At ease, disease: AIDS jokes as sick humor. *American Behavioral Scientist, 30,* 72–81.

Dundes, A. (1987b). *Cracking jokes: Studies of sick humor cycles and stereotypes.* Berkeley, CA: Ten Speed Press.

Dunn, T. F., & Goldstein, L. G. (1959). Test difficulty, validity, and reliability as a function of selected multiple-choice item construction principles. *Educational and Psychological Measurement, 19,* 171–179.

Dworkin, E. S., & Efran, J. S. (1967). The angered: Their susceptibility to varieties of humor. *Journal of Personality and Social Psychology, 6,* 233–236.

Easton, A. (1994). Talk and laughter in New Zealand women's and men's speech. *Wellington Working Papers in Linguistics, 6,* 1–25.

Ebel, R. L. (1951). Writing the test item. In E. F. Lindquist (Ed.), *Educational measurement* (1st ed., pp. 185–249). Washington, DC: American Council on Education.

Eble, K. E. (1994). *The craft of teaching* (3rd ed.). San Francisco: Jossey-Bass.

Esler, M. D. (1998). Mental stress, panic disorder and the heart. *Stress Medicine, 14,* 237–243.

Evans, W. (1984). Test wiseness: An examination of cue-using strategies. *Journal of Experimental Education, 52,* 141–144.

Fancy, A. (1999). This hour has too many minutes (an interrupted lecture): The case for edu-prop drama. *Journal on Excellence in College Teaching, 10,* 95–123.

Farhi, P. (2000). The jocularity of television ads: Commercials aimed at guys go for the funny bone—Don't laugh ladies. *The Washington Post,* July 19, C1, C8.

Farhi, P. (2002). Oh, the profanity! *The Washington Post,* April 21, G1, G4,

Foot, H. C., & Chapman, A. J. (1976). The social responsiveness of young children in humourous situations. In A. J. Chapman & H. C. Foot (Eds.), *Humour and laughter: Theory, research, and applications* (pp. 141–175, 187–214). London: Wiley.

Forabosco, G. (1992). Cognitive aspects of the humor process: The concept of incongruity. *HUMOR: International Journal of Humor Research, 5,* 45–68.

Frecknall, P. (1994). Good humor: A qualitative study of uses of humor in everyday life. *Psychology: A Journal of Human Behavior, 31,* 12–21.

Freud, S. (1905). *Jokes and their relation to the unconscious.* London: Hogarth Press.

Freud, S. (1959). Humour. In J. Strachey (Ed.), *Collected papers of Sigmund Freud* (Vol. 5). New York: Basic Books.

Freud, S. (1960). *Jokes and their relation to the unconscious.* New York: Norton.

Fry, W. F., Jr. (1971). Mirth and oxygen saturtion levels of peripheral blood. *Psychotherapy and Psychosomatics, 19*(1), 76–84.

Fry, W. F., Jr. (1984). *Learning with humor.* Paper presented at the annual International Conference on Humor, Tel Aviv, Israel.

Fry, W. F., Jr. (1986). Humor, physiology, and the aging process. In L. Nahemow, K. A. McCluskey-Fawcettt, & P. E. McGhee (Eds.), *Humor and aging* (pp. 81–98). Orlando, FL: Academic Press.

Fry, W. F., Jr. (1992). The physiological effects of humor, mirth, and laughter. *Journal of the American Medical Association, 267,* 1857–1858.

Fry, W. F., Jr., (1994). The biology of humor. *HUMOR: International Journal of Humor Research, 7,* 111–126.

Fry, W. F., Jr., & Rader, C. (1977). The respiratory components of mirthful laughter. *Journal of Biological Psychology, 19,* 39–50.

Fry, W. F., Jr., & Savin, W. M. (1988). Mirthful laughter and blood pressure. *HUMOR: International Journal of Humor Research, 1,* 49–62.

Fry, W. F., Jr., & Stoft, P. E. (1971). Mirth and oxygen saturation levels of peripheral blood. *Psychotherapy and Psychosomatics, 19,* 76–84.

Galloway, G., & Cropley, A. (1999). Benefits of humor for mental health: Empirical directions for further research. *HUMOR: International Journal of Humor Research, 12,* 301–314.

Gardner, H. (1983). *Frames of mind.* New York: Basic Books.

Gardner, H. (1993). *Multiple intelligences: The theory in practice.* New York: Basic Books.

Gardner, H. (1995). Reflections on multiple intelligences: Myths and messages. *Phi Delta Kappan, 77,* 200–209.

Goldstein, J. H. (1976). Theoretical notes on humor. *Journal of Communication, 26,* 104–112.

Goldstein, J. H., Harmon, J., McGhee, P. E., & Karasik, R. (1975). Test of an information processing model of humor: Physiological response changes during problem and riddle solving. *Journal of General Psychology, 92,* 59–68.

Goodheart, A. (1994). *Laughter therapy.* Santa Barbara, CA: Stress Less Press.

Green, K. (1984). Effects of item characteristics on multiple-choice item difficulty. *Educational and Psychological Measurement, 44,* 551–561.

Gruner, C. R. (1978). *Understanding laughter: The workings of wit and humor.* Chicago: Nelson-Hall.

Haiman, J. (1998). *Talk is cheap: Sarcasm, alienation, and the evolution of language.* New York: Oxford University Press.

Hakel, M. D. (Ed.). (1998). *Beyond multiple choice: Evaluating alternatives to traditional testing for selection.* Mahwah, NJ: Laurence Erlbaum Associates.

Haladyna, T. M. (1992). Context-dependent item sets. *Educational Measurement: Issues and Practice, 11*(1), 21–25.

Haladyna, T. M. (1997). *Writing test items to evaluate higher order thinking.* Needham Heights, MA: Allyn & Bacon.

Haladyna, T. M. (1999). *Developing and validating multiple-choice test items.* (2nd ed.). Mahwah, NJ: Lawrence Erlbaum Associates.

Haladyna, T. M., & Downing, S. M. (1989a). A taxonomy of multiple-choice item-writing rules. *Applied Measurement in Education, 1,* 37–50.

Haladyna, T. M., & Downing, S. M. (1989b). The validity of a taxonomy of multiple-choice item-writing rules. *Applied Measurement in Education, 1,* 51–78.

Hay, J. (2001). The pragmatics of humor support. *HUMOR: International Journal of Humor Research, 14,* 55–82.

Hedl, J. J., Jr., Hedl, J. L., & Weaver, D. B. (1981, April). *The effects of humor on anxiety and performance.* Paper presented at the annual meeting of the American Educational Research Association, Los Angeles, CA.

Helitzer, M. (1987). *Comedy writing secrets: How to think funny, write funny, act funny, and get paid for it.* Cincinnati, OH: Writer's Digest Books.

Herzog, T. R. (1999). Gender differences in humor appreciation revisited. *HUMOR: International Journal of Humor Research, 12,* 411–423.

Herzog, T. R., & Anderson, M. R. (2000). Joke cruelty, emotional responsiveness, and joke appreciation. *HUMOR: International Journal of Humor Research, 13,* 333–351.

Herzog, T. R., & Karafa, J. A. (1998). Preferences for sick versus nonsick humor. *HUMOR: International Journal of Humor Research, 11,* 291–312.

Herzog, T. R., & Larwin, D. A. (1988). The appreciation of humor in captioned cartoons. *Journal of Psychology, 122,* 597–607.

Hudak, D., Dale, J., Hudak, M., & DeGood, D. (1991). Effects of humorous stimuli and sense of humor on discomfort. *Psychological Reports, 69,* 779–786.

Hunter, M. (1982). *Mastery learning.* El Segundo, CA: TIP Publications.

Hutcheon, L. (1995). *Irony's edge.* New York: Rouledge.

Itami, J., Nobori, M., & Teshima, H. (1994). Laughter and immunity. *Japanese Journal of Psychosomatic Medicine, 34,* 565–571.

Johnson, A. M. (1990). A study of humor and the right hemisphere. *Perceptual and Motor Skills, 70,* 995–1002.

Jones, P. D., & Kaufman, G. G. (1975). The differential formation of response sets by specific determiners. *Educational and Psychological Measurement, 35,* 821–833.

Kant, I. (1790). *Kritik der urteilskraft. [A Treaty on Judgment].* Berlin, Germany: Lagarde.

Kataria, M., Wilson, S., & Buxman, K. (1999, June). *Where east meets west: Laughter therapy.* Workshop presented at the annual meeting of the International Society of Humor Studies, Oakland, CA.

Kehl, D. G. (2000). Varieties of risible experience: Grades of laughter and their function in modern American literature. *HUMOR: International Journal of Humor Research, 13,* 379–393.

Kelley, M. L., Jarvie, G. J., Middlebrook, J. L., McNeer, M. F., & Drabman, R. S. (1984). Decreasing burned children's pain behavior: Impacting the trauma of hydrotherapy. *Journal of Applied Behavior Analysis, 17,* 147–158.

Kenealy, P., & Monseth, A. (1994). Music and IQ tests. *The Psychologist, 7,* 346.

Kline, L. W. (1907). The psychology of humor. *American Journal of Psychology, 18,* 421–441.

Korotkov, D., & Hannah, T. E. (1994). Extraversion and emotionality as proposed superordinate stress moderators: A prospective analysis. *Personality and Individual Differences, 16,* 787–792.

Kuhlman, T. (1984). *Humor and psychotherapy.* Homewood, IL: Dorsey Press.

Kuhn, C. C. (1994). The stages of laughter. *Journal of Nursing Jocularity, 4*(2), 34–35.

Kuiper, N. A., & Martin, R. A. (1993). Humor and self concept. *HUMOR: International Journal of Humor Research, 6,* 251–270.

Kuiper, N. A., Martin, R. A., & Dance, K. (1992). Sense of humor and enhanced quality of life. *Personality and Individual Differences, 13,* 1273–1283.

Labott, S. M., Ahleman, S., Wolever, M. E., & Martin, R. B. (1990). The physiological and psychological effects of the expression and inhibition of emotion. *Behavioral Medicine, 16,* 182–189.

Labott, S. M., & Martin, R. B. (1987). The stress-moderating effects of weeping and humor. *Journal of Human Stress, 13,* 159–164.

Labott, S. M., & Martin, R. B. (1990). Emotional coping, age, and physical disorder. *Behavioral Medicine, 16,* 53–61.

LaFave, L. (1972). Humor judgments as a function of reference groups and identification classes. In J. H. Goldstein & P. E. McGhee (Eds.), *The psychology of humor: Theoretical perspectives and empirical issues* (pp. 195–210). New York: Academic Press.

LaFave, L., Haddad, J., & Marshall, N. (1974). Humor judgments as a function of identification classes. *Sociology and Social Research, 58,* 184–194.

Lambert, R. B., & Lambert, N. K. (1995). The effects of humor on secretory Immunoglobulin A levels in school-aged children. *Pediatric Nursing, 21,* 16–19.

Lefcourt, H. J., Davidson, K., Prkachin, K. M., & Mills, D. E. (1997). Humor as a stress moderator in the prediction of blood pressure obtained during five stressful tasks. *Journal of Research in Personality, 31,* 523–542.

Lefcourt, H. M., Davidson-Katz, K., & Kueneman, K. (1990). Humor and immune system functioning. *HUMOR: International Journal of Humor Research, 3,* 305–322.

Lefcourt, H. M., Davidson-Katz, K., Shepherd, R., & Phillips, M. (1995). Perspective-taking humor: Accounting for stress moderation. *Journal of Social and Clinical Psychology, 14,* 373–391.

Lefcourt, H. M., & Martin, R. A. (1986). *Humor and life stress.* NY: Springer-Verlag.

Lefcourt, H. M., & Thomas, S. (1998). Humor and stress revisited. In W. Ruch (Ed.), *The sense of humor: Explorations of a personality characteristic* (Humor Research Series, Vol. 3). Berlin, Germany: Morton de Gruyter.

Lehman, K. M., Burke, K. L., Martin, R., Sultan, J., Czech, D. R. (2001). A reformulation of the moderating effects of productive humor. *HUMOR: International Journal of Humor Research, 14,* 131–161.

Leiber, D. B. (1986). Laughter and humor in critical care. *Dimensions of Critical Care Nursing, 5*(3), 162–170.

Leng, X., & Shaw, G. L. (1991). Toward a neural theory of higher brain function using music as a window. *Concepts in Neuroscience, 2,* 229–258.

Liechty, R. D. (1987). Humor and the surgeon. *Archives of Surgery, 122,* 519–522.

Linn, R. L., & Gronlund, N. E. (2000). *Measurement and assessment in teaching* (8th ed.) Upper Saddle River, NJ: Merrill.

Lipman, S. (2002). Humor and 9–11. *The Humor Connection, 16*(1), 6.

Lloyd, E. L. (1938). The respiratory mechanism in laughter. *Journal of General Psychology, 10,* 179–189.

Locke, S. E. (1984). Life change stress, psychiatric symptoms, and natural killer cell activity. *Psychosomatic Medicine, 6,* 441–453.

Lowman, J. (1995). *Mastering the techniques of teaching* (2nd ed.). San Francisco: Jossey-Bass.

MacIntosh, H. G., & Morrison, R. B. (1969). *Objective testing.* London: University of London Press.

Makri-Tsilipakou, M. (1994). Laughing their way: Gender and conversational mirth. *Working Papers in Language, Gender and Sexism, 4*(1), 15–50.

Martin, R. A. (2001). Humor, laughter, and physical health: Methodological issues and research findings. *Psychological Bulletin, 127,* 504–519.

Martin, R. A., & Dobbin, J. P. (1988). Sense of humor, hassles, and immunoglobulin A: Evidence for a stress-moderating effects of humor. *International Journal of Psychiatry in Medicine, 18,* 93–105.

Martin, R. A., Kuiper, N. A., Olinger, L. J., & Dance, D. A. (1993). Humor, coping with stress, self-concept, and psychological well-being. *HUMOR: International Journal of Humor Research, 6,* 89–104.

Martin, R., A., & Lefcourt, H. M. (1983). The sense of humor as a moderator of the relationship between stressors and mood. *Journal of Personality and Social Psychology, 45,* 1313–1324.

May, R. (1953). *Man's search for himself.* New York: Norton.

McClelland, D. C., Alexander, C., & Marks, E. (1980). The need for power, stress, immune function, and illness among male prisoners. *Journal of Abnormal Psychology, 10*, 93–102.

McClelland, D. C., & Cheriff, A. D. (1997). The immunoenhancing effects of humor on secretory IgA and resistance to respiratory infections. *Psychology and Health, 12*, 329–344.

McGhee, P. E. (1979). *Humor: It's origin and development.* San Francisco: Freeman.

McGhee, P. E. (1999). *Health, healing, and the amuse system: Humor as survival training* (3rd ed.). Dubuque, IA: Kendall/Hunt.

McGhee, P. E. (2002, February). *Comprehensive review of humor research.* Paper presented at the annual meeting of the Association for Applied and Therapeutic Humor, Baltimore, MD.

McGhee, P. E., & Johnson, S. F. (1975). The role of fantasy and reality cues in children's appreciation of incongruity humor. *Merril-Palmer Quarterly, 12*, 19–30.

McGuire, P. A. (1999). More psychologists are finding that discrete uses of humor promote healing in their patients. *APA Monitor, 30*(3), 1.

McKeachie, W. J. (1994). *Teaching tips: Strategies, research, and theory for college and university teachers* (9th edition). Lexington, MA: DC Health.

McMorris, R. F., Boothroyd, R. A., & Pietrangelo, D. J. (1997). Humor in educational testing: A review and discussion. *Applied Measurement in Education, 10*, 269–297.

McMorris, R. F., Brown, J. A., Snyder, G. W., & Pruzek, R. M. (1972). Effects of violating item construction principles. *Journal of Educational Measurement, 9*, 287–295.

McMorris, R. F., Kim, Y., & Li, X. (2001, July). *International students' experiences with and reactions to humor in university classes and tests.* Paper presented at the annual meeting of the International Society of Humor Studies, College Park, MD.

Mehrens, W. A., & Lehmann, I. J. (1991). *Measurement and evaluation education and psychology* (4th ed.). Fort Worth, TX: Harcourt Brace Jovanovich.

Mentzer, T. L. (1982). Response biases in multiple-choice test item files. *Educational and Psychological Measurement, 42*, 437–448.

Millman, J., Bishop, C. H., & Ebel, R. L. (1965). An analysis of test-wiseness. *Educational and Psychological Measurement, 25*, 707–726.

Milsum, J. H. (1985). A model of the eustress system for health/illness. *Behavioral Science, 30*, 179–186.

Mindess, H., Miller, C., Turek, J., Bender, A., & Corbin, S. (1985). *The Antioch Humor Test: Making sense of humor.* New York: Avon Books.

Mintz, L. E. (1999). American humor as unifying and divisive. *HUMOR: International Journal of Humor Research, 12*, 237–252.

Mittwoch-Jaffe, T., Shalit, F., Srendi, B, & Yehuda, S. (1995). Modification of cytokine secretion following mild emotional stimuli. *Neuroreport, 6,* 789–792.

Mueller, D. J., (1975). An assessment of the effectiveness of complex alternatives in multiple-choice achievement test items. *Educational and Psychological Measurement, 35,* 135–141.

Mundorf, N., Bhatia, A., Zillmann, D., Lester, P., & Robertson, S. (1988). Gender differences in humor appreciation. *HUMOR: International Journal of Humor Research, 1,* 231–243.

Nelms, J. (2001). *A descriptive analysis of the uses and functions of sarcasm in the classroom discourse of higher education.* Unpublished doctoral dissertation, University of Florida, Gainesville.

Nevo, O., Keinan, G., & Teshimovsky-Arditi, M. (1993). Humor and pain tolerance. *HUMOR: International Journal of Humor Research, 6,* 71–88.

Newman, J., Rosenbach, J. H., Burns, K. L., Latimer, B. C., Matocha, H. R., & Vogt, E. R. (1995). An experimental test of "the Mozart effect": Does listening to his music improve spatial ability? *Perceptual and Motor Skills, 81,* 1379–1387.

Nezu, A. M., Nezu, C. M., & Blissett, S. E. (1988). Sense of humor as a moderator of the relation between stressful events and psychological distress: A prospective analysis. *Journal of Personality and Social Psychology, 54,* 699–714.

Niepel, M., Rudolph, V., Schützwohl, A., & Meyer, W-U. (1994). Temporal characteristics of the surprise reaction induced by schema-discrepant visual and auditory events. *Cognition and Emotion, 8(5),* 433–452.

Nitko, A. J. (1984). Review of Roid and Haladyna's *A technology for test item writing. Journal of Educational Measurement, 21,* 201–204.

Njus, D. M., Nitschke, W., & Bryant, F. B. (1996). Positive affect, negative affect, and the moderating effect of writing on sIgA antibody levels. *Psychology and Health, 12,* 135–148.

O'Connell, W. E. (1960). The adaptive function of wit and humor. *Journal of Abnormal and Social Psychology, 61,* 263–270.

O'Connell, W. E. (1976). Freudian humour: The Eupsychia of everyday life. In H. C. Foot & A. J. Chapman (Eds.), *Humour and laughter: Theory, research and applications* (pp. 313–330). London: Wiley.

O'Leary, A. (1990). Stress, emotion, and human immune function. *Psychological Bulletin, 108,* 363–382.

Olson, J. M., Maio, G. R., & Hobden, K. L. (1999). The (null) effects of exposure to disparagement humor on stereotypes and attitudes. *HUMOR: International Journal of Humor Research, 12,* 195–219.

O'Quin, K., & Derks, P. L. (1997). Humor and creativity: A review of the empirical literature. In M. Runco (Ed.), *Creativity research handbook* (pp. 223–252). Cresskill, NJ: Hampton Press.

Oppliger, P. A., & Sherblom, J. (1988). Late night with David Letterman: A humorous balance. *Communication Research Reports, 5*(2), 193–196.

Overholser, J. C. (1992). Sense of humor when coping with life stress. *Personality and Individual Differences, 13,* 799–804.

Pascarella, T., & Terenzini, P. (1991). *How college affects students.* San Francisco: Jossey-Bass.

Paskind, H. A. (1932). Effects of laughter on muscle tone. *Archives of Neurological Psychiatry, 28,* 623–628.

Perlmutter, D. D. (2000). Tracing the origin of humor. *HUMOR: International Journal of Humor Research, 13,* 457–468.

Perret, G. (1982a). *Comedy writing step by step.* New York: Samuel French.

Perret, G. (1982b). *How to write and sell your sense of humor.* Cincinnati, OH: Writer's Digest Books.

Perret, G. (1990). *Comedy writing workbook.* New York: Sterling Publishing.

Perret, G. (1993). *Successful stand-up comedy.* Hollywood, CA: Samuel French Trade.

Perret, G. (1998). *Business humor: Jokes and how to deliver them.* New York: Sterling Publishing.

Peterson, K. (1992). Use of humor in AIDS prevention, in the treatment of HIV positive persons, and in the remediation of care-giver burnout. In M. R. Seligson & K. E. Peterson (Eds.), *AIDS prevention and treatment: Hope, humor, and healing.* Bristol, PA: Hemisphere.

Plake, B. S., & Huntley, R. M. (1984). Can relevant grammatical clues result in invalid test items? *Educational and Psychological Measurement, 44,* 687–696.

Popham. W. J. (1999). *Classroom assessment* (2nd ed.). Boston: Allyn & Bacon.

Porterfield, A. L. (1987). Does sense of humor moderate the impact of life stress on psychological and physical well-being? *Journal of Research in Personality, 21,* 306–317.

Prerost, E. (1988). Use of humor and guided imagery in therapy to alleviate stress. *Journal of Mental Health Counseling, 10*(1), 16–22.

Prerost, F. J. (1984). Reactions to humorous sexual stimuli as a function of sexual activeness and satisfaction. *Psychology: A Quarterly Journal of Human Behavior, 21,* 23–27.

Prerost, F. J., & Ruma, C. (1987). Exposure to humorous stimuli as an adjunct to muscle relaxation training. *Psychology: A Quarterly Journal of Human Behavior, 24,* 70–74.

Provine, R. R. (1992). Contagious laughter: Laughter is a sufficient stimulus for laughs and smiles. *Bulletin of the Psychonomic Society, 30,* 1–4.

Provine, R. R. (1996). Contagious yawning and laughter: Significance for sensory feature detection, motor pattern generation, imitation, and the evolution of social behavior. In C. M. Heyes & B. G. Galef (Eds.), *Social learning in animals: The roots of culture* (pp. 179–208). New York: Academic Press.

Provine, R. R. (2000). *Laughter: A scientific investigation*. New York: Viking Penguin.

Provine, R. R., & Fischer, K. R. (1989). Laughing, smiling, and talking: Relation to sleeping and social context in humans. *Ethology, 89,* 295–305.

Raskin, V. (1985). *Semantic mechanisms of humor*. Boston: Reidel.

Rauscher, F. H., Shaw, G. L., & Ky, K. N. (1993). Music and spatial task performance. *Nature, 365,* 611.

Rauscher, F. H., Shaw, G. L., & Ky, K. N. (1995). Listening to Mozart enhances spatial-temporal reasoning: Towards a neurophysiological basis. *Neuroscience Letters, 185,* 44–47.

Rideout, B. E., & Laubach, C. M. (1996). EEG correlates of enhanced spatial performance following exposure to music. *Perceptual and Motor Skills, 82,* 427–432.

Rishel, M. A. (2002). *Writing humor: Creativity and the comic mind*. Detroit, MI: Wayne State University Press.

Rosen, M. J. (Ed.). (1989). *Collecting himself: James Thurber, on writing and writers, humor and himself*. New York: Harper and Row.

Rosenberg, L. (1991). A qualitative investigation of the use of humor by emergency personnel as a strategy for coping with stress. *Journal of Emergency Nursing, 17,* 197–203.

Rothbart, M. K. (1976). Incongruity, problem solving and laughter. In A. J. Chapman & H. C. Foot (Eds.), *Humour and laughter: Theory, research, and applications* (pp. 37–54). London: Wiley.

Rotton, J., & Shats, M. (1996). Effects of state humor, expectancies, and choice on postsurgical mood and self-medication: A field experiment. *Journal of Applied Social Psychology, 26,* 1775–1794.

Ruch, G. M., & Charles, J. W. (1928). A comparison of five types of objective tests in elementary psychology. *Journal of Applied Psychology, 12,* 398–403.

Ruch, G. M., & Stoddard, G. D. (1925). Comparative reliabilities of objective examinations. *Journal of Educational Psychology, 16,* 89–103.

Ruch, W., & Hehl, F-J. (1988). Attitudes to sex, sexual behavior, and enjoyment of humour. *Personality and Individual Differences, 9,* 983–994.

Sarason, S. B. (1999). *Teaching as a performing art*. New York: Teachers College Press

Sarnacki, R. (1979). An examination of test-wiseness in the cognitive test domain. *Review of Educational Research, 49,* 252–279.

Sarnthein, J., Stein, A. V., Rappelsberger, P., Petsche, H., Rauscher, R. H., & Shaw, G. L. (1997). Persistent patterns of brain activity: An EEG coherence study of the positive effect of music on spatial-temporal reasoning. *Neurological Research, 19*(2), 107–116.

Schmitt, N. (1990). Patients' perception of laughter in a rehabilitation hospital. *Rehabilitation Nursing, 15,* 143–146.

Sheehan, P. (1972). A functional analysis of the role of visual imagery in unexpected recall. In P. Sheehan (Ed.), *The function and nature of imagery* (pp. 149–174). New York: Academic Press.

Sherman, K. M. (1998). Healing with humor. *Seminars in Perioperative Nursing, 7*(2), 128–137.

Sierra, M., & Berrios, G. E. (1999). Flashbulb memories and other repetitive images: A psychiatric perspective. *Comprehensive Psychiatry, 40,* 115–125.

Singer, D. L. (1968). Aggression arousal, hostile humor, and catharsis. *Journal of Personality and Social Psychology Monograph Supplement, 8,* 1–14.

Slakter, M. J., Koehler, R. A., & Hampton, S. H. (1970). Grade level, sex, and selected aspects of test-wiseness. *Journal of Educational Measurement, 7,* 119–122

Smith, J. R., Foot, H. C., & Chapman, A. J. (1977). Nonverbal communication among friends and strangers sharing humour. In: A. J. Chapman & H. C. Foot (Eds.) *It's a funny thing, humour* (pp. 417–420). Oxford, England: Pergamon Press.

Smith, R. E., Ascough, J. C., Ettinger, R. F., & Nelson, D. A. (1971). Humor, anxiety, and task performance. *Journal of Personality and Social Psychology, 19,* 243–246.

Søbstad, F. (1990). *Førskolebarn og humor* Trondheim, Universitetet I Trondheim, Pedagogisk Institutt, Rapport nr. 1.

Søbstad, F. (2001, June). *Contagious laughter.* Paper presented at the annual meeting of the International Society of Humor Studies, College Park, MD.

Sousou, S. D. (1997). Effects of melody and lyrics on mood and memory. *Perceptual and Motor Skills, 85,* 31–40.

Stough, C., Kerkin, B., Bates, T., & Mangan, G. (1994). Music and IQ tests. *The Psychologist, 7,* 253.

Strang, H. R. (1977). The effects of technical and unfamiliar options on guessing on multiple-choice test items. *Journal of Educational Measurement, 14,* 253–260.

Stratton, V., & Zalanowski, A. (1994). Affective impact of music vs. lyrics. *Empirical Studies of the Arts, 12,* 173–184.

Suls, J. M. (1972). A two-stage model for the appreciation of jokes and cartoons: An information-processing analysis. In J. H. Goldstein, H. Jeffrey, & P. E. McGhee (Eds.), *The psychology of humor: Theoretical perspectives and empirical issues* (pp. 81–100). New York: Academic Press.

Suls, J. M. (1983). Cognitive processes in humor appreciation. In P. E. McGhee & J. H. Goldstein (Eds.), *Handbook of humor research: Vol. I, Basic Issues* (pp. 39–58). New York: Springer-Verlag.

Svebak, S. (1982). The effect of mirthfulness upon the amount of discordant right-left occipital EEG alpha. *Motivation and Emotion, 6,* 133–143.

Svebak, S., Christioffersen, B., & Aasarød, K. (2001, July). *A two-year prospective study of survival among patients with end stage renal failure: The significance of sense of humor.* Paper presented at the annual meeting of the International Society of Humor Studies, College Park, MD.

Swanson, D. B., & Case, S. M. (1993). Trends in written assessment: A strongly biased perspective. In R. Harden, I. Hart, & H. Mulholland (Eds.), *Approaches to the assessment of clinical competence: Part 1* (pp. 38–53). Norwich, England: Page Brothers.

Swanson, D. B., Norman, G. R., & Linn, R. L. (1995). Performance-based assessment: Lessons from the health professions. *Educational Researcher, 24*(5), 5–11, 35.

Talbot, L. A., & Lumden, D. B. (2000). On the association between humor and burnout. *HUMOR: International Journal of Humor Research, 13,* 419–428.

Tan, S. A., Tan, L. G., Berk, L. S., Lukeman, S. T., & Lukman, L. F. (1997). Mirthful laughter, an effective adjunct in cardiac rehabilitation. *Canadian Journal of Cardiology, 13,* Supplement B, 190B.

Thorson, J. A. (1985). A funny thing happened on the way to the morgue: Some thoughts on humor and death, and a taxonomy of the humor associated with death. *Death Studies, 9,* 201–216.

Timpson, W. M., & Tobin, D. N. (1982). *Teaching as performing: A guide to energizing your public presentation.* Englewood Cliffs, NJ: Prentice-Hall.

Timpson, W. M., Burgoyne, S., Jones, C. S., & Jones, W. (1997). *Teaching and performing: Ideas for energizing your classes.* Madison, WI: Magna Publications.

Tomasi, T. B. (1976). *The immune system of secretions.* Englewood Cliffs, NJ: Prentice Hall.

Trebek, A., & Barsocchini, P. (1990). *The Jeopardy! book.* New York: Harper Perennial.

Trebek, A., & Griffin, M. (1992). *The Jeopardy! challenge.* New York: Harper Perennial.

Trice, A. D., & Price-Greathouse, J. (1986). Joking under the drill: A validity study of the humor coping scale. *Journal of Social Behavior and Personality, 1,* 265–266.

Veatch, T. C. (1998). A theory of humor. *HUMOR: International Journal of Humor Research, 11,* 161–215.

Weaver, J., & Zillmann, D. (1994). Effect of humor and tragedy on discomfort tolerance. *Perceptual and Motor Skills, 78,* 632–634.

Weisenberg, M., Raz, T., & Hener, T. (1998). The influence of film-induced mood on pain perception. *Pain, 76,* 365–375.

Weisenberg, M., Tepper, I., & Schwarzwald, J. (1995). Humor as a cognitive technique for increasing pain tolerance. *Pain, 63,* 207–212.

Weller, T. (1987). *Cvltvre made stupid.* Boston: Houghton Mifflin.

Wesman, A. G. (1971). Writing the test item. In R. L. Thorndike (Ed.), *Educational measurement* (2nd ed., pp. 81–129). Washington, DC: American Council on Education.

White, S., & Camarena, P. (1989). Laughter as a stress reducer in small groups. *HUMOR: International Journal of Humor Research, 2,* 73–79.

White, S., & Winzelberg, A. (1992). Laughter and stress. *HUMOR: International Journal of Humor Research, 5,* 343–355.

Wicker, F. W., Barron, W. L., III, & Willis, A. C. (1980). Disparagement humor: Dispositions and resolutions. *Journal of Personality and Social Psychology, 37,* 701–709.

Wicker, F. W., Thorelli, I. M., Barron, W. L., III, & Ponder, M. R. (1981). Relationships among affective and cognitive factors in humor. *Journal of Research in Personality, 15,* 359–370.

Winograd, E., & Neisser, U. (Eds.). (1992). *Affect and accuracy in recall: Studies of flashbulb memories.* Cambridge, UK: Cambridge University Press.

Wise, B. (1989). Comparison of immune response to mirth and to distress in women at risk for recurrent breast cancer. *Dissertation Abstracts International, 49*(7), 2918.

Woods, R. (1977). Multiple-choice: A state of the art report. *Evaluation in Education: International Progress, 1,* 191–280.

Wooten, P. (1996). Humor: An antidote for stress. *Holistic Nursing Practice, 10*(2), 49–56.

Wooten, P., & Dunkelblau, E. (2002). Tragedy, laughter, and survival. *The Humor Connection, 16*(1), 3–4.

Worthen, B. R., White K. R., Fan, X., & Sudweeks, R. R. (1999). *Measurement and assessment in schools* (2nd ed.). New York: Addison Wesley Longman.

Yoshino, S., Fujimori, J., & Kohda, M. (1996). Effects of mirthful laughter on neuroendocrine and immune systems in patients with rheumatoid arthritis [letter]. *Journal of Rheumatology, 23,* 793–794.

Yovetich, N. A., Dale, J. A., & Hudak, M. A. (1990). Benefits of humor in reduction of threat-induced anxiety. *Psychological Reports, 66,* 51–58.

Zajonc, R. B. (1965). Social facilitation. *Science, 149,* 269–274.

Zand, J., Spreen, A. N., & LaValle, J. B. (1999). *Smart medicine for healthier living.* Garden City Park, NY: Avery Publishing.

Ziegler, J. (1995). Immune system may benefit from the ability to laugh. *Journal of the National Cancer Institute, 98,* 342–343.

Zillmann, D. (1983). Disparagement humor. In P. E. McGhee & J. H. Goldstein (Eds.), *Handbook of humor research* (pp. 85–108). New York: Springer-Verlag.

Zillmann, D., Rockwell, S., Schweitzer, K., & Sundar, S. S. (1993). Does humor facilitate coping with physical discomfort? *Motivation and Emotion, 17,* 1–21.

Ziv, A. (1976). Facilitating effects of humor on creativity. *Journal of Educational Psychology, 68,* 318–322.

Ziv, A. (1983). The influence of humorous atmosphere on divergent thinking. *Contemporary Educational Psychology, 68,* 68–75.